# ENSNARED in a SPIDER'S WEB
## A WORLD WAR II POW HELD BY THE JAPANESE

# ENSNARED
## in a
# SPIDER'S WEB

## A WORLD WAR II POW HELD BY THE JAPANESE

### Morgan Thomas Jones, Jr.
#### with
### Linda Dudik, PhD

SANTA FE

© 2009 by Morgan Thomas Jones, Jr. All Rights Reserved.

No part of this book may be reproduced in any form or by any electronic or mechanical means including information storage and retrieval systems without permission in writing from the publisher, except by a reviewer who may quote brief passages in a review.

Sunstone books may be purchased for educational, business, or sales promotional use. For information please write: Special Markets Department, Sunstone Press, P.O. Box 2321, Santa Fe, New Mexico 87504-2321.

Book design • Vicki Ahl
Body typeface • Palatino Linotype
Printed on acid free paper

---

Library of Congress Cataloging-in-Publication Data

Jones, Morgan Thomas, 1916-
  Ensnared in a spider's web : a World War II POW held by the Japanese / by Morgan Thomas Jones, Jr., with Linda Dudik.
    p. cm.
  ISBN 978-0-86534-732-8 (softcover : alk. paper)
 1. World War, 1939-1945--Prisoners and prisons, Japanese. 2. Prisoners of war--Philippines--Biography. 3. Prisoners of war--United States--Biography. 4. Prisoners of war--Japan--Biography. 5. World War, 1939-1945--Personal narratives, American. 6. Camp O'Donnell. 7. Jones, Morgan Thomas, 1916-  I. Dudik, Linda. II. Title.
  D805.P6J66 2009
  940.54'7252092--dc22

                         2009030316

---

**WWW.SUNSTONEPRESS.COM**
SUNSTONE PRESS / POST OFFICE BOX 2321 / SANTA FE, NM 87504-2321 /USA
(505) 988-4418 / ORDERS ONLY (800) 243-5644 / FAX (505) 988-1025

# Ensnared in a Spider's Web

# Contents

Prologue / 9
1. The Spinning of the Web / 11
2. Fort Bliss / 21
3. Conscription / 25
4. Busted = Promoted / 29
5. Augmenting My Income / 34
6. Opportunities Declined / 39
7. An Excursion / 44
8. Another Excursion / 53
9. Our First Cruise / 59
10. Fort Stotsenberg / 64
11. This Is It / 75
12. The 515th CA(AA) Is Activated / 81
13. Bataan / 92
14. Surrender(ed) / 104
15. O'Donnell / 114
16. The Bataan Death March / 122
17. More O'Donnell / 125
18. Cabanatuan / 131
19. Cabanatuan-Odds and Ends / 155
20. Las Pinas / 173
21. Haro Maru / 198
22. Formosa / 211
23. Melbourne Maru / 216
24. Japan / 219
25. Kosaka / 228
26. Senso Owari / 250
27. American Food / 255
28. Another Free Cruise and Old Friends / 258
29. Our Last Free Cruise / 266
30. Home at Last / 272
31. Return to Kosaka / 297

Addendum / 312

"We rejoice in our suffering, knowing that suffering produces endurance, and endurance produces character, and character produces hope, and hope does not disappoint us, because God's love has been poured into our hearts through the Holy Spirit which has been given to us."

—Romans 5, Verse 3

# Prologue

Never have so many American military prisoners of war been so brutally and so callously treated as were those held by the Japanese during World War II. The Japanese acted with premeditation. Throughout the prisoners' captivity, beginning with the Bataan Death March, during their internment in various camps, and then on the prisoners' trip to Japan and forced labor there, the Japanese annihilated those who had been forced to surrender.

The only episode in United States history that resembles the story of these World War II POWs is that of Civil War prisoners held at Andersonville, Georgia, a stockade for Union enlisted soldiers. Confederates moved prisoners into the enclosure before barracks, cooking facilities, and hospitals had been readied. At one point, the thirty-acre enclosure held nearly 30,000 men. Of the

49,485 prisoners confined there from February 1864 to the end of the war in April 1865, nearly 13,000 died of disease, exposure, and malnutrition. Following the war, a military commission hung the prison's commander, Major Henry Wirz, after his conviction for murdering prisoners.

In all probability, the Japanese never heard of Andersonville. The conditions in Camp O'Donnell, north of Manila, were quite similar to Andersonville, though. Prisoners were housed in barracks, but water was extremely limited as were sanitary facilities. What little food the Japanese gave the Americans proved foreign to most of the men. The atrocities and barbarism the Japanese subjected their prisoners to in route to Camp O'Donnell, the infamous Bataan Death March, made the men's situation even worse than Andersonville. Initially, it is estimated that 10,000 Americans were surrendered to the Japanese on April 9, 1942. Of that number, 8,500 are believed to have survived that march. They were in such pitiful condition, however, that the likely death of many more was a foregone conclusion. The Japanese did their utmost to exterminate the recently vanquished.

I was one of those men surrendered at Bataan and taken to Camp O'Donnell. For the next three years and four months, I survived various prison camps as well as an arduous journey to Japan toward the end of the war on two of the vessels we prisoners called "Hell Ships." That name by itself should convey to you what the forty-eight-day journey to Japan was like for us. What follows in these chapters is my story of those years.

# 1

# The Spinning of the Web

When I enrolled in 1934 at Texas Tech College in Lubbock, I had the option of taking two years of Physical Education, Reserve Officers Training Corp (R.O.T.C.), or Band. I was a little allergic to exercise and I had no desire to play war. Since I had been in the high school band, I chose the last option. Little did I know that I avoided the military only temporarily and that my choice of the band would factor into my early Army career. Some sage once suggested that, "Life is a tangled web." If so, I walked into the web shortly after my graduation in 1938 from Texas Tech.

At first, the thought of war seemed distant to me. In the middle of the Great Depression, when jobs were extremely hard to come by, I accepted one that appeared to be secure. I had an Economics professor to thank for that. He had required all of his students to take any test offered by prospective employers, especially one by the United States government. I did as he asked. Because of that, on graduation day early in June 1938 I received a telegram from Uncle Sam offering me a position in Amarillo, Texas in one of the many programs started by Franklin D. Roosevelt. As it turned out, my job did not last long. The fiscal year ended on June 30$^{th}$, and since Congress did not get around to funding the budget on time, many of us were laid off on that date.

I returned to my hometown, Clovis, New Mexico, where I hired out on the Santa Fe Railroad. I had worked on the railroad during the summer between my sophomore and junior years of college. Soon after arriving home, however, Congress passed the budget and I received a telegram calling me back to work for the government. By that time, though, I was making the same salary with the railroad that I would have made with the Amarillo job, so I declined the offer. Little did I realize that the web was widening.

In the railroad industry, as in many other businesses, the majority of positions worked on a seniority basis. A new employee was always assigned to the bottom of the list until such time as one's seniority and ability allowed the individual to bid on a position that became vacant. Until such time, an employee worked "on the extra board," meaning the person filled a temporarily vacant position. After a year on the extra board, I finally secured a permanent job as Ticket Clerk, selling tickets at night for the passenger trains. In the entire passenger depot, there were no advertisements except those related to railroad services, but this soon changed. Because of the war in Europe that broke out in September of 1939, the Santa Fe allowed a large government poster to be hung. It was quite prophetic, not only the type of poster but also its location, right across from the ticket office which had only one customer window. I could not escape seeing that poster. It stared me in the face each day, every time I opened the window. It looked right into my eyes. The poster was a huge picture of a stern Uncle Sam, pointing straight at me with the legendary demand under the picture, "I WANT YOU." Those familiar with it will remember that from whatever angle you looked at that poster, Uncle Sam's finger and eyes stared right at you. I was forced to look at it every time I waited on a patron buying or pricing tickets. Little did I know that with Uncle Sam's haunting face and gesture, the web was pulling me in more and more.

Congress had legislated the first peacetime draft in American history to begin on September 15, 1940. The year of a man's birth determined his place on the draft list, or in other words, when he would be called for service. When newspapers printed the dates, I saw that mine, 1916, was way up near the top of the list. The draft law became another silken thread in the web.

As the draft began, the Santa Fe assigned me on December 1st to the position of Ticket Agent in Roswell, New Mexico. The hours and pay were much better than my railroad job in Clovis. In less than three months after the draft's beginning, though, I received a notice, forwarded by my parents, that I was to show up for a physical, the first step toward my conscription. The medical exam was to be taken in Clovis. I called the draft board and asked permission to take the physical in Roswell. The board approved my request. I passed the exam, even though I was considerably overweight. In retrospect, if I had taken the physical from the draft board's doctor in Clovis, who knew me, he probably would have failed me. I believe that physician, out of consideration for my family, would have not passed me. My choice of Roswell became another thread in the web pulling me into my fate.

About the same time I received my draft notice, a regiment of the New Mexico National Guard, the 200th Coast Artillery (Antiaircraft) received the news that it would be called into Federal service on January 6, 1941. The Regiment included two batteries from Clovis—Battery E, a .50-caliber machine gun unit and 2nd

Battalion Headquarters Battery. Those in this regiment were to serve for one year, the period decreed by the draft for men conscripted into the military.

After apparently very little thought, I decided to evade the draft and, if possible, join the National Guard. On Monday, December 23rd, I received word that both of my parents were in two different hospitals with the flu. Concerned about them, and wanting to explore the possibility of joining one of the Clovis National Guard units, I asked my boss to allow me to catch the passenger train from Roswell to Clovis when my shift ended on Christmas Eve. I promised to return to Roswell by freight train in time to work the passenger trains on Christmas night. He gave me his permission to make this quick trip

I arrived in Clovis before 1:00 am and I went home for the night. On Christmas morning I visited each of my parents. I found both of them well on the way to recovery. I explained the certainty that I would be drafted soon, but I added that I planned first to join the National Guard where I presumed I would be with some friends and acquaintances. While they did not like the idea of their little boy being a soldier, they agreed with my decision.

I immediately went to the Armory to see if I could sign up that day, Christmas Day. It turned out that I knew both of the Command Officers at the Armory. I went in to see the head of the Battalion Headquarters Battery since I was better acquainted with him than the other Commanding Officer. I asked him if I could join his unit and he was quite happy to have a warm body. I pushed my luck even more, requesting to be made a sergeant. I did not know anything about rank or duties, but that position sounded better than that of a private. The Commander explained that all such jobs were filled, but he offered to make me a corporal; later, when draftees arrived, he would be able to make me a sergeant. Instead of taking him up on this offer, I went over to Battery E since I had seen two men I knew and joined it without asking for any rank. Without realizing it, I had thrown out another thread that would pull me into the web.

I hurried back to the railroad and caught a freight train to Roswell to cover my job that night. I was a little late opening up the ticket office, but the boss knew my situation. Luckily, the traffic was light because of the holiday. Little did I know that this was the first of a number of Christmases that would be completely out of the ordinary.

One never knows what road should be taken, and usually the options are never clear. The more options there are, the more likely it is that the wrong road will be chosen. Due to the hours I worked, I often spent time after my shift at the local bowling alley where I had made a few friends. On this Christmas night, alone in the city, I ended up there once again. I ran into one of my friends and told him about my last twenty-four hours, including my enlistment in the National Guard. He was quite upset with me. It turned out that he was an officer in a local unit of another National Guard Regiment that was to be called into federal service later than the 200th. My friend told me he could have given me a better offer with his unit. This was long before Murphy's Law. After the war, when I returned home, I was told that my friend's Regiment had been wiped out in Italy. I have never returned to Roswell, so I am not sure if this indeed was its fate. I do know that I had several other choices that I did not take. In the end, they all turned out badly. But I digress. The spider is still busy and the web continues to grow.

When I returned to work, I asked for a leave of absence from my job to go into the military. I also arranged for an auditor to make sure the cash and deposits equaled the number of tickets sold. Additionally, my books needed to be balanced on my last day of work, December 31, 1940.

Needless to say, my books did not balance. In frustration, I tore up the sheets of paper I had been working with and started all over. Again, the numbers did not add up, so I finally forced a balance by changing the figures. On December 31$^{st}$ the auditor arrived to begin his work. He labored over my books for several hours. The auditor eventually looked up at me and asked if I balanced. I assured him I did, but then I did confess that I had not been able to show that balance so I had forced one. The auditor tried again to do what I had not been able to, yet even he could not get the figures to come out right. Since I had worked with him before, and we were thus well acquainted, the auditor finally told me to take off. He would keep at it until he found what was wrong and get word to me. In that era, if a railroad employee had too much cash in his till, the railroad kept the excess money; if the person was short, the Santa Fe took it out of his wages.

When I went into the Division Office to pick up my leave of absence form, I happened to run into the Division Superintendent. He knew me and proceeded to bawl me out for joining the National Guard. The man told me he could have obtained a deferment to keep me out of the military. I should have come to his office to ask for it. If I had requested the deferment, I could have joined a Railroad Battalion, one that originated in Clovis, at a later date. At that time, however, no one offered me such an alternative, and I do not know even today the details of this unit.

The draft law had originally required a one-year period of service, regardless of whether one went into the regular military or into the National Guard. Within a few months, however, this was extended to eighteen months; not long after that, Congress decreed that the service would be "for the duration." My leave of absence from the railroad was only for twelve months, but because of Uncle Sam's recent decisions on the length of service, the Santa Fe Railroad automatically extended my leave. I could have gotten a deferment since I worked in an industry, the railroads, which was crucial to the war effort. Instead I had enlisted in the National Guard. I wanted the excitement of a different world and I also wanted to get my year of military service over with.

Men in both units of the National Guard, including myself, reported to the Armory on January 6, 1941. With the exception of one or two weekend passes before we were shipped overseas, we were never to sleep in our homes again for many years. I am now caught in the web.

Once in the military, the first experience we had was a physical examination. Our first medical check-up after we had received our draft notice had been a state physical, but this exam at the Armory was a federal one. Aside from a few minor glitches, I recall everyone passing it. The man who stood in the line in front of me was W.A. Noffsker, the supply sergeant. He had been in the National Guard for a long time. W.A. had been working in a local bank, and the doctor told him he was underweight, meaning he would not be passing the physical. W.A. protested. "Doc, I have been working inside. If I get outside, exercise, and eat hearty, I will gain weight." The doctor considered this for a moment and told him to go eat a lot of bananas, then come back after lunch, at which time the doctor would look at him again. I was next in line. The doctor told me I was overweight. Taking my cue from W.A., I replied, "Doc, I have been working inside. If I get outside and get a lot of exercise, I will lose weight." The physician apparently was short of people so he passed me. After lunch, W.A. returned to the Armory and this time he passed the physical. The doctor who checked W.A. then, however, was the draft board physician. If he had seen me earlier that day, I would not have passed. Once we were officially in the National Guard unit, we were issued uniforms and fatigue suits. My outfits would have been a good fit if I had been about twenty pounds lighter.

After lunch, the Captain's orderly came looking for me. He

told me I was to report to the Captain. I immediately thought they were going to promote me, or perhaps give me an easy job because of my friendship with two of the officers. When I arrived at the Captain's office, I spoke to the officers I knew. Failing to understand military courtesies, I informally asked the Captain, "You wanted to see me, Bill?" He understood my lack of protocol and informed me that I was to be the bugler. "What the hell are you talking about," I shot back. "I don't know how to play the bugle." The Captain turned to one of the lieutenants and asked, "I thought you said he played in the high school band?" Lieutenant Cash Skarda said I had. I then went into a long recital, explaining that I had played a clarinet, which is a reed instrument. A bugle is a brass instrument. Nevertheless, the Captain ordered the First Sergeant to give me a bugle and a book of bugle calls. I was also told where to go so that I could practice. I had not been in the military for even six hours when I found myself volunteered and promoted. I saw my new position as a promotion since I would wear a side arm rather than carry a rifle.

Knowing I would not be a bugler for very long, I aggravated my relationship with the First Sergeant even more when I asked if I could be issued a rifle and also practice marching in addition to all of the other drills. An old Army man, the First Sergeant thought I was stupid for asking to march. The first thing I knew, though, I was out marching up and down the street with a rifle on my shoulder and a .45 automatic on my hip. I learned to "about face" and to march "to the rear." I also learned numerous other commands that a private without an inside job must know. I think I made a good impression on the First Sergeant. Learning to play the bugle took a little longer.

For that, I was shown to a little room in the corner of the Armory. Because of the background I had in band, I knew how to read the music. Making the correct sounds come out of the bugle, however, was an entirely different skill. The bugle does not have any keys. One changes the tone and brings the proper sounds out of the bugle with pressure from the lips.

After a couple of days, I thought I was good enough to make the officers understand that I was not a bugler, so just before noon one day I went into the kitchen and sought out the Mess Sergeant, Bud Kiely. I knew him by name and sight, but I really was not well acquainted with him. Disturbing him as he was performing his duties, I asked the sergeant if he was ready for me to play "Mess Call." Bud sternly replied, "No, I am not, Private. Sit down and eat this piece of pie. I will tell you when to play the call." That was the start of a very close friendship. More importantly, I found out that Bud and the First Sergeant were good buddies. We soon had a threesome going.

But again I digress. Sergeant Kiely told me to sound Mess. All of the men dropped what they were doing and rushed to get in line for chow. They did not really recognize the call I gave, but since it was a little late for noon mess, they all came running when they heard the bugle. Bud asked me what I had played since it really sounded terrible. The officers did not say a word, except to tell me to continue to practice on my new instrument. Before the week was up, I was able to give a reasonable interpretation of all the calls.

I felt that I earned every bit of the approximately $4.75 due me out of the $21 a month I received. Of course, the military also gave me clothing and all of the food I could stomach. Realize, though, that my pay was a comedown from the approximately $75 a month I had been making with the railroad.

Bud Kiely (left) and I at Fort Bliss in February 1941.

# 2

# Fort Bliss

On January 14, 1941, the two batteries from Clovis boarded a special train for El Paso, Texas. As I noted earlier, the 1st Sergeant and the Mess Sergeant were old buddies. Because I had become a good friend of the Mess Sergeant, the pair of buddies became a trio. Taking advantage of rank, we three occupied the best facilities the train had to offer for enlisted men. We enjoyed the privacy of a drawing room. It could actually sleep five persons, but in our case only three used it. This is where I learned the saying, "rank has its privileges." We arrived at El Paso the next morning. Trucks took us to Fort Bliss, an old Army post. All of the buildings at Fort Bliss were made of brick. This Army installation was the home of the First Calvary.

The area assigned to us was across the highway from the old post. It was a sea of platforms; tents needed to be erected on them. Putting tents over the wooden framework turned out to be our first chore. The tents had wooden floors and wooden sides that went about three or four feet up from the floor. Wire siding went from the top of the framework to about seven feet from the floor. The sides of the tent could be rolled up in warm weather; we had a small, gas heater for the cold weather. Each succeeding tent was a few yards up the hill from the preceding tent. The mess hall and kitchen were at the foot of the first street, with the latrine and showers at the top of each battery, behind the last street. A tent could sleep eight men, or a squad.

Odd balls, such as the Mess Sergeant, the cooks, the bugler, and the company clerk, were assigned the first tent in the second row, opposite the Company Headquarters. That tent was also the one nearest the mess hall. Once we finished setting up the tents, we picked up our metal cots, sheets, blankets, pillows, towels, etc. We tried to make ourselves at home, for how long we did not know. Sand and rocks surrounded us. The company streets were brownish, white clay. The day had been a busy and tiring one by the time we had erected the tents, drew our supplies, and cleaned everything up. We were quite ready for our first meal in our new home.

As time passed, we found out that there was room in our area for five regiments, all of which were to be housed at the base of Mount Franklin, which was soon renamed Mount Hamilton after our 1st Sergeant, Jim Hamilton. I am sure that each of the other regiments also named the mountain after their 1st Sergeant. We never knew the exact number of men at Fort Bliss. In the new area, there were close to ten thousand in just four or five of the other anti-aircraft regimental units; this was after draftees brought us up to authorized strength.

Our regiment consisted of Regimental Headquarters, 1st Battalion Headquarters, Battery A (search lights), B, C, and D

Batteries (3-inch anti-aircraft guns), Headquarters 2nd Battalion, Battery E (.50 caliber anti-aircraft guns), and Batteries F, G, and H (37-mm.guns). The 2nd Battalion Headquarters was below us, fronting the highway. As one went up the mountain, E Battery was followed by F Battery from Carlsbad, New Mexico. G and H Batteries were south of us, near Regimental Headquarters, which was above the batteries.

The main highway from El Paso to eastern New Mexico separated the old Fort Bliss from the new Fort Bliss. Mount Franklin looked down upon and was parallel to the main highway. Such details, while of no relevance by themselves, will eventually prove relevant to my story, such as it is.

We stayed at Fort Bliss for almost eight months. The Army trained us to be good, strong, disciplined soldiers, which wasn't easy given the terrain in which we trained and the fact that we came from civilian life. Rocks, sand, and clay bordered the western side of Mount Franklin, while nothing but sagebrush and sand bordered the northern and eastern edge of the camp. As far as one could see, the same sand and sagebrush surrounded us. We operated in this terrain whenever we went out on eight-hour, or overnight, forced marches. Sometimes we were out for a week, living in the sand, during which time the cooks received training in preparing food in the sand and open air. Because not all of the units had the same type of equipment, they did not train in the same manner, except, of course, for the opportunity to wander under the boiling sun and over the sand and sagebrush. Since I was more used to the sun than the cold, I did not suffer as much during the summer as I did in the winter when the blustery wind blew off of Mount Hamilton. It rained by the buckets full during the winter. These maneuvers, however, proved good for us and they nearly succeeded in making men out of many of us.

Several of our platoon sergeants were spit and polish, old

Army men. They did not have patience with civilians, or with many of the antics some of us "citizen soldiers" tried to get away with. Fortunately, all of our officers were from the same civilian group. The original fifty-four men in Battery E were farmers, railroaders, bankers, post office employees, clothing store clerks, and grocers. A similar group of twenty-seven civilians made up the other battery from Clovis.

I have special praise for some of our officers. We had one private who simply could not march in step. During one terrible rainstorm, we were sitting in our tents trying to keep warm. We heard someone counting cadence. Eventually, we looked out to see who was dumb enough to be out in the rain doing this. We saw Lieutenant Jordan, one of our favorites, walking with a lowly private, trying to teach him how to march in step.

One of the dubious benefits of being the battery bugler was that once every two months that individual had to participate in Regimental Guard duties. This lasted twenty-four hours a day for a week. The guards were from the bugler's own battery. The bugler had to blow all of the calls everyday, and every night, for the entire seven days. By the time our battery was assigned guard duty, I had mastered the bugle and really was not any worse than any of the others. During this period I had not been idle in locating another prospect to replace me as bugler.

Probably one of the most important topics privates discussed was the difference in salary between our previous jobs and our present wages. In my case, I had had a fairly good job for that time, and certainly one I did not worry about losing unless I really messed up big time. The twenty-one dollars a month I now made as a private, in addition to my food and clothing, was not to be ignored in those Depression days. It turned out to be, however, just a little more than twenty percent of my monthly pre-military salary of over seventy dollars.

## 3

# Conscription

Due to the fact that Jim Hamilton, our 1st Sergeant, was an old Army man, he had the knowledge and ability to recruit draftees into our Regiment who otherwise might have ended up in the 1st Calvary or another AA outfit. Consequently, when we heard that someone from Clovis had been drafted and stationed at the original Fort Bliss to await assignment, Jim and Bud would join me to pay him a visit. We would see if our friend would like to get assigned to our unit. Little did we know what we were doing to that individual.

While I do not remember others in the battery talking Jim into going over and getting other men transferred into our organization, I do recall that we talked several men into asking for our Regiment. After this was done, Jim arranged, through Regimental Headquarters, for the recruit to be assigned to our battery. I especially rued the day when we convinced my friend Bob Stephens to ask for our Regiment.

Bob had been my next-door neighbor in Clovis for as long as I could remember. While I also knew Jim and Bud because they were from Clovis, Bob and I were much closer. We had grown up together. Three years older than me, he had also worked for the railroad in Clovis where he was a brakeman and conductor. When Jim, Bud, and I visited Bob to see if he would like to join our Regiment, he was not sure. I knew he disliked horses, and I also knew that the old Fort Bliss was home to the 1st Calvary. I pointed out that he could very well end up being assigned to the horse cavalry. We finally convinced him to ask for the 200th Coast Artillery (AA). Jim did the rest, and to my undying sorrow, Bob ended up with us in E Battery. Is the spider more active? You will read more on Bob later in my story.

Our battery strength was fifty-four men when we arrived at Fort Bliss. With the addition of the draftees, we reached a strength of about two hundred men. The majority of our draftees were from New Mexico, with a sprinkling of men mostly from the eastern part of the United States. The 2nd Battalion Headquarters Battery was originally twenty-seven men from the Clovis area. But the draftees assigned to it more than doubled that number.

As I recall, the build-up of the new Fort Bliss included three or four other anti-aircraft units. The one next to us was from Arkansas. All of the AA units underwent basically the same training. We later found out, though, that we were in competition with each other. All units seemed to have been given the same opportunity to perform guard duty at various times. Periodically, we had to assume guard duty for the entire camp. For example, we guarded the ammunition dump and the supply areas. A week of all night, twelve-hour guard duty (two hours on and two hours off) was followed by our return to our Regiment to complete whatever training schedule had been posted for that day. This did not make for much fun.

Eventually, the Regiment reached the number of men authorized in the Table of Organization. At that time, about fifty percent of our men were Mexican Americans and American Indians who were mostly from New Mexico. We had one Indian who never spoke a word of English; other Indians in our unit claimed that he could not speak English. I will tell you more about him later. Some men escaped the web.

Soon after the draftees joined us, Bud, the Mess Sergeant, came down with a good case of pneumonia. He was sent to the base hospital in the old section of Fort Bliss since the new area did not have a hospital. Because of Bud's absence, I stepped in as acting Mess Sergeant. I made up the daily menu. Since the coffee was so poor, I would include hot chocolate due to the fact that it was winter and very cold. I received no respect from the cooks. I would always hear the cooks laughing about my spelling. Oscar Ruckman, one of the cooks, would say, "Jones went to college and does not know to spell 'coffee.'" Those cooks just refused to make the hot chocolate I requested.

Since I did not want to make a career of being a bugler, with the consent of the 1st Sergeant I trained another man, Buren Johnston, to be my successor. Writing now, fifty years later, I still do not know how I chose him for my job, but Johnston was one of the original men in the Battery from Clovis.

With the incoming draftees, the batteries were able to fill out their Table of Organization and as such they promoted some of the men. I became a corporal and I was given a squad. We received the title of "Communication Section." That was a well-earned promotion thanks to the 1st Sergeant, but it did interfere with my other duties. Once Bud was out of the hospital, he and I pretty much had the run of the place because as Mess Sergeant, he did not have to train in the field and I helped out wherever my assistance was needed. The Supply Sergeant was also an old friend from Clovis, and his tent was next to that of the 1st Sergeant. My tent was directly across from the supply tent, so I often ended up helping out the Supply Sergeant.

We had a company clerk, Wilson Jones, who had handled the paperwork for the Regiment for several years. With the influx of draftees, however, Jones found that he had more clerical work than he could handle. Since I had learned how to type in high school, I became an extra clerk. I also helped the Supply Sergeant, W.A. Noffsker, issue provisions to the new men. Probably the best extra duty I had, though, and the one that involved the most money, was when I paid the various bills the Battery incurred. Usually, on the first day of the month I would requisition a vehicle to go to El Paso to pay the Company's bills. Depending on who accompanied me on these trips, I would ask for a certain type of vehicle. If only Bud went with me, I used a jeep. Jim, who was big and tall, though, did not like to ride in that type of a vehicle. If the 1st Sergeant Jim decided he needed a change in menu, he, Bud, and I would leave around noon and enjoy a respite from Army food with lunch at a good restaurant. After a relaxing meal, we paid the bills and returned to camp where we turned in our vehicle. These side duties prevented me from having to do K.P. (Kitchen Patrol) and other arduous duties.

## 4

## Busted = Promoted

One of these trips to El Paso occasioned my first reduction in rank. When I went one day in July to pay the Company bills, I requisitioned a Jeep since only Bud accompanied me. After I took care of business and we had lunch in El Paso, Bud and I decided to visit a bar a little bit north of Fort Bliss. This establishment was "off limits" to military personnel, no doubt because of too many altercations by unruly soldiers. Bud and I were aware of its reputation, but we felt a need to avail ourselves of the cool libation it offered in such a miserably hot area.

With a cold drink in one hand, I busied myself playing a marble machine. I thought Bud was right behind me, watching and waiting his turn. I soon felt a tap on my shoulder. When I turned around, the Military Police stood there, asking me for my ID. After he took my name, rank, serial number, and organization, the MP released me to return to camp. I looked for Bud, but he was nowhere in sight. I continued to look for him on the trip back to Fort Bliss, but I did not set sight on him. I later found out that Bud had walked the couple of miles back to the Battery after seeing the MP approach me.

I returned the Jeep to the motor pool and walked back to the Battery. Unknown to me, MP Headquarters had notified Regimental Headquarters, which in turn had notified my Battery Commander, of my unauthorized visit to the bar. I had incurred the wrath of the Base Commander. Before I could find Bud, the 1st Sergeant found me. He invited me into the C.O.'s office. Captain Reardon, the Battery Commander, informed me that I could get him into more trouble than he could get me out of.

Word had come down that I was to be reduced in rank. I would once again be a private. Captain Reardon had sympathy for me, but he had been less than happy with my attitude. I had continually failed to sew on my corporal stripes even though two lieutenants had suggested to me that I do that. I also had a propensity to agitate some of these lower-ranking officers. At that time, all of our lieutenants had been civilians with limited experience as Army officers.

They had been, in most cases, just like the enlisted men. Before going into the military, they had been clerks, farmers, and bankers. Most of the lieutenants had only limited experience in leading a rag-tag group of non-military men, although the recruits were later trained in the spit and polish of the army. Since some of these officers were rather pompous and pretentious, I felt it necessary to help educate them. I would walk on the right side of the lieutenant until he remembered that the enlisted man should be on his left. I would walk out of step, and without thought on his part, the lieutenant would skip step to get in step with me.

My friend Jim, the 1st Sergeant and an old Army man, tried

to head off my demotion. He told the C.O. that he had already disciplined me by restricting me to quarters for three days. Such punishment would, ironically, have benefited me since I would not have left camp that weekend to spend some of my monthly salary of $54. The disciplinary action would have saved me money. When this was relayed, however, to Regimental Headquarters, they would not buy it. On Friday I was busted back to a private. On Monday, though, I was promoted to Private First Class, Specialist Third. That position paid $56 a month, so I was now earning more than before I was busted, but the new rank meant I lost control of the squad and I became one of the working men in the group.

My way of handling the men as corporal was to lead. By this, I mean that when it came time to load or unload heavy equipment in or out of the trucks, I would shout, "Okay men, let's go." I would then grab a medium-sized piece of equipment and throw it on the truck. Once the men began to do the same, I would stand back and watch them. They finally caught on and got a laugh out of my leadership method, but they then refused to do what I ordered unless I helped, too.

We were somewhat of a happy family. There were cliques, but I am not aware of any enmity between groups in our Battery. Of course, we all had our closer friends with whom we spent our off-duty time, especially when we went to El Paso or Juarez. Bud, Jim, and I spent time with each other more than with any other group. Many times Noffsker and the cooks joined us.

We trained both inside and outside. We were usually inside during the winter rains; we would strip our guns as we learned how to take them apart, clean them, and put them back together, without ending up with extra pieces. In warmer weather, although it might not necessarily be good weather, we would be out on the range where we played soldier. We learned how to sleep under the stars and eat out of the mobile kitchen. The first experience the cooks had with the field stoves proved difficult for them, but with training they soon had the food back to normal. We quickly learned that if we did not clean our mess kit well after a meal, we would soon have a bout of diarrhea.

I do not recall anyone being unable to stand the rigors of the desert marches. I certainly was not in as good physical shape as many of the others since I had always been on the heavy side. My dislike of physical activity did not help. I also must admit that our work and the heat really wore me out, but I still managed to keep up with the others. In most instances, I tried to prove to myself that, if necessary, I could keep up with the other men.

In many respects, before the draftees arrived, this first year of Army life seemed like a lark to the majority of our original group composed of enlistees such as myself and those who had been in the National Guard before we had signed up. But to a few of the older men, who were married, Army life posed somewhat of a hardship. They were separated from their families and, generally, their military pay did not equal their civilian income. On the other hand, a good number of the draftees accepted their conscription as their duty, and they tried to make the best of it. To understand how most draftees handled Army life, one could just look at the experiences of two of my friends from civilian life who also served in my Battery. One hated it from the start; he complained and fought it. The other laughed about his new life and tried to enjoy himself in spite of difficulties he encountered.

Even though Army life seemed strange to me, I fell in the later group. As a Boy Scout, I had enjoyed all of the activities except the campouts and, sleeping on the cold ground with only one 1918 Army blanket, I tried to enjoy a good night's sleep. I did not, therefore, like the exercises when we slept out in the desert. The time in camp was not too bad, and I tried to find enjoyment in what I had to put up with.

I did miss chocolate, though. Even though I was close to the cooks and the Mess Sergeant, and I had the run of the kitchen, I could not talk the cooks into baking any kind of cake aside from white sheet cakes. Being a chocolate nut, I finally wrote my mother to ask her to send me the recipe for her chocolate cake. She thought I was crazy but still mailed it to me. With the help of the cooks, we multiplied the ingredients to make a number of sheet cakes to serve approximately two hundred men in the Battery. With the usual lack of forethought, the cakes were baked on Friday evening and, since there was no time to let them cool, they had to be put on the shelves without icing.

The following morning, the General came through for inspection. When he saw the cakes, he explained, "Baking gingerbread for the men is unusual, but it is a very good idea. Keep up the good work." As it turned out, we had not included enough chocolate or cocoa in the ingredients. As a result, the cakes were not as dark as they should have been. After icing them, though, they were well received by the men. Later, the cooks added more cocoa to the recipe and the cakes turned out much better.

# 5

# Augmenting My Income

I do not remember if it was Bud or Jim's idea to build a dice table, but that is what Bud and I did. It was about six feet long and four feet wide. We set it up on payday in the one extra tent we had. We ran an honest game for several months, yet for some reason we never made much money off the table.

In between paydays, we stored the table in the supply tent. Supply Sergeant Noffsker slept in there and we parked the table between his bed and the wall of the tent. During several inspections, the Inspecting Officer would ask Noffsker what was beside his cot. He replied that they were civilian clothes belonging to the 1st Sergeant and several others; they kept them in the box so that the clothes would stay pressed and cleaned.

If too many people heard about the table, we were afraid that the brass would learn of its existence and then we would get into trouble. As it turned out, though, we never had any problems. Most of the men would play a little, although a few were heavy gamblers. As I recall, not many American Indians participated. By keeping the game within the Battery, we limited our players. Jim, Bud, and I split the money we made three ways. Jim's name could not be included as one of the owners.

We did fairly well for about three months until, in the fourth month, we lost money. It was not a heavy loss, but enough of a one to make Jim mad at Bud and I. He accused us of holding out on him. Jim made us get rid of the table by chopping it up. For a couple of months, Bud and I were on the outs with Jim until he got over it and let us back into his good graces.

After the fiasco with the crap table, Bud and I raffled off a small radio. We tried to be very honest. All of the tickets went into a hat and we let each man who had bought some tickets pull one out. Whoever owned the last ticket in the hat would own the radio. I pulled out the last ticket. Surprisingly, it turned out to be mine. When the next payday arrived, we tried to let someone else win the radio. Again, we followed the same procedure to determine who the winner would be. This time, Bud drew the last ticket out of the hat. To no one's surprise, it turned out to be Bud's. We had run an honest game but in spite of this fact, we were unable to sell more chances on the radio.

It was about this time that I received an education in drinking. One of the cooks in another Battery kept coming over to our kitchen to borrow vanilla extract. Bud finally cut him off and refused to give him anymore. According to Bud, this cook was drinking all of the vanilla extract he could get his hands on. This was usually at the latter part of the month, near payday. The next month, this same cook borrowed lemon extract. After this happened a few more times, Bud again cut him off. Eventually, all of the Mess Sergeants did the same. In trying to understand what was happening, I tried the vanilla and lemon extracts. The vanilla was not too bad, but the lemon was terrible. Since alcohol—be it beer, wine, or gin—was very cheap in nearby Juarez, I could not understand why the cook drank the vanilla and lemon extracts. This proved to be my first exposure to an alcoholic.

Five Points, on the way to El Paso, had the nearest good café outside of the post. On one of the trips Bud, Jim, and I made to that city, a waitress I had known in Clovis served us. I had met her during my 11 pm to 7 am shift when I ate in a small café just off of Santa Fe property. Several times during those encounters, I had seen her with a black eye or other black and blue marks on her arms and face. When I had asked what had happened to her, she had told me that her boyfriend had beaten her up. When I met her again in Five Points, and asked what she was doing in the area, she told me that she had followed her boyfriend from Clovis. It turned out that he was a cook in the other Clovis Battery.

Soldiers like to make trouble for the non-coms (non-commissioned officers) above them and we were no exceptions. In most instances, you pull tricks not on those you dislike but on those you like to agitate. After I had been busted and assigned to another squad, we had a Corporal Wiggins who we liked but who also gave us problems. He really pushed us for inspections. The corporal was bucking for a promotion to sergeant. On inspection day, Wiggins pushed, pushed, pushed until our dress, bunks, and footlockers were perfect. Then the corporal would lie on his bunk to take a nap, but not before he warned us to wake him up before the inspector reached our tent. One day we stuck a little shoe polish on the insole of Wiggins' shoe, between the upper and the sole, right at the bottom of his arch. Then we lit the shoe polish with a match. In a few minutes it started getting warm through the upper and soon it get very hot. This woke him. Wiggins jumped up, stomping his foot. The corporal realized what had happened and he jerked his shoe off, dug out the polish, and hopped around on his hot foot. Of course, we had the timing down so the corporal could clean up the mess and his bunk before the inspection. Naturally, no one knew who had given him the hot foot. Corporal Wiggins was a good sport. When more promotions were in the wind, the corporal kept boasting that his "promotion to sergeant was in the bag." This led us to put a pair of sergeant stripes in a small paper bag, which we stuffed under his pillow. While Wiggins did not move up a rank that time, he did eventually make sergeant.

We pulled the biggest trick on our superiors during one very rainy inspection day. As I mentioned earlier, our streets were composed of clay-like dirt. Once on our boots, it made a mess of anything our feet touched. Since our tents were close to the kitchen on that particular Saturday inspection day, I went to the mess hall where I got a big bucket of hot water. We splashed it over the floor of the tent and swept the excess water through the cracks in the floor. When the Inspector started to come into our tent, he saw the still wet floor. He commended us and announced that he would not dirty up such a clean floor. The Inspector left without looking at anything from the doorway. As a result of that, we tried the same trick several more times when the weather cooperated. We did not, on those days, spend much time preparing our gear or bunks. Unfortunately, weather did not always cooperate, so sometimes we had to be ready for inspections.

During this time one of the men in our Battery, Joe Schovanec, contracted polio. Our Battery was quarantined for several weeks. No one could come in or go out. We were allowed to order and receive items from the Post Exchange. Friends would also contact us to inquire as to our needs and then throw items to us, so we did not suffer. Most fortunately, Joe recovered without any lasting negative effects. I wish I could say the same for my relationship with Jim.

My big problem with the 1st Sergeant continued for the entire time we were together, which would be until 1943. Jim would not let anyone smoke at the meal table. This seemed strange since he was a very heavy smoker, usually of Bull Durham. Jim rolled his own cigarettes and almost always had one in his mouth, except when he was at a meal table or when he addressed an officer. Our 1st Sergeant always followed military protocol when he found himself in the presence of any officer, but privately his feelings towards a few of them were anything but respectful. I think that Jim had been in the National Guard since World War I. As such, he was probably one of the oldest men in the regiment. Even though we had many excellent officers, many did not act as officers and gentlemen should. Because of their attitude, many of us could not fault Jim.

# 6

# Opportunities Declined

As it turned out, I had two opportunities to avoid disaster. Late in the spring of 1941 the Air Corps elicited applications from those desiring to be Officers and Gentlemen. Our Captain and one of the Lieutenants suggested that I go over and take the necessary tests. In fact, they made arrangements for me to apply. As directed, I took the written exam with about thirty other enlisted men. I was one of twelve who passed; we were then required to take a physical. I think only two passed and I was not one of them. The doctor told me to lose two pounds a week for six weeks, after which I could return for another weigh in. Since I was not too thrilled with the entire operation, I did not try to lose any weight. If the Air Corps did not want me the way I was, it could do without, and as it turned out, it did just that. Did I escape the web or did the spider get closer to its prey?

About this same time, Jim asked Bud and I if we would like to go over to Biggs Field to visit an old friend of his who was a 1st Sergeant in a Tow Target Detachment. We did so one day and watched Jim and his buddy have a good reunion. It turned out that Jim's friend, years ago, had also lived in Clovis. Before our visit was over, this 1st Sergeant invited Bud and I to transfer to his organization, offering us both a promotion. I never understood the why and wherefore of this. I did not think Jim was trying to get rid of us. In fact, he seemed upset that we would leave him. Fortunately, we declined what appeared to be a good offer. Later, after the war, we learned that this outfit had been wiped out in Africa. We never learned the details, though. Did I escape a more deadly web? Would that spider have been a more lethal one?

During the time I spent with my Battery, I received two weekend passes which I used to go back to visit my parents in Clovis. These did not turn out to be very productive trips since I could not catch the bus until late Friday afternoon; I arrived in Clovis very late that night. I slept in on Saturday morning with just the rest of that day and Sunday morning in Clovis. I went to church with only Mother as Dad had to work. I caught a bus back to Fort Bliss after the service. During one of these trips, I found out that after the Railroad Auditor's hard work, he had finally balanced the books I had left him the last day in December. It turned out that I was $3.41 short. Dad paid the railroad what I owed. As I mentioned earlier, in those days if you were short in your accounts, you had to make the difference up with money out of your own pocket; if you were over, you did not get to keep it. When I returned to the railroad several years later, I found out this system had changed. During the war, there was too much of a turnover in help, the unions were stronger, and if the railroad wanted someone to sell tickets, it had to take what it could get. These wartime employees would not take a job if they had to pay when books did not balance.

If an account was short, the railroad absorbed the loss. In any event, because I had little time in Clovis if I availed myself of the weekend passes, I ended up spending most of my free days at the Fort. Music occupied some of my time.

During my first few months at Fort Bliss, I recruited a trainee to take my place as bugler. In some ways I relished the job since it gave me a little freedom at times when I would otherwise have been caught up in more arduous duties. I also admitted to myself that I had become rather proficient with the bugle. I became as good as most of the other buglers in the Regiment, but I would have to admit that I was not as good as the Band Bugler. Regardless of my official duties, I was glad to be in my Battery and not another one.

Battery "A" was the Searchlight Battery. It had what was the precursor to radar. A truck towed a large, trailer-like machine that measured about six feet or so wide, possibly ten or twelve feet long, and perhaps ten feet high. It was equipped with a ledge where the operators sat. These soldiers would twirl steering wheels while they looked at scopes or dials; I also recall that they wore headsets. Cables ran from this piece of equipment to each of the searchlights; the cables would move the light in the direction where the radar-like machine indicated the target would be. These searchlights were similar to those used today to attract attention to special events such as an opening of a store. In some respects, it seemed as though that Battery had it a little easier than the rest of the Regiment, but in other ways I guess it may have had a more difficult time. A great deal of the training of those men had to be at night. The Tow Target Detachment from Biggs Field flew missions after dusk to give targets to the searchlights.

When we were out in the field learning how to handle our .50-caliber, 37mm, or 3-inch guns, the Tow Target Detachment would fly targets over us. These targets were long, white socks towed behind an airplane from Biggs Field. As far as I know, our Regiment was pretty good at hitting the targets. Neither my Regiment nor any of the others ever hit a plane, but one of the other AA Regiments did come close to doing that, so close that the pilot aborted the mission.

It was about this time of the year, in the late summer, that we received word that our Regiment was going on a full week's exercise. At first, we thought this was going to take place in Louisiana since a large Army exercise was suppose be held there in the near future. A trip to Louisiana sounded like fun, but as with most rumors, this one did not turn out to be true.

Soon after this, on August 1st, I was again promoted to Corporal. Recall that Private First Class, Specialist Third paid more than Corporal, so my promotion reduced my pay by $2.00 a month, but rank is supposed to have its privileges. I could not, though, find any at this two-stripe rank. At the behest of the Captain, I sewed on my stripes. I still did not see the purpose in doing this, however. I guess I thought everyone in our battery knew I was a Corporal, so they certainly did not need to see my stripes. For those not in my Battery, or in the Army, it would not matter to them what my rank was.

Whenever we went to town, or off the post for any reason, we almost always wore civilian clothes. We did this so we would be comfortable, but we also did it so we would be treated better. One of the biggest surprises we had encountered in downtown El Paso were signs in many of the stores and bars that read, "No Soldiers or Dogs Allowed." We could not believe that anyone would be so callous. We later learned that since Fort Bliss had been a very old Army post, many of the "Regular Army" men had been less than desirable customers in the bars where the soldiers often created disturbances that resulted in property damage. But I believe the new soldiers set a better example and so, as time went by, many of the signs disappeared.

El Paso was not the only city I visited. One of my acquaintances was Daniel Jopling, a 2nd Lieutenant from Fort Sumner, New Mexico, about sixty miles west of Clovis. He and I had become friends in 1933 when we were in a band made up of musicians from all over the state. Dan owned a car and several times Bud and I would borrow it, with the understanding that we would fill the tank up with gas when we returned the car. We always drove to Las Cruses, about sixty miles from our camp. Because we had to get around Mt. Franklin, we would first drive south to El Paso and then north again, along the west side of the mountain.

In those years, Las Cruces was a small town. Most of the time we would stop in a little village called Mesilla Park, just short of Las Cruces. The purpose of our trip was to get away from soldiers and have a good Mexican meal and libations appropriate for the occasion. Mesilla was a very old village; it predated the Civil War. In fact, during that conflict there were clashes between the North and the South for possession of the New Mexican territory. Union soldiers were sent from Santa Fe and Albuquerque to secure it for the North. Several battles were fought over Mesilla and the area north of it and Old Albuquerque. None of the battles lasted long. Usually the Northern forces won since the distance involved and the logistics did not favor the South. The Lewis and Clark Expedition, the Santa Fe Trail, and other caravans going to Oregon and California by the more northern routes had all resulted in the Union building forts along the Santa Fe Trail. This gave the North a big advantage in holding onto the territory.

Shortly after August 1, 1941, we received orders to police up the equipment, guns, trucks, communications, mobile kitchen, etc. We also, of course, got ourselves ready—uniforms, haircuts, and packs.

## 7

# An Excursion

On the appointed day, away we went, the entire Regiment—down through El Paso, around Mt. Franklin, north to Las Cruses, then to Deming, and finally to Hot Springs, or as it was later called, "Truth or Consequences." There really is a town in New Mexico with that name. Hot Springs changed its name in 1950 to a television show, "Truth or Consequences." The Master of Ceremonies of the program, Art Linkletter, offered to do his show anywhere in the United States if the town changed its name in honor of his show. After Hot Springs, we went on to Albuquerque and Santa Fe.

In some ways, it proved rather hard to ride in the back of the Army trucks. I have no idea how many vehicles we had in the convoy, but it was an extremely long one and they probably numbered over three hundred. We drove in sections, with a time span between each section that actually made it several convoys of shorter length. If it was too hot, we could roll up the side curtains, but then it would be even hotter inside. It was also windy and dirty, but the breeze helped. The trucks' springs were not quite Mercedes Benz quality. In spite of these drawbacks, all in all I believe it was good training for everyone, from the top officers to the lowest private.

At each overnight stop, we set up our tents, guns, and searchlights as we played Army. We did this for the benefit of any parents, friends, or other interested people who came out to see us. We displayed our equipment and tents at the county fair grounds, but in Albuquerque we used the state fair grounds. In effect, we hosted an open house. If one of the Batteries happened to be drawn from the town in which we were spending the night, the soldiers from there would be given a short leave to visit family and friends. Because of the size of the state and the miles involved, we did not visit several of the towns, such as Gallup, Taos, and Clovis, which had furnished Batteries.

The Regiment took a shortcut on our way south and missed several towns. On the last night of this excursion, we tied up at Ruidoso, a village that at that time was a summer and winter resort. It is located in the Capitan Mountains. El Capitan Mountain itself is over 10,000 feet high. In 1941 Ruidoso was a winter ski resort with one ski run and in the summer wealthy families from Texas and Oklahoma mostly populated it; they sought a cool place where they could avoid the heat. The motels and cabins were rather inferior by today's standards. I was very happy to spend the night in Ruidoso since Bud and I were broke. Because we had no money, we would have to eat in camp and also do without libations since Bud and I could not even afford a beer. I told Bud that with any luck at all we could spend the evening sharing a bottle of Johnnie Walker Scotch. He did not understand what I meant. I then told Bud about my only previous visit to Ruidoso.

It had occurred in November of 1940 when a dentist friend of mine and I decided it was time we learned how to ski. That was a new sport in those days, at least in New Mexico. I believe only three ski runs existed in the whole state, and Ruidoso was the nearest one to us since it was about 180 miles from Clovis. (The other two were in Taos and the Albuquerque area.) On the first weekend in November, on a Friday afternoon, we headed for Ruidoso. Once there, we found a motel, had a good dinner, and visited what nightspots we could find. We got a good night's rest to prepare us for our new experience the following day. On Saturday morning we stopped at a liquor store to purchase a bottle of Johnnie Walker Red Label to warm us up. After we rented the necessary equipment, we returned to the motel and experimented with our new toys. When we were halfway comfortable with the skis, we set out for the ski run.

It was a beautiful, bright crisp day with cold sunshine and plenty of snow. There were no lifts or chairs at the village's one ski run so we trudged up the trail. We watched many neophytes come down the run, most of them on their back or on the seat of their pants. I realized I had failed to leave the bottle of Scotch in the cabin. It was in the pocket of my jacket, and I knew what was going to happen on my first trip down the run. After reaching the top of the run, I waited until all eyes were on the people going down. I then threw the bottle in a deep snowdrift behind a tall pine tree.

Learning to ski, especially down a steep slope, proved to be extremely hard work since we had to walk back up the trail beside the run. In many instances we rolled down, head over heels, instead of smoothly gliding down. Because of the number of people like us who were learning how to ski, after one unpleasant trip down the run we decided to call it a day when we were at the bottom of the hill. My friend and I decided to leave the bottle where it was well hidden and recover it the next day. This one had been an exhausting day.

Sunday morning was a rather cold, blustery, and cloudy day. Because of the weather, coupled with our aches and pains, we decided we had enough skiing for this trip. After breakfast we headed home. We completely forgot our bottle of Scotch until we were well away from Ruidoso.

Now, ten months after I had hidden the bottle behind the tree in a big snowdrift, I told Bud the sad story. I suggested that we try to find the ski run to see if, by any chance, the bottle was still there. Ruidoso itself was devoid of snow during our Regiment's summer encampment, but we could see snow up the many canyons that stretch out from the village. Even though it was August, at an altitude of over 8,000 feet there was still snow in those deep gorges because of the tall pine trees that protected the snow from the sun. We stopped in a store to ask about the location of the ski run. It turned out that we were within a mile of it, so off we went.

Once there, we climbed up the trail with some difficulty. The gradually melting snow on each side of the path made it wet and slippery. The ski run itself was completely clear of snow, although when we finally reached the top, we found considerable snow still on the ground. After looking behind several trees, I finally spotted the bottle—two inches of the neck stuck up through the snow. Bud and I were a little dubious as to whether or not the bottle was actually full of scotch. I felt positive it was since my dentist friend and I had each taken only one drink out of the bottle. The bottle we found certainly looked like the one that had been hidden ten months before. Surrounded by snow, the bottle was delightfully cold. Needless to say, Bud and I really enjoyed our last night of the convoy through the state of New Mexico.

Early the next morning, the Regiment started back to Fort

Bliss, only about 150 miles away. This was one time Bud and I were really happy to see our camp again. We still had a lot to do before we could be released for the weekend. We needed to unpack and then clean up our equipment, our gear, and ourselves. With the exception of a few who had girlfriends in Juarez or El Paso, I recall that most of us were glad to stay in camp for the weekend and rest.

Within a few days, we were all back to normal. As we complained about the abnormally hot weather, we heard a rumor that the Arkansas National Guard Anti-Aircraft Regiment, camped next to us, was to be sent to Alaska. While the hot weather made such a destination sound like a good idea, the majority of us were glad that the Arkansas Regiment might get that order and not the New Mexican one. I think most of us would have liked to have taken a cruise to Alaska, but an extended visit did not sound that glamorous. Within a few days there was a lot of activity in the Arkansas Regiment and soon it was gone. We did not think much about its departure other than being grateful that it was them and not us. All at once, though, our Regiment was restricted to camp. We soon learned that we, too, were to go on a trip. Rumor had it that our destination was the Philippines.

We were not allowed to leave camp, make a long distance phone call, or send a Western Union message. As the validity of the rumor became apparent, I wanted to contact my family, but how could I do that with these restrictions? I am sure the brass figured out a way to contact their families, and so did I. Since we could make local calls, I called the agent at the Santa Fe Railroad in El Paso. I did not know this man personally, just his name. I asked him to call my father, who worked for the Santa Fe in Clovis, with the message that his son was about to take a cruise over the Pacific Ocean. Through the El Paso agent, I also requested that my father contact families of other Clovis soldiers.

The same day I called that agent, I received a Western Union message from my father. He was alerting other families about our orders and they planned to come down to Fort Bliss that weekend. Sure enough, on that Saturday, a great number of parents and families started showing up at camp about noon. Years later, I do not remember if they stayed in El Paso overnight. The important thing was that most of the men from Clovis were able to see their parents. This was true for not only members of our Battery, but for men from all of the batteries. My message to my father had gotten through.

We were very excited as we busied ourselves getting ready to pack up and move out. We felt sorry for the Arkansas Regiment, bound for Alaska. With few exceptions, almost all of the men were extremely happy that we were going to a warm area. Since New Mexico has a varied climate, from deserts to mountains that rise to over 14,000 feet, most of the men from our state were more accustomed to a warm climate than to a extremely cold one. The Regiment also had a large number of Mexican Americans who were quite excited about our orders. They were anxious to try out their Spanish on Filipino natives.

At this time, the Regiment made everyone aware of a little known section of Army regulations. Section Eight allowed a soldier to be released from active duty if there was a "hardship." This could be due to family considerations or his inability to understand English. Being extremely dumb, or as we also put, not having the ability to get both oars in the water or not living with a full deck, could also qualify a soldier for a hardship release. Several men from our battery were issued Section Eight discharges, primarily because of the hardship their military service imposed on their families. One man in particular, however, outsmarted the entire Battery. I mentioned earlier that one Indian had been assigned permanent K.P. because he could not speak. Even his Indian friends, and he had only a few because of his language problem, told officers that they had never heard him speak. As a consequence, the Army granted this Indian a hardship discharge. When he left Fort Bliss, several men from our battery (also discharged and heading home) were on the same bus the Indian took as he left camp.

The bus route followed the highway that separated old and new Fort Bliss. The New Mexico state line was not too many miles north of the camp. Anyone heading for eastern New Mexico, one of the nearby Indian reservations, or north to Ruidoso, Roswell, or Clovis, took this bus. Not long after these men returned home, those of us back at Fort Bliss received some news. It seems that after the bus passed the state line between Texas and New Mexico, the Indian took a deep breath, turned to the men from Clovis, and exclaimed, "It sure is good to be able to talk again." The Indian and others in our regiment might be out of the Army, but I was still in it. As it turned out, I received some new military orders relating to our upcoming departure.

Our 1st Sergeant, Jim Hamilton, called me into his office a few days later. He told me to report to the C.O. at the 2nd Battalion Headquarters. Inquisitive by nature, I wanted to know why. Jim, an old Army man, was quite blunt in his reply. He told me to do as I was told and to not ask any foolish questions. (I later found out that Jim did not know why I received these orders, so he could not have explained them to me even if he had wanted to.)

When I reported as instructed, the C.O. told me that he had found out from Lieutenant Skarda that, when I was a civilian, I had worked for the railroad. (Lieutenant Skarda was already responsible for expanding my Army duties. He had suggested I would make a good bugler because I had played a clarinet in my high school band seven years before I had joined the National Guard. Now the lieutenant was unwittingly moving me in another direction.) When I verified the information the C.O. had on me, he directed me to sit down and fill out a large number of government Bills of Lading.

These covered the 2nd Battalion's movement from El Paso to San Francisco. (This reminded me of the mix-up I had already been in with respect to my expertise with a clarinet; that did not necessarily translate into expertise with a bugle.) I told the C.O. that I had not worked with Bills of Lading at the railroad. This did not make any difference to the Army, however.

I sat down and filled out the forms. After studying the sheets, I was finally able to fill in all of the Bills of Lading. This paperwork took me several hours to do since it covered the entire battalion, men and equipment. When I completed this task, the 1st Sergeant gave me a pat on the back and sent me back to my battery. Since none of the forms were returned to me, I apparently had filled them out correctly, or reasonable correctly. Of course, Jim caught me as soon as I returned. He wanted to know what I had been doing. Once Jim was sure that I had not been out drinking all that time, he was satisfied. Little did I know that this chore with the Bills of Lading would result in another reduction in my rank.

The next few days were rather hectic. We cleaned up the camp in preparation for our departure and packed our personal possessions as well as our equipment. Fortunately, in most cases we had already given to our parents or families some of the things that we did not want to take overseas. We also loaded the trucks up with all of the big equipment, securely tying the items down.

A day or two before our departure, I was again called down to 2nd Battalion Headquarters. This time the Battery Commander told me that he had both good news and bad news for me. The Battalion Sergeant Major was being promoted to Regimental Sergeant Major. I was to be transferred to his new Battery. I assumed that someone in the Battery was being promoted to Battalion Sergeant Major and I was to be moved in to take over the vacancy created by that promotion. The Commander then told me that I would be busted back to private and lose my two stripes that I had become so proud of, but he also promised me that I would be promoted again when we reached the Philippine Islands. I never understood why I could not be promoted when I was transferred, but I guess the usual Army red tape had something to do with it. As it turned out, the current Battalion Sergeant Major was also not going to be promoted until we reached the islands.

Finally, the Battery Commander told me that I was being promoted to 2nd Battalion Sergeant Major. With his perverted sense of humor, he had given me the good news last. Because of all of this, I was busted back to private before we left Fort Bliss. With my actual transfer to the new battery once we reached the Philippines, as a Staff Sergeant I would be given three stripes up and a rocker connected to the stripes. (This is a reference to the appearance of the emblem denoting my rank.) This all happened because of comments by Lieutenant Skarda which had resulted in me being made a bugler and later a Battalion Sergeant Major.

# 8

# Another Excursion

During the last week of August 1941, we loaded our trucks onto flatcars and ourselves onto Pullman cars as we headed for San Francisco. Since I was still in Battery E, Bud, Jim, and I shared a drawing room as we had on our first train trip when we had headed to Fort Bliss. There was one drawing room in each Pullman car. In the other cars, the ranking non-coms shared the space, with five men in a drawing room. The officers were on their own, and I do not know what accommodations they ended up with. Even though the drawing car could sleep five, only Bud, Jim, and I shared our car.

Since Bud was still the Mess Sergeant, his official duties occupied him. His number one responsibility was to post the day's menu, and, when Bud was not occupied with our poker games, he also oversaw the baggage car that was set up as a kitchen. Bud

*53*

ordered meals for the three of us, with a soldier assigned to K.P. delivering the meal and later picking up the dishes. The rest of the troops had to take what was on the menu. In our case, rank once again had its privileges. There is no doubt we ate well. Jim, as 1st Sergeant, was responsible for the morning reports. He had the Company Clerk check the Company Roster daily to see if anyone had fallen off of the train.

The mood of the entire group was one of anticipation. I am sure some felt great trepidation. Those who were married were not as happy about the move, no doubt, as the single men. In fact, after we had been informed of our destination several men tried every trick they had ever heard of to get admittance to the hospital. For example, they rubbed large quantities of soap under their armpits to raise their body's temperature, they swallowed complete bags of Bull Durham tobacco, and they acted as if they were crazy. I am not sure what their problem was. Perhaps they were fearful of the voyage across the Pacific, or maybe they did not like military duty, or it could be that they did not want to leave home. In a couple of cases, they were successful in avoiding service. They probably were smarter than the rest of us. I believe one man was hospitalized. At least one other soldier went AWOL (Absent Without Official Leave) on the day we entrained. We will return to his story in a later chapter. As for the rest of us, when we left Fort Bliss we enjoyed the respite from training. We knew we were on another excursion to parts unknown, and we were going to make the most of it.

We rode the Southern Pacific Railroad tracks along the southern border of New Mexico and Arizona. The train stopped first in Yuma, Arizona where we detrained, did some exercises, and marched through the town. Fortunately, Yuma was a very small town back then. Although it was early in the morning, it was exceedingly hot. After the brisk march, we devoured breakfast, entrained again, and set off to California. The train ride proved to be a slow one since the regular passenger and freight trains had priority. We must have visited every siding between El Paso and San Francisco.

Our next stop was Indio. Recall that it was late August when we set out on this excursion. While the train ride itself had not been unbearable, when we pulled into Indio it was exceeding hot even though it was the early evening. By this time, most of the troops had run out of liquid refreshments. Bud and I, with our knowledge of railroading, knew that Indio was probably a crew change stop, which meant that we would have time to run to the nearest bar for supplies. As soon as the train pulled in, Bud and I headed through the railroad yards looking for the nearest grocery store, bar, or the yard offices where we knew someone would direct us to one of these establishments. Sure enough, we located a place where we obtained four cases of beer and four bottles of liquor. Bud and I headed back to the train. As it started pulling out of Indio with the two of us running after it, about twenty boxcars and flatcars separated Bud and I from our passenger car. We threw the beer onto the flatcar that was coupled in front of the kitchen car that preceded our passenger car. As our passenger car, which was moving, got even with us, we boarded it, hurried through the kitchen car, and then jumped onto the flatcar to retrieve the beer. But Bud and I had not been alone on our excursion into town. Others had seen us arrive back at the train with our liquid refreshments. We discovered that some unknown individuals had already appropriated two cases. The other two, however, were still on the flatcar where we had thrown them.

Even though there had been a partial exodus of men from the train when we had stopped in Indio, the next day at morning roll call everyone had made it back. I remember that we passed through Los Angeles very early in the morning. The progress of the train, however, was slow and uncertain since it was still routed to the sidings to make room for other trains, carrying more important cargo. In fact, our progress was so slow that we were just going through the fertile San Joaquin Valley way after dark that night. By then, everyone had tired of the train ride and hoped for some type of excitement. I thought of a way to oblige them.

We received news that when we arrived in San Francisco the next morning we would have to return to the Army all of our unused food supplies. The Batteries would not receive any credit for these items. This upset the officers since the Company had purchased the food for the trip. In more than one way, the officer in charge of the mess and kitchen was beside himself. He had overimbibed, and the heat in the hot, humid Central Valley had slightly overcome him.

As we sped between sidings, we sometimes passed a few homes near the tracks, but these were visible only if there were lights in the windows. I mentioned to Lieutenant Byars that the lights indicated the homes of track laborers, whose houses were near the tracks. Their duties were to keep tracks together and in shape for the movement of the trains. These men worked hard in the heat of the day for relatively little pay. I suggested that we contribute to their well being by throwing off the groceries we were ordered to return to the Army. The lieutenant thought this was a wonderful idea. Seeing some lights near the track, he picked up a sack of flour and threw it out of the baggage car. He mentioned, "They are not going to shoot me in the back," referring to a practice in World War I where enlisted men shot officers they disliked. In Lieutenant Byars case, such action was not necessary since he was well liked and a good officer. It turned out that sack was the first and last one we disposed of in that manner. After the lieutenant tossed it out, the track looked like a snowstorm had hit it because the flour sack had burst in flight. Within a short time, we managed to dispose of nearly all of the other surplus groceries. Every time Lieutenant Byars threw something out the door, he made the same statement about not being shot in the back. We saved just enough for the breakfast menu that Bud had posted.

We arrived in San Francisco early on Wednesday morning, September 3, 1941. After detraining, we were loaded on trucks and driven to a pier on San Francisco Bay. We boarded ferry-type boats and caught our first glimpse of the fabled Alcatraz penitentiary. We docked at Angel Island, in the middle of San Francisco Bay, where Fort McDowell was to be our island retreat for several days. The boat trip had given us our first, good view of the famed Golden Gate Bridge. It was quite a sight and we were impressed.

Our stay on Angel Island allowed us time to reflect on our train trip. I am sure that some of the men had never been on a train before. The experience was not a new one for me since my father worked on the railroad. As such, our family traveled free on the Santa Fe line. I had been riding trains since I was six weeks old. What was new to me, however, was the trip from El Paso to San Francisco. I had never been north of Los Angeles. I would also interject that trains I had been on before this trip were a little more luxurious and comfortable than our troop train, but I really could not complain about the style or service I experienced on this trip. It was just the dogged speed of the train, which took over three days to go from El Paso to San Francisco, that bothered me. The other soldiers and I wondered what the railroad's section men thought when they found all of the canned food along the right of way. We hoped they were able to use the items and that the food gave them something to talk about during their day's work.

Once on Angel Island, we understood that we were entering a new phase of our lives. A trip across the Pacific on a huge ship would be a part of it. Odds were that none of the men had ever taken such a voyage before. Personally, I was worried about getting seasick. We lived day to day, not knowing when orders to ship out would be given. More important things were on our mind most of the time, such as enjoying liberty in San Francisco. While we waited for that, we took pleasure in the delightful weather on Angel Island. It was typical Bay Area weather—sunny days that began with foggy mornings and ended with cool, foggy nights. Such weather proved to be a welcome relief after the heat of Fort Bliss and the train trip.

We wondered how long we would be on the island and if we would be able to go into San Francisco. We sweated out the first question day by day, but the second one was answered quickly. We were all given a one-day leave in the city. Bud and I departed in the middle of the morning and returned to Fort McDowell before dark. I do not think it mattered to us if we spent the evening in the city since we were practically broke. The two of us really only had enough money for food and bus fare for some sightseeing.

All of us were told to check the "duty board" every evening for our instructions, if there were any, for the next day. I was unlucky enough to be assigned K.P. (Kitchen Police) duty at one point. It proved to be a rather long day for me. I had to get up before first call to organize breakfast for the men and clean that up after they ate. I did have a short break before getting lunch ready and another short break after that meal. I then went back to the Mess Hall to prepare for the evening meal, cleaned that up, and then I was done. Luckily, I only had that one K.P. assignment. The worst part of that duty was the walk back and forth, up and down the hill to the Mess Hall from our barracks. I was surprised, as others probably were, that Angel Island was hilly. It did have lots of trees and good roads. When time permitted, it would have been interesting to explore the island. How could I possibly complain, though, about K.P. duty? I had been in the Army for over eight months, and this was the first time I had received such an assignment. Because of the number of men in our Battalion, a machine washed the dishes instead of arms and elbows deep in dishwater.

# 9

## Our First Cruise

We were billeted on Angel Island for four days. On the fifth, the Army again loaded us on small boats with all of our gear. Once on the mainland, a truck took us to the berth of what appeared to be a huge boat. It was the *S.S. President Coolidge*, a ship belonging to the American President Lines. Even though someone would assume from its name that it was a Navy ship, the *Coolidge* was privately owned. But in 1941 when we sailed on it, the ship was under contract to the U.S. government. A luxury vessel, it had been halfway converted to a troopship. Many of what had been public rooms used by vacationing passengers on prior voyages had been converted to house soldiers; extra cots had also been put into several of the cabins. My group was quartered in the ship's "Tea Room." When the *Coolidge* had sailed as a passenger liner on a voyage to Honolulu or the Orient, the Tea Room had served as a light refreshment spot for paying passengers. For us soldiers, however, this large ballroom type of facility had been set up with bunks, five high. Just enough space existed between the rows to squeeze by another person. This room alone accommodated between four hundred and five hundred men. The soldiers assigned to staterooms had it a little better. While they were jammed in like bedbugs, each stateroom did have a private toilet and shower. Those of us in the Tea Room used the toilets that were on deck for the public, had there been any civilians on the ship. Upon its return from this trip to the Philippines, the ship was reconverted to a passenger liner.

Our cruise began on September 8, 1941, and while I am not positive on this, I seem to recall that the 1st Battalion and Regimental Headquarters had sailed on another ship a few days before us. I do know that there was a mob of excited soldiers on the *Coolidge* as we pulled out of San Francisco Bay early that evening. Once we passed under the Golden Gate Bridge, we headed west, out into the Pacific Ocean. I remember the up and down motion of the ship as we hit each breaker. Farther out, we ran into the swells. To preclude the possibility of seasickness, I went to bed early, grateful to be in a horizontal position. I was lucky in that I had the top bunk of the five in the tier. Because of the windows and the height my bunk, I got the benefit of the cool ocean breeze. For what seemed like several hours, the ship continued to move up and down. Much to my dismay, just as I was getting used to the ocean's swells, we started rocking sideways. I have always been susceptible to motion sickness. My family had often visited Long Beach and from there we had sailed on the "big white ship" to Avalon on the island of Catalina. I always became ill on those trips. And even though I traveled on trains quite a bit, I would at times become sick on those trips, too. The hour we had left San Francisco, however, proved to be very propitious since it was bedtime when we started to rock bank and forth. I avoided becoming seasick, no doubt, because the ship's motion put me to sleep.

As our ship sailed westward, we were not kept informed about aspects of the journey nor were we told our destination. Our main form of entertainment, as I recall, was playing cards or shooting dice. It proved difficult at times to get through the passageways due to the dice games in the halls. We also spent considerable time lining up for our meals. Just getting through the stuffy, inner passageways proved difficult, and the dining rooms were not any better when it came to air quality. Unless a soldier was exceedingly hungry, the smell of food in the hot room could overcome a man. Although the food itself was more than sufficient and edible, it still lacked the elements of home cooking. It also seemed as if we just finished a meal in the dining room when it was time to line up again for the next one. Fortunately, most of the line was on the outside deck of the ship where we benefited from the cool sea breeze.

I believe we saw land again on the fifth morning. Rumor had it that what we sighted was one of the Hawaiian Islands. Anxious soldiers crowded the ship's rails. We were finally informed that soldiers desiring a shore pass would receive one. We docked about 8:00 am Hawaiian time; shore leave would last until 4:00 pm. By the time we disembarked, we had figured out that we were docked in Honolulu on the island of Oahu. We walked to the main part of town. Even though a shipload of soldiers had arrived, we still saw many white, sailor uniforms. We felt extremely happy to be able to stretch our legs and get away from the motion of the ship. Bud and I, along with several others, dined at Wo Fats, which was, even then, a famous restaurant. We visited all the tourist traps, wrote some postcards home, and arrived back at our ship within the allotted time. The weather was nice, and we probably thought that we had seen Oahu, but with my later visits to the island, I learned that we had hardly scratched the surface. The *Coolidge* departed Honolulu shortly after 4:00 pm. We would not see land again until September 25th.

The remainder of the cruise turned out to be more enjoyable than the early part of the trip. A few rain showers fell now and then. We were a single ship, and we moved pretty fast in terms of ocean travel. Although not part of a convoy, we did have two escort vessels accompany us. Daily, our main interest focused on attempts to spot these ships. We regularly sighted a cruiser. It came close enough for us to identify it as the *U.S.S. Astoria*. At times we also observed a destroyer, but we were never close enough to see its name. Usually the *Astoria* stayed on the starboard side of our ship, but it would go back and forth on both sides of the *Coolidge*. Rarely could we see the destroyer. One day we apparently had an alert as the *Astoria* raced in front of us and disappeared for several hours. The destroyer followed suit. We did not see the *Astoria* until the next day. We were not sure if anything had really happened, either good or bad.

Many years later, I lived next door to Rear Admiral Carlton Jones. After the war, he had been Governor of Guam, spent several years in the Pentagon, and had also testified many times before Congress. Even though Jones was retired by the time we were neighbors, he was still wrapped up in the Navy. The admiral liked to talk about it, everything from the Naval Academy to what was wrong with the present-day fleet. Once when we visited, I told him that the *Coolidge*, on our voyage that fall of 1941, was probably the first or second ship to be protected by the Navy before the United States entered the war in the Pacific. I mentioned sighting the *Astoria*. The admiral immediately corrected me, insisting that the *Astoria* was not part of the Atlantic fleet at that time. I bowed to his superior knowledge. Later in the evening, he brought the subject up again. Jones told me I was probably correct in my statement about the *Astoria*. He had been thinking of the *U.S.S. Augusta* that had been in the Atlantic before the war.

Being somewhat of an agitator, I asked Jones where he was when Admiral Halsey went the wrong way during the last major Naval battle in the Philippines. (In the Leyte campaign in October of 1944, Halsey, abandoning the 7th fleet, had sailed away from Leyte to seek out a Japanese ship to the north, This decision became a controversial one.) Admiral Jones replied, "I was with him." Jones told me he commanded a destroyer at that time under Halsey. He also detailed for me where every aircraft carrier, battleship, cruiser, and destroyer had been during the entire foray by Halsey.

Taking everything into consideration, our cruise from Honolulu to Manila was not too bad. We became accustomed to the luxury of the cruise ship, crowded as it was. As we neared the Philippines, which consists of some seven thousand islands, it became rather muggy. The ocean breeze, however, helped to keep it pleasant. We sailed through the San Bernardino Strait, in Leyte Gulf, which later became famous as the site of just about the last big sea battle of WW II. We landed in Manila on September 26, 1941 and were promptly (as promptly as the Army can be) on our way to what we soon learned was Fort Stotsenberg. The military loaded us on ordinary buses for the less than one hundred mile trip to the fort. As we left the docks in Manila, we saw some of our equipment unloaded from the *Coolidge*. One of the big cranes accidentally dropped, into Manila Bay, one of our big 3-inch guns.

# 10

# Fort Stotsenberg

The bus ride from Manila to the fort proved quite educational. As we passed through the city and then into its outskirts, it was interesting to see the construction of the homes. In Manila, they resembled our houses in the states, although many of them had tin roofs and they were crowded together. On the outskirts and in the countryside, the homes were usually on stilts. The houses themselves, with thatched roofs, did not seem to be very large, just two or three rooms. The interior was lit with fluorescent lights rather than incandescent bulbs. Many children played under the raised homes. Chickens ran loose. We saw an occasional goat tied to one of the house's stilts.

Upon our arrival at Fort Stotsenberg, we were assigned a camp area, barracks, and office buildings. All of these had been recently constructed of native material, which seemed appropriate for the occasion. The barracks, in fact all of the buildings in our area, had been built about two feet off of the ground. Light and airy, the barracks had wooden floors. The upper parts of the walls were open, but they had shutters that could be closed during inclement weather. The best part of life in these Army accommodations was that we could hire "bunk boys" who would take care of not only our beds but also our clothing and the entire barracks. The local Filipino boys took our uniforms to their mothers who washed and pressed them. We paid the boys one peso a week, and we immediately caught a lot of flak from the old timers (the Regular Army soldiers who had been stationed in the Philippines way before our arrival there). Those men were paying their boys only fifty centavos a week. We thought their labor well worth the peso since we would, by necessity, change uniforms several times a day. The weather was pleasant but, depending on the time of year, intermittent showers could fall followed by humid, muggy weather. During the rainy season, we experienced hard, driving rain. At other times the weather was hot. We arrived during the dry season; no doubt that timing was premeditated.

We soon learned that we were all wearing shirts and pants (our cotton khaki uniforms) which were too large. When the Filipino women laundered our uniforms, they beat them on flat rocks to get the dirt out. Soon my shirt cuffs covered my hands. Our bunk boys told us where we could buy tailored uniforms. Of much better quality and fit than the Army-issued ones, these locally made uniforms made a soldier look very smart. My bunk boy also educated me on the type of civilian clothing I should purchase. Made of a white cloth called sharkskin, this clothing was attractive and not too expensive.

The nearest village was Angeles (pronounced "Anhayles"), only a few kilometers from camp. Our bunk boy lived there. He advised us on places to eat in Angeles. Our favorite one was

Chicken Charlie's. It was located in an old house, but not one built on stilts. The eatery resembled a very worn-out house in the States. At Chicken Charlie's, for one peso, we would get a sandwich. It consisted of one-half of a fried chicken and two thick slices of bread. French fries accompanied the sandwich. The Philippine beer, San Miguel, was also good. A lumberyard stood next door to Chicken Charlie's. In it, I found something I wanted to purchase and send home. It was a large chest with carved legs and end panels, with a huge lid on which was carved the Last Supper. It was beautiful and cost only a little over one hundred American dollars. I put the chest in the back of my mind until I had saved enough to purchase it.

On October $1^{st}$ I was promoted to Battalion Sergeant Major, with the rank of Staff Sergeant. This translated into a monthly salary of $72.00. I never found out why I had been busted to private before leaving the States, but I did learn when I was promoted again that one could not understand some of the decisions made by the Army. This promotion also prompted my transfer to the $2^{nd}$ Battalion Headquarters. I was given a nice, new desk with my new job. It stood just outside of the office belonging to the Battalion's Commanding Officer. The office was in a new building adjacent to the barracks of both E Battery and Headquarters $2^{nd}$ Battalion Battery. Since I did not want to disturb bunking assignments in my new Battery, I remained in the same barracks I had been assigned to upon my arrival at Fort Stotsenberg. This arrangement required that I take morning exercises with E Battery, but as a rule, those exercises did not last long. Before breakfast I would check in at Battalion Headquarters to see if anything was up, then I left for chow, and finally I went back to the office to work.

When I took over as Sergeant Major, the instructions I received were even more limited than when I had become bugler. At least then I had been given a horn and a book of calls. In my new position as Sergeant Major, however, I received no instructions or statement of my duties. All I had was a desk and a book of Army regulations. I knew the Commanding Officer, Lieutenant Colonel John Luikart, well. As a civilian, he had been the Postmaster in Clovis. Luikart had lived just a block west of my parent's home. He had four daughters, one of whom was my age and in my classes at school. I found Luikart to be a very nice gentleman. He had served in the Army during World War I and after that, he had been in the New Mexico National Guard for many years. I do not think that Colonel Luikart promoted me to Sergeant Major, but I am sure that he had to approve of the promotion. Of course, in spite of my transfer I could still socialize with my friend Bud, and I drew on a practice he had employed when confronted with Army authority figures.

Bud was never at a loss for words. In any conversation, regardless of the rank of the person he was speaking with, Bud always had something to say. Many times he quoted some Army regulation. Bud would talk fast and rather unintelligibly. With few exceptions, the person with whom Bud was speaking was a civilian in National Guard/Army clothing, so that individual was not completely knowledgeable of what Army regulation Bud had quoted. Rather than appear to be dumb, the person with whom Bud was speaking would abruptly finish the conversation. Remembering how my friend had fooled so many officers by this ruse, with my book of Army regulations in hand, I tried to recall some of Bud's conversations. I soon found that in my new duties, nothing helped me more than that book.

I never completely understood what those new duties consisted of. It became uncanny how many times I would be reading the book on Army regulations when Colonel Luikart would come out of his office, or call me into it, to ask me to find the exact regulation that covered a particular subject. It became more common for one of the other Battalion officers to ask for a particular page and section number of the regulations that related to a situation they confronted. Many times the subject requested by the Colonel was something I had recently read so I could immediately quote it for him. As a result of this good timing, I guess he thought I knew what I was doing. By osmosis, I found out that Regimental Headquarters sent me instructions and information that I was to relay to Colonel Luikart. Usually, he would then pass them down to the Batteries under us. In effect, I was an administrative assistant to the Colonel. As such, I became very familiar with the military structure.

Regimental Headquarters stood at the top our triangle, with a direct line down to each Battalion Headquarters. Under Regimental were the Band and Medical Corps. Four Batteries were under each Battalion Headquarters. 1st Battalion had A Battery, Searchlights B, C, and D Batteries, and 3-inch antiaircraft guns. 2nd Battalion had Battery E, .50-caliber antiaircraft machine guns, F, G, and H Batteries, 37 mm antiaircraft guns. Colonel Sage was Regimental Commander, with Lieutenant Colonel Peck commanding the 1st Battalion and Luikart the 2nd.

Altogether, the New Mexico National Guard had almost 2,000 men stationed in the Philippines. Our primary responsibility was to protect Clark Field, the major airfield in the islands. There were several smaller airfields. In addition to Clark Field, Luzon (the main island where Manila, the capital, was located) had at least three more. The larger islands also had at least one airfield. Of the 7,000 islands that comprised the archipelago, there might have been ten more airfields.

Our Regiment was the only antiaircraft unit in the islands, although one more was located on Corregidor, an island south of Luzon. Two units of antiaircraft guns, the 59th and the 60th, both Regular Army, were on Corregidor. At Clark Field, our guns were dispersed around the field. The bigger the gun, the greater distance it was from the airfield. The .50-caliber machine guns were positioned a short distance off of the field's perimeter. The 37 mm guns were a little farther out, and the 3-inch guns farthest out from the field. (The three inches referred to the bore of the gun; they could shoot the highest. The 37 mm and the .50-caliber guns could not reach too high; in theory, they could, however, go after straffers.) The searchlights were at an even greater distance so they could pinpoint any incoming planes before they reached the 3-inch gun positions.

In addition to positioning the guns in the best possible location to protect the airfield, we also spent the month of October getting acquainted with the area and acclimated to the tropics. Additionally, we did dry runs on each segment of the Batteries where we practiced as if we were firing the guns. The Army showed us the usual pornographic movies meant to protect the health of the soldiers. We also endured rounds of shots to guard us against various illnesses. It was strange to watch a large number of grown men line up for these shots. Some keeled over in a dead faint when the needle went into their arm. This scene appeared especially bizarre if the man was a large individual or one of the bullies.

With a boosted immune system, Jim, Bud and I would take a recon car. With it, we made trips into the backcountry and the jungle. The first time we had gone about four miles into the jungle when we came upon a little hut where a native Negrito tribesman lived with his wife and children. Their only clothing consisted of dirty "g" strings. Their little hut, with a dirt floor, had just one room; the sides and roof were made of native grass. The roof had a small hole to allow smoke to escape. The man was hardly five feet tall. He carried a bow and arrow, but he could hardly see. His eyes were in terrible shape from living in the hut without proper ventilation. We put an empty, Lucky Strike cigarette package onto a little tree. Using hand and arm signs, we asked him to shoot the big red emblem on the package. I did not think he would be able to do this because of his poor eyesight. But while the first arrow missed the mark, the second one pinned the empty package to the tree. We gave him some pesos, which he seemed happy with, as we departed. We drove deeper into the jungle, and finally we ended up in such dense plant growth that the recon car could not go any further. We decided that on the next weekend we would requisition a jeep and see how far we could go. Perhaps it would be where no civilized man had ever been.

This picture was taken in the Phillippines, November 1941.
Captain William Reardon is on the left,
Bud Kiely is in the middle, and I am driving.

The following Saturday afternoon, Jim, Bud, and I did as we had planned. Once we returned to the spot where we had turned back the week before, we continued on for a mile or so. At several points one of us had to get out of the jeep to hold back bamboo or other jungle vines so we could continue. The three of us finally got to what appeared to be the end of the trail. We felt sure that we had penetrated deeper into the jungle than any non-native ever had. Inching along, we finally turned a little corner where, above us, a sign that read "Hollywood Blvd." had been nailed to a bamboo grove. How disappointing! After driving another quarter of a mile, we turned a second corner to spot another sign, "Dottie's Blvd." That one obviously referred to Dorothy Lamour. So much for exploration.

At least the next day, Sunday, we enjoyed quite a treat. We would always have ice cream that day. The only problem was that the mess crew never learned to set it out early to soften it. The ice cream had evidently been packed in dry ice. The cooks left it packed until nearly everyone had finished their meal. Then the cooks would drag out the ice cream, at which point they proceeded to dig and dig at the dessert. They tried to scoop it out but were only able to slice off a little at the top. It took about fifteen minutes before they could finally dig out a dish for each man.

Even trips into the jungle and Sunday's treat could not relieve the boredom I felt at my job. One day while I tried to look busy at my desk, I looked through the Fort Stotsenberg phone book. I did not know I would see several names, all of them belonging to generals, that I would recognize. But I certainly was not going to call them. I finally spotted the name of a 2$^{nd}$ lieutenant, R.E.L. Michie. When I had enrolled in college back in 1934, Texas Tech was only in its ninth year. That did not stop the college, however, from bragging, as all true Texans do, that it was the largest college in the United States, not in respect to enrollment but in square miles. Texas Tech only had five buildings, excluding two dormitories, but they were widely spaced, with about one mile between the two buildings. The college did not have fraternities or sororities, but it did have social clubs. A friend of mine in one of the clubs was named Robert E. Lee Michie.

On impulse, that evening I called the number in the book and asked for Lieutenant Michie. When he came to the phone, I inquired as to whether he had attended college in Lubbock, Texas. When he replied that he had, I then asked if he had belonged to a particular club. Michie again answered in the affirmative. He wanted to know who I was. I made some disparaging remarks about officers and told him that I was Private Jones, but I did not give my full name. Michie became somewhat upset at a private calling an officer the type of names I had just used. At that point I gave the lieutenant my full name. At first, he did not recognize it. It was only after I repeated it that he finally woke up. A few days later Michie invited me over to his quarters where we had a good reunion. He was an Air Force pilot. Unfortunately, we were never able to get together again due to circumstances beyond our control.

The passage of one month to the next translated into some major changes. October had been quite pleasant. We had been able to go to Angeles in the evenings if we so desired. Some of the men had even received weekend passes for Manila. One or two alerts had been called, and all of the gun crews spent twenty-four hours in the field. With the coming of November, however, we were put on "full alert." Gun crews spent the entire time in the field. The actual crews on the guns alternated in shifts. Sometimes my job meant very little work and at other times I was very busy issuing orders from the Colonel to the Captains. I sent out runners when the phones did not work. In rereading letters I mailed to my parents in October and November of 1941, I can see now that we really expected to see action any day. But at that time, it did not soak into my feeble brain what all of this meant, or where the spider, which would ensnare me in its net, was.

During this period, construction crews also worked continuously to bring in more water and sewer lines. A huge ditch had been dug just outside of Battalion Headquarters. A soldier had to jump over it to get to the P.X. The ditch measured at least five feet in depth and over four feet in width at the very top. Since I often met Jim and Bud at the P.X. for lunch, I jumped the ditch because the route over it proved to be the shortest distance to lunch from my office. Bud and Jim, however, walked around to a little bridge. Some Chinese ran the restaurant inside of the P.X. While the food, a mixture of Chinese and Filipino, was good, it seemed that whatever items we ordered tasted the same, although one time our meal might be soup and another time it might be fried food. The ingredients always seemed to be identical.

Because of the looming war clouds, to which I was oblivious, the brass decided that men twenty-eight years and older would be sent home. I do not know what the rationale was, except that possibly they were perceived as too old to fight. About two hundred men in our Regiment made the first list, including several soldiers from our Battery. Some of them were from Clovis, my hometown. More were scheduled to return to the States on the next ship. Bob Stephens, who had been my next-door neighbor in Clovis, was to be on the next list for departure. Jim, Bud, and I had talked him into joining our Regiment when he was drafted.

We were still on a twenty-four hour alert as these men prepared to leave the islands. Some soldiers who were not assigned to gun crews slipped away to Angeles for a meal at Chicken Charlie's. I also tried to go by the lumberyard to check on the large, carved chest that I had wanted to buy. On one of these trips, some sort of an election was going on, with the lumberyard designated as one of the polling places. Officials even allowed us to vote. I never knew what we voted on since the ballot was printed in the local dialect.

Jim, Bud, and I thought this alert business was rather silly.

The guns had never been fired since we left Fort Bliss, but all of the crews were on the guns twenty-four hours each day. Surely, we thought, we would get some practice on the guns soon. If and when we did fire the guns, because the rest of the Fort was on twenty-four hour alert, someone would think a war was starting.

74

# 11

## This Is It

On the morning of December 8, 1941, Bud and I were taking exercise with the Battery. When we were just about through, Jim came out of his office. He motioned to us to see him when we were finished. After we were dismissed from the exercises, we did so. Jim told us that the Japanese had bombed Pearl Harbor. You must remember that the Philippines is west of the International Date Line, so while it was December 7th in Hawaii and in the States, it was the 8th where we were. I immediately went to my desk and within a few minutes Colonel Luikart rushed in. He ordered me to get all of the Battalion's officers into his office. How big the spider had become; the web's sticky threads were so close to ensnaring me.

I got on the phone and also sent some runners out to a couple of the Batteries. Soon all of the officers reported as ordered. Colonel

Luikart shared with the men the information he had received from Regimental Headquarters on the sneak attack by the Japanese airplanes and the apparent loss of the majority of our Pacific Fleet. While I had the Regiment and each Battalion's Table of Organization available to me, I had never studied the lists. Our officers included five captains, some twelve or fourteen 1st lieutenants, and one 2nd lieutenant. That 2nd lieutenant piped up and asked if they could test fire the guns. Colonel Luikart very expressly ordered that we were not to fire until fired upon, and no guns were to be test fired. The lieutenant responded by pointing out that none of the guns had been fired since we had left the States in September. The "head spacing" of the 37 mm and .50-caliber machineguns would need adjusting to be able to fire. Again, Colonel Luikart reiterated that General MacArthur had ordered everyone not to fire until fired upon. The Colonel then dismissed all of the officers, telling them to return to their posts.

    Most of the officers were quite upset. They even mentioned the one 3-inch gun that had fallen into Manila Bay during the unloading of our equipment, but it was to no avail. The orders would stand. With that, I had nothing to do except sit at my desk and wait for the phone to ring. I also wished that I had been with the twenty-eight year old soldiers who had gone home. I have to admit, though, that I was not really worried. I do not think many of the other men were, either. We felt this way because of our lack of knowledge and our ignorance of the consequences to us once America became involved in the war. We were ready to do what we had been training for since the first of the year.

    Commercial radios were all over the area, including one I owned that I kept in my office. Reports came in that Manila was being bombed, or that Clark Field was under attack. Since we were in the Philippines and on the spot, we knew these stories were the result of hysteria. The Colonel went to lunch with his peers. When he returned, he told me to take a similar break. Bud, Jim, and I went to the P.X. restaurant about fifty yards from my office. It was a large room, with its high ceiling framed in by screens. The waiter took our order and when the food arrived, he wanted his money. Jim, in his gruff way, told the waiter that we would pay when we were finished, in case we wanted more. He also added, though, that maybe we would be bombed before we finished. Jim sent the waiter, talking to himself, away.

As we ate, I faced Clark Field. About halfway through our meal, I urged my friends to "look at those damn fools running on the airfield." Normally, one does not run in such humid climate. About that time, the bombs started to drop. Then we heard guns going off all around us. We jumped up and took off running. I do not remember what Bud and Jim did. I dashed towards my office, thinking only of getting my tin helmet. I jumped a big, deep ditch under construction and grabbed my tin hat. I ran outside and crawled under the very fragile nipa shack. I never thought about the nice, safe ditch.

When the bombing stopped, I came out from under the shack. But about that time the strafers started to come in. I had a fairly good field of vision. I pulled out my .45, intending to blast the strafing planes. First, however, I had to take off all of the plastic wrapping I had on my automatic. I had wanted to protect the gun to avoid having to clean and oil it everyday. As I was about to fire, it occurred to me that I probably could not hit the side of a barn door with the .45-caliber automatic. Seeing a rifle beside a recon car, with the owner underneath the vehicle, I thought that if I used my gun, I would have to clean it afterwards. But if I used this man's rifle, I would not have to do so with his. I am sure you can understand my actions from that point on. It seemed that the planes were coming in from my right, strafing the field about one hundred yards north of my spot. Because of the distance, I was not too concerned about my safety. There were two men nearby, one under the vehicle and another one under my office. I used their rifles to fire at the Japanese planes, probably to no avail.

Since we had been told not to fire unless fired upon, we could not test our antiaircraft guns. In spite of this, one officer in our Battalion disobeyed orders and test fired his guns, so his were the only ones that could fire when the men on the guns first pulled the triggers. Of course, everyone heard the test firing, and Colonel Luikart wanted to know who the culprit was. The Colonel realized from the sound of the gun that it was someone in his Battalion. Luikart ordered me to find out who the guilty party was and bring him in from the field. It turned out to be the only 2$^{nd}$ Lieutenant in our Battalion, Lieutenant Thorpe. Before Luikart could see him, though, the Japanese were all over us.

Our Regiment has been cited as the first American unit, in the Philippines when the war began, to return fire to the enemy. We have been credited with bringing down seven or eight of the strafers. That did little good. Our B-17 bombers had been out on patrol most of the morning and had returned to refuel right before the Japanese attacked. The planes were all lined up, very pretty, on Clark Field, not only the B-17s but also our P-40 fighters. Soon after the Japanese bombers and strafers hit the field, we were almost completely out of an air force. A few planes still stood on Luzon's Nichols Field and Iba Field, and some planes were on the other islands, but not on Clark Field.

We had not practiced with our 3-inch guns, or any of the other guns, since our arrival in the islands. These guns were also World War I-1918 issue, as was the ammunition. Since the guns could not reach the height of the incoming bombers, they were useless. We should have been allowed to test fire the other guns to calibrate them and adjust the head spacing. To make matters worse, we were still wearing 1918 helmets in spite of all of the high power bullets flying around. The helmets were the flat type and any bullets would go right through them. With five hours warning before the Japanese attacked, it was inexcusable that we were caught with our pants down. There is not much reason to keep beating a dead horse, though. This lack of preparedness has been examined from many sides for over fifty years.

As for Lieutenant Thorpe, the $2^{nd}$ Lieutenant who had disobeyed orders and test fired his guns, after all of the bombing and strafing the Colonel announced that Thorpe would receive a court martial. Events moved so fast, however, that I know there was not time to carry out on that threat. Instead of facing a court martial, I think the lieutenant should have been given a commendation since he had the only guns that could be fired accurately without adjustment. Within a few minutes of the Japanese attack, however, all of the guns were active.

We lost several men that first day. $1^{st}$ Lieutenant Byars, who had announced more than once that he would not be shot in the back as officers were in WW I, was one of the wounded. According to General Jonathan Wainwright, who commanded American forces in the Philippines after General Douglas MacArthur left the islands, 193 men were killed and injured on December $8^{th}$. The events of that day really brought it home to us that we were not playing tag anymore—this was for keeps. As for the two men whose rifles I had borrowed, I was as scared as they were. But when I crawled out from under the grass shack, I realized that the bombing was not in our area. It was probably one thousand yards from where we were. When the strafing had started, I had been able to see where the American fighter planes were, also about one thousand yards from my position. The two men from whom I had borrowed rifles were still not able to see what was happening. I have always wondered who they were and what they thought when they found their guns empty and dirty.

I was too busy after the Japanese left to help with the wounded or with the cleanup. I had to send messengers out to each position to find out the casualties. I then coordinated the information I received for the Colonel and Regimental Headquarters.

# 12

# The 515th CC (AA) Is Activated

At this point, of the two thousand members of the 200th Coast Artillery Regiment from New Mexico, we had about fifteen hundred left. Some had stayed behind in the States when we shipped out, and a large group of those who had been at least twenty-eight years old had returned home just before the war began for us. Aside from two other regiments of antiaircraft batteries, the 59th and the 60th that were on Corregidor, the 200th was the only antiaircraft regiment in the Philippines. On the 8th, in the middle of the afternoon, we received orders to send about one-third of our men to Manila to pick up more antiaircraft guns. These soldiers were to form another regiment. Orders were issued to each company commander to assign one out of every three men under him to the new unit.

Lieutenant Colonel Luikart was chosen to be its Commanding Officer. When I received the roster of who was being sent to the antiaircraft regiment, in most cases I saw them to be the goof offs and undesirables. I did not like to think that was the case in all instances, however, because I also was one of those on the list to move out. Of course, I did not know for sure who was actually selecting the soldiers who were to go to Manila. I am sure that the company commanders had their say, but probably the 1st Sergeants selected the men. Jim was assigned to the new regiment, as was Bud. Both were from Battery E. I was assigned from Battalion Headquarters. We had roughly five hundred men initially assigned to the Provisional 200th (CA) Antiaircraft Regiment. Since the departing soldiers had to gather equipment and personal belongings, the new convoy did not assemble until after dark, about 9 pm, as I recall.

Away we went towards Manila, with more than the usual confusion. We had everything with us but the guns, which we were to pick up in Manila. Back in Washington, D.C., Congress had by now declared war. Because of this, and also because of the alerts and the general confusion as to whether or not the Japanese were going to bomb us again, mass hysteria and confusion existed throughout the countryside. Blackouts had been ordered on the highways. All of this combined to make the trip to Manila a long and tiresome one. We got lost several times since none of the drivers had driven on these roads and they had no maps to guide them. Additionally, the drivers were completely disoriented by the black night that resulted not only from the lack of lights but also from a moonless night. Finally, we arrived on the outskirts of the city. It was as active and busy as it would have been in the middle of the day. Rifle and pistol shots rang out. If anyone exposed a light, shots were fired in reaction to it.

Apparently, the natives were restless. The shooting scared us, even though we seldom heard or saw what they were shooting at or the direction in which the shots were fired. About midnight, we were finally directed to the Manila Polo Club. This would have been a very plush place to establish our headquarters, but we were instructed to bed down only for the night. We would find a more permanent home the next morning. Again, luck was with us; if anyone had played polo on the field recently, at least someone had cleaned up after the horses. The night was still not a very comfortable one because of the intermittent gunshots. Since the field, however, was almost the size of a football field, only wider, we had ample space.

Civilian residents in Manila were very excited. With talk of spies, fifth columnists, and rebels, the Filipinos brought out every weapon they owned. At night, every time a house light went on, shots would be fired. Innocent civilians who stayed out late at night, going to or coming from work, could become targets. Thanks to the poor eyesight of the shooters, however, very few people were injured.

After a very small and poor breakfast the next morning, we were directed to the Walled City. This was the old, original city of Manila. The walls were at least twenty-four feet high. There were actually two earthen walls near each other, their tops covered with vegetation, concrete, and stone. The tops of these walls were wide enough for barracks and other buildings to be erected on them. Huge openings were spaced around the walls for entrance and egress. A regular city existed within these walls, with streets, houses, automobiles, and businesses. A large, green space, pretty and serene, surrounded the Walled City. Usually, throngs of citizens walked through this park. Now, though, Filipinos rushed across the expansive area, with no time for fun and play.

We were assigned to some of the barracks on top of the walls. If there should be an air strike, we were also told where we should go. (The air raid warning horns emitted the most mournful sound I have ever heard from such a horn, but at least it was loud and clear.) We also received orders as to where we should go for our meals. The next day, the soldiers who were to operate the antiaircraft artillery were told where to go to get the guns. They were to set them up around Nichols Field, on the outskirts of the city. As one would expect, both ammunition and guns dated from 1918.

The first thing I did was to locate a facility from where I could send a message to my parents. I found a Western Union office in the Walled City. In my message, I told my parents that I was okay, as were all of the other men from Clovis. I also advised them not to worry. As the message was distributed around Clovis, it was well received, but the addendum to not worry proved to be of no avail.

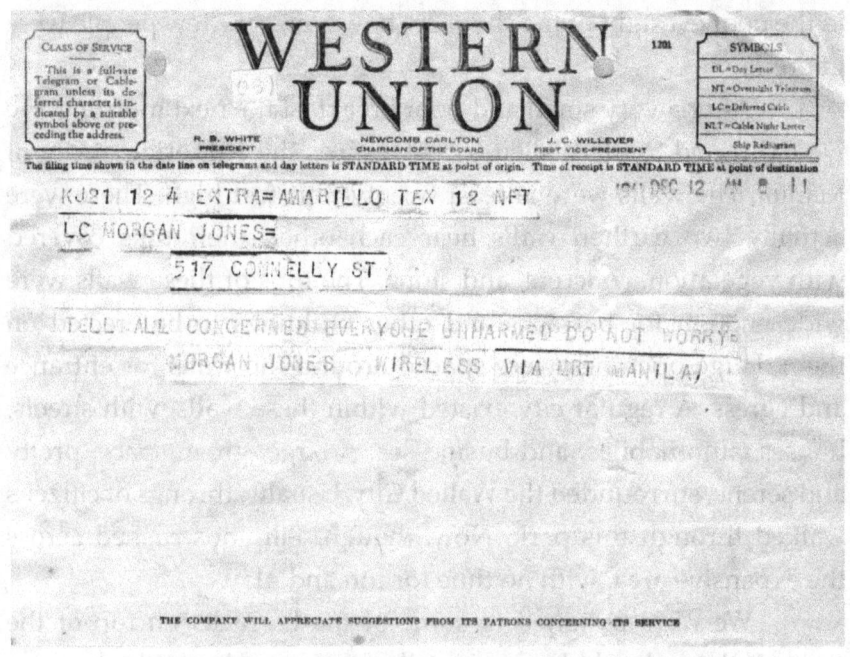

**The telegram I sent my parents from Manila
four days after the war began.**

During the day, we experienced several air raid warnings. They usually proved to be false alarms, although the Japanese did reconnaissance a few times each day. They did more damage to our nerves than to anything else. During one of these alerts, when I reported to the shelter (a tunnel to which we had been assigned), I discovered that it was also the shelter for USAFE (U.S. Army Far East) Headquarters. MacArthur and all of his staff were there. These shelters were within the actual walls of the city. Unless a bomb was dropped at the entrance, there was no way anyone could be hurt.

On my first trip into this shelter, I sat among a great number of stars and bars, generals on down to a few non-coms. Because it was extremely hot in the tunnel, after about fifteen minutes I decided to go outside to see what was happening and to cool off. I was very surprised to find General MacArthur standing outside talking to a one-star general. He stood in his usual pose, with a corncob pipe in his mouth, his hands stuck in his hip pockets, looking up at the sky. I immediately reasoned that if MacArthur was not scared, there was no reason I should be. But to be on the safe side, I kept my eye on him. I stayed outside until the all clear sounded, as did MacArthur. In future alerts, I followed the same routine. On the outside, I always stood between MacArthur and the entrance of the shelter. I figured if he started running for the safety of the tunnel, I would be about ten steps ahead of him. This system worked very well since we had several daily alerts. Daily temperatures were also much more bearable outside of the shelter than inside of it. A bomb never dropped, however, near our part of town.

The Japanese had really torn up Clark Field and had destroyed most of our planes with their initial attack. They had also done some damage to Iba and Nichols Fields. Subsequent attacks did not do as much destruction. Since we did not have many B-17 bombers, and only a small supply of P-40 fighters, we were unable to do more than delay the landings by their ground forces even when it was evident where they would land. While the Japanese continued air raids on Manila, Clark Field, and Subic Bay (principally a Naval installation), the enemy did not inflict much damage in their attacks.

Beginning with our first night in the barracks, we heard the sound of gunfire and even an occasional bullet as it ricocheted through a nearby building. We would jump from our bunks and hit the deck, but that response did not last long. We found it was practically impossible to zero in on the level of our bunks since we were so elevated above ground level. It proved difficult to get a good night's sleep.

After a few days, the official name of our regiment changed from the Provisional 200th to 515th CA (Antiaircraft). Rumor had it that the unit would be filled with Filipinos, but the exigencies of war apparently dictated that untrained, antiaircraft soldiers should not be used. Instead, the brass decided to put the men they had in the field and on the line.

Rumors flew every day as to what was happening and where, but most of the rumors were unconfirmed. *The Manila Bulletin* newspaper had an English edition that we Americans consumed each day. Since troops in the 515th were scattered and without transportation except for the brass, I did not get out to any of the gun emplacements. I spent my time filling out reports given to me by the Colonel after his return from inspecting.

As the air raid alerts increased in number, I and the other men from my Regiment continued to use General MacArthur's bomb shelter. Never had I seen so many stars and chicken colonels. (A "chicken colonel" is a full colonel; his insignia is a little eagle while a lieutenant colonel has a silver oak leaf as an insignia.) Three, two, and one-star generals were a dime a dozen in that tunnel. I became ashamed at the lack of courage they exhibited. As for me, I was scared, but I was a civilian soldier. It was the brass' job to make war, not love, and I was amazed at what I heard and saw during what little time I spent in that tunnel.

When MacArthur was there (and there were only a few times he was not present during an air raid), he always stood outside of the tunnel, exhibiting no fear. No one seemed to be in charge of the bomb shelter, so people could do as they pleased. Since the inside of the tunnel was unbearably hot and humid, and the air did not circulate, I followed my plan to stay between MacArthur and the tunnel entrance. One or two officers (probably his aides) accompanied him outside, but he seldom spoke to them. After watching MacArthur, I sensed no reason to call him "Dugout Doug." I admired him for his bravado.

The Japanese started their landings on December 10th. Foot soldiers, along with their artillery and vehicles, initially landed at Lingayen Gulf and Aparri. Lingayen Gulf is located in the northwest corner of Luzon. Aparri is in the extreme northern tip of the island, quite a few kilometers from Lingayen Gulf. Shortly thereafter, other enemy troops started arriving on the islands of Panay and Mindanao. The landings were hard fought for a few days, but eventually strength overcame determination. The American Army was woefully unprepared. If we had had at least one more year before the war started, we would have been halfway prepared.

MacArthur had been asking for more troops to help defend the Philippines. He, and most of the Army staff knew what was going to happen, but politicians in Washington, D.C. would not let the American people know the true facts. Actually, MacArthur was not the highest-ranking military officer on active duty in the islands the year before the war started. He was a consultant trying to make an Army for the Filipinos.

The Philippine military consisted of the Army and the Constabulary. This latter group was made up of slightly trained or newly recruited soldiers. The Philippine Army and Constabulary were very poor soldiers, although there were some exceptions. They simply had not had enough time to learn even the basic commands. Many were not accustomed to wearing shoes. The large, Army-issued footwear hurt their feet. At the first sign of trouble, these soldiers were more likely to take to the hills, removing their shoes and carrying their rifle upside down. One could not really criticize them for their actions. Probably none of them had received any type of military discipline prior to joining the Army, although the Constabulary had had some training.

There was another group of Filipinos called the "Philippine Scouts." They had been trained by American officers and were also commanded by American officers. The Scouts trained with American forces and were excellent soldiers.

In the several months before December 8th, as the movements of the Japanese war machine became more apparent, the bureaucracy in Washington finally seemed to listen to MacArthur. That was why the 200th Coast Artillery had been sent to the islands. When the war actually broke out, additional troops were on the way, with even more scheduled to arrive. Not only were ground forces to be sent, but air power as well. Washington appointed MacArthur head of the Far East, but as usual with the government, the additional supplies and troops proved too little, too late, at least a year too late. By December, we had the 59th CA (Antiaircraft), the 60th CA (Antiaircraft) on Corregidor, the 4th Marine Division (that had just arrived from China shortly before the Japanese attacked the Philippines), support groups on Corregidor, the 200th CA (Antiaircraft), the 515th CA (Antiaircraft), the 31st Infantry, the Regular Army, two Anti-Tank Battalions that had been activated National Guard units (the 192nd and the 194th with their support groups), a decimated Air Force (which included not only the air crews but the support staff as well), and lastly, a small contingent of Navy to back up the Philippine troops.

I must admit that I was amazed to see so many generals and colonels in the islands. Back in the States, I don't think I had ever actually seen a general, in person, more than once. Aside from getting ready for the next move, there was not much for me to do. Several times Bud and I went over to the main portion of Fort Stotsenberg, which included Clark Field, to see how the other half lived. One day we ran into General Wainwright. He looked like the very image of a general, but it would not have hurt him to gain about twenty pounds. Wainwright carried a swagger stick in his right hand, so when we saluted him, he returned the salute with his left hand.

Off of Luzon, Corregidor was well defended, but there were problems that would later be apparent to defenders of the Philippines. It was a very old outpost, built and armed to protect Manila Bay and Manila City. Many of its guns were on fixed sites, pointing out to sea. They were positioned to pulverize enemy ships and preclude their entry into the bay. Just south of the main gun placements, stood two more installations with more guns. They were ill prepared, however, to direct their biggest guns north, east, or south. The northern part of the island, where Lingayen Gulf and Aparri were, was the closest point enemy forces could advance from by foot. Whether one looked at American forces on Luzon or on Corregidor, we were woefully unprepared.

Several years before, a defensive plan, "War Plan Orange," had been formulated in the event of a surprise attack on Luzon. If American forces could not repel the invaders, military forces were to withdraw into the Bataan peninsula and put up their defense there until assistance arrived from the States. As sound as the plan was, several bugs appeared in its implementation.

The Philippine Army and the American 31$^{st}$ Infantry, as well as some antitank and other units, fought valiantly that first day and night. At first, it appeared that they would succeed in rebuffing the Japanese, but the enemy's greater manpower ultimately wore our forces down, gradually forcing them to withdraw. Meanwhile, what little Air Force we had would continually be a thorn in the sides of the Japanese, but without sufficient planes, it could not destroy all of the troopships. Little by little, as more Japanese troops landed, they pushed the united island defenders back from the coastline.

On December 23$^{rd}$, my new regiment was officially named the 515$^{th}$ CA (Antiaircraft). Now with two antiaircraft regiments (which together constituted a brigade), some promotions were in order. Colonel Sage became a one-star general. Peck and Luikart, the two lieutenant colonels who were originally in the 200$^{th}$ CA (Antiaircraft), were promoted to full colonels. Two majors became lieutenant colonels and some captains became majors.

To deter Japanese bombing of Manila, MacArthur decided to declare it an "open city." In other words, Manila would not be defended. With this proclamation, MacArthur hoped to preclude the destruction of a city that he loved. All of our troops started moving out of Manila, with instructions to head for Bataan.

Shortly after Christmas, we evacuated Manila in the dark of night. A mass exodus occurred as trucks and troops moved out. Within at least twelve hours, no American or native troops were to be in Manila. As my last official act in the Walled City, I went to the Quartermaster Supply Depot to draw a large order of canned goods. Since we were going out in the field, to Bataan, we did not know when we would be able to get another meal. With a vehicle at my disposal, I felt I should be prepared for any eventuality in the matter of food. I thought that we should have some back-up supplies in case we had to miss a meal or two. The supply depot, however, absolutely refused to issue me any food without a requisition or orders. This big supply warehouse was full of food. There was no way the military could get rid of it all. There was absolutely no reason why it could not put out any canned goods, other than old Army regulations that demanded a piece of paper. Even though the military was going to move out the next morning, and leave everything behind, the supply depot refused to budge an inch. I am sure the Filipinos were able to salvage what was left.

Although I was unsuccessful in procuring a large amount of goods, I did manage to avail myself of one case of peaches. With the fruit, my personal belongings, and a safe containing the Battalion's papers, the Headquarters' office was soon loaded up. I had been left behind with a jeep to bring up the rear with whatever scattered Battalion personnel and personal belongings was left. Off we went on another excursion.

# 13

# Bataan

On December 28th we finally made our way to Bataan and to milepost 138.5 (actually, kilometer post 138.5) that was our assigned Battalion Headquarters. We were not very far into the Bataan peninsula that was north and west of Manila. The southern tip of Bataan, across the bay from that city, was just about even with Manila. The island of Corregidor was a few kilometers south of Bataan. Off of the southern side of Corregidor stood two, small fortified islands, Fort Mills and Fort Drum. The peninsula had been selected as the line of defense because there was only one road in and out of Bataan. It was on the eastern side of the peninsula, next to the western side of Manila Bay. The Pacific Ocean stood just a few kilometers west of the road. Nothing but mountain and jungle, uninhabitable and practically impenetrable, stood between the ocean and the road. Our objective in this position was to help defend Bataan Field, one of two small airfields carved out of the jungle.

Meanwhile, the Japanese pushed their offensive south from Lingayen. They had also landed on the eastern side of Luzon, below Manila, and were making their way towards that city. From their airplanes, the Japanese could see American and Filipino forces moving from all directions into Bataan. Our various units were gradually pushed back, but they were able to delay the Japanese long enough so that all of the American and Island troops could enter Bataan. Our defenses were so shot up that elements of the 200th guarded the last bridge into the peninsula until all of our troops made it to the safety of that area. After the last elements made it safely over the bridge, engineers blew it up. That gave us a few days to prepare for the defense of the peninsula.

Even as we made our way into Bataan, I had not really experienced war. With the bombing and strafing, I will admit that at times I was scared, but I did not yet really know what war was. Certainly, I would not be too critical of a person who was afraid of all of the noise, the bombs, or the whine of the bullets slapping through the jungle. While I was frightened, I felt my Maker was going to take care of me. I would categorize myself as an average soldier, one who did not take foolish chances. I performed my duties and certainly did not see myself as a hero.

Out at the gun emplacements, the war was separating the men from the boys, with a lot of surprises as to who the men were. To my great surprise and shock, a few of the spit and polish, hardnosed sergeants were the first in the bomb shelter or the first to hide under a tree. Not all of the non-coms were poor soldiers when under fire, but surprisingly, enough were. Some of the officers also fell into this category. On the other hand, some of the biggest goof offs proved to be the best wartime soldiers. One man in particular, Corporal Wolfenbarger, a member of Battery E, had not even been trained in the use of the .50-caliber machine guns, but when the regular gunner hit the dugout, this man stepped in the cradle of the gun and started firing at the staffers who flew over Clark Field.

These .50-caliber antiaircraft guns had a cradle shaped like a question mark attached to the gun. To get into the cradle, a man had to lean back to elevate the muzzle of the weapon. When a target entered the crosshairs, the gun would be fired. The soldier operating the gun had to take into consideration the elevation of the weapon as well as the height of the target and its speed. Corporal Wolfenbarger would shout, "Hey, this is fun, the most fun I have had in a long time." He just kept shooting and shooting. All of us on Bataan, in these early weeks of the war, were implementing a war plan drawn up years before.

Military strategists had devised War Plan Orange in the early 1930s to defend the Philippines, in particular Luzon. Should an enemy succeed in landing troops on the island that American forces could not repulse, the military would withdraw into Bataan. With sufficient supplies, medicine, ammunition, and food, the peninsula could be held for at least six months, until aid reached the islands. In theory, it was a good plan. But the brass had counted on one more year before the enemy attacked the Philippines. The consensus in Washington and in Manila was that, with an additional year of preparation, the islands could be defended without any problems. This would be especially true with the arrival of more planes, Army personnel, and Naval ships. This, therefore, was the reasoning behind the move into Bataan of the entire military based on Luzon.

Logistically, it proved to be a nightmare getting all of the scattered men onto that strip of land. While that was happening, military forces delayed the Japanese who had landed on the eastern coast of Luzon below Manila. Others fought to preclude enemy landings in the north and northeastern parts of the island. All of this gave the main military force time to withdraw into Bataan.

To add to the confusion, many, many civilian Filipinos followed the troops onto the peninsula. A large number of these people, no doubt, were family members of the men in the Philippine Army, Constabulary, or the Scouts. I am sure that the soldiers who protected the last bridge into Bataan would not have been given any orders to stop the influx of civilians. There were good and bad aspects to the civilians being in such close proximity to the bombing, the strafing, and the hand-to-hand combat.

I personally did not shoot any weapons during this time. I occupied myself with administrative duties and taking care that the daily bombings did not find me. After a few weeks, when the Japanese finally started their push against American defenses, on January 2$^{nd}$ our headquarters moved further south to KP 150 because the front line was too close for comfort and soldiers in my unit were not supposed to be on the front line.

Down the middle of Bataan, running north and south, stood a range of mountains. A decent, paved road had been carved out on the eastern side of Bataan; it ran the full-length of the peninsula. On the western side of Bataan, a very poor road covered a short distance; it lead to a somewhat better road that extended slightly over halfway up the peninsula. In the middle of Bataan, there was only one road; it ran east to west. Thick jungle covered the entire area. Two small airfields, Bataan and Cabcaben, had been partially leveled out for use by what few light planes we had left. These airfields were on the bay side of Bataan. We ended up between these two dirt airfields.

About three weeks later, on the 26$^{th}$, we moved further south to KP 161.5 where our guns protected Cabcaben, the more southern of the two airfields. Most of the time the antiaircraft guns were not too busy. There were daily bombing runs by enemy planes, both light and heavy bombers. We always went to the shelters even though we were never sure if the enemy's target was Bataan or Corregidor. The planes flew too high for our 3-inch guns. The strafers and spotters proved to be more of a nuisance than a threat because their accuracy was so poor. There was not much left of our Air Force. The planes themselves were gradually self-destructing since the pilots damaged them on takeoffs and landings due to the conditions of the airfields. What we had left operated out of these two makeshift fields.

Someone had the brilliant idea to hook radar up to the 3-inch antiaircraft guns. The plan was then to zero in on enemy planes during the nightly raids, knocking them down. Rumor had it that the first time this idea was put into action, the guns did hit a plane but the cables between the guns and the radar were too short. The concussion from the guns put the radar out of action forever.

By holding off the Japanese, we were, in effect, stopping them from using Manila Bay as a military staging area. Corregidor was heavily fortified, but the majority of its guns were pointed west to defend the bay. There was no problem keeping the invaders out of Manila Bay, and that meant that it took the Japanese much longer to seize the Philippines.

As I recall, we had approximately 10,000 American troops and possibly 12,000 Philippine Scouts (both infantry and cavalry). In addition, there must have been about 60,000 Philippine Army and Constabulary forces. The Constabulary had been organized more as a police force than as a military one, and as I mentioned earlier, both the Philippine Army and Constabulary had very little military training. Both had been rushed into service because of military needs. While their intentions were excellent, in most instances their abilities were next to zero.

The American defenders consisted of displaced Navy and Air Force forces as well as one regiment of trained infantry, the 31st Infantry. We also had two anti-tank battalions (the 192nd Battalion and the 194th Battalion) that had been National Guard units, as had the two antiaircraft regiments. The remaining forces were made up of engineers, air warning units, the medical staff, and other peripheral units.

Of course, as in most wars, comfort was non-existent. For all practical purposes, we camped out from when the war started early in December until a few weeks after the battle for Bataan was over in April. Our first camp on Bataan was near Pilar, the second near Bataan Field, and the third near Cabcaben Field. We thought we were in good shape if we could scavenge a cot or mosquito net. If our sleeping accommodations were not rough enough, we had been in Bataan for just a little over a week when our rations were cut in half.

The first priority of the USAFE (United States Army Far East) seemed to be to hold off the Japanese as long as it could to forestall the enemy's advance south. Australia, especially, was in danger. Japan had already seized Hong Kong and the Singapore area. On Bataan, we heard daily rumors that help was on the way. Someone always had a radio and with it we listened to San Francisco, a Manila station, and even one in Tokyo that featured Tokyo Rose. She talked about our girlfriends and wives. Because of the source, however, we could not always believe what we heard about the progress of the war from either the Manila or from the Tokyo radio station. We also received a daily dose of propaganda, urging us to surrender, from leaflets dropped by a small enemy plane. Apparently our holding action did not prevent the Japanese from going down the Malay Peninsula and on to Singapore. We knew little as to what was happening in the rest of the world.

Within a month after our rations had been cut in half, they were decreased again, this time by another half. We were, therefore, on quarter-rations. Rumors circulated about how well the troops on Corregidor ate. Some submarines had been able to run the enemy blockade to bring supplies to that island. We never knew if what had been brought in was shared with men on Bataan. I think morale reached its lowest point when we heard that Washington had ordered MacArthur to Australia. His wife and son, of course, accompanied him. We were not against the decision that they should go, but the departure of the general's staff and the President of the Philippines was a different matter.

As I mentioned earlier, the influx of civilians to the peninsula, before Bataan was sealed off, proved to be a little thorn in our side. It meant less food for the military but there was a positive aspect to their presence. Quite a few of the civilian women set up little cafes where they sold some food, mainly hotcakes. For topping, the women sometimes used sweetened, condensed milk. We found out, however, that too much of that resulted in diarrhea. They also used chocolate syrup, made from sugar and a coloring, as a topping.

While observing the women, we noticed they had a strange method of smoking. They used long, thin, dark brown cigarettes, but after tapping off the ash, they stuck the burning end of the cigarette in their mouth. Of course we had to try that, too, and it did warm our mouth. All of the women wore long dresses, ones that did not quite touch the ground. About half of them had babies on their backs. One day while we were talking with several of the women, trying to buy food from them, one woman squatted down. She continued to smoke and talk to us. In a few moments, a little puddle of liquid came rolling down the path. We often wondered what happened to all of the civilians, especially the women and children.

Once we started running out of food, we first ate horses and cavalry mules. Horses' oats and some carabao followed, but few of those animals were left since the men had already been eating them. Some individuals captured iguanas, which were supposed to taste good, and snakes, but I was not lucky enough to have any of those two items come my way.

After the initial push by the Japanese Army, in which we lost some ground, a lull occurred in the fighting. This push had lasted for about six weeks. The lull was apparently due to the Japanese bringing in more troops to try to finish us off. It was not completely quiet, though. Some skirmishes occurred, but the fighting was limited. During that period, as I mentioned earlier, we went from full rations to half rations and then to quarter rations. At the same time, we were rapidly depleting our medical supplies. Two hospitals had been established in the jungle. During the first phase of the fighting, the hospitals were able to take care of the wounded. During the lull in ground fighting, however, from about the middle of February to the first week in April, the hospitals started filling up with men suffering from malaria, dysentery, dengue fever, diarrhea, and malnutrition.

It was about this time that the two New Mexico National Guard regiments and their draftees were notified that so-called "battlefield promotions" could be recommended for about thirty men. I write this tongue-in-cheek since, with the exception of hiding from the bomb drops and strafing, none of us had really seen any hand-to-hand combat or front line duty, although some members of our regiments nearest the front lines did occasionally experience a few sniper problems from Japanese soldiers who had infiltrated our area.

I think promotions for those thirty men began with an elevated rank of no lower than a three-stripe sergeant. As it turned out, I was designated to become a second lieutenant. In the latter part of March, the two regiments received the authority to promote fifteen on the list; the other fifteen were to be promoted after the first of April. My name was on that second list for April. As it turned out, circumstances that month did not permit the last fifteen to be promoted. Again, was fate for me or against me? We can only wait to see the outcome on the final day of the war. The spider's threads are pulling me even closer to my fate, into the web.

Up to this point, my life during the war could have turned out very differently if I had just made some different decisions. There had been more than one opportunity to change what became my destiny. I could have taken R.O.T.C. in college; I would have thus entered the Army as an officer. Instead of joining the Clovis National Guard as a private, I could have waited to be drafted and then apply for a deferment because of my work on the railroad. At Fort Bliss, I had opportunities to join the Roswell National Guard that ended up in Europe, to transfer to the Tow Target detachment that went to Africa, or I could have pursued a transfer to the Air Corps. While at Fort Bliss, I also could have been promoted to Battalion Sergeant Major. While in Bataan, I might have been in that first promotion group and thus I would have become a second lieutenant in March.

But if I had tried to become an officer at the very beginning of my military service, there was no guarantee that I would have been accepted into the R.O.T.C. program and that I would not have washed out. I would have also lost track of friends who were enlisted men. While the deferment might have been possible, I did not want to give up my plan to become a soldier and a hero. The opportunities for transfer at Fort Bliss did not necessarily mean I would have survived military service in either Europe or Africa. As for the Air Corps, while I had always wanted to fly, I also was susceptible to motion sickness; additionally, I really did not try to lose weight as the doctor had wanted me to and return for another weigh-in. As for promotions either in Texas or on Bataan, as an officer I would have had an easier time as a prisoner of war since the Japanese required very few officers to work. But I also might have been sent to Japan at a different time than I was, and on a different ship, perhaps one of the vessels that were bombed or sunk en route to Japan. I could have been lost at sea. A different path would have changed not only my life during the war but also the rest of my life, for better or worse.

In spite of these considerations, I found myself on Bataan as a non-com, one of over ten thousand Americans trying to hold back the Japanese. Probably one of the good things about the enemy's invasion, and I am sure it was premeditated, was that we were in the middle of the seasonal dry spell in the Philippines. In anticipation of the approaching wet season, we started building bamboo cabins behind and below Cabcaben airfield. We began from scratch, cutting down, for our corner posts, bamboo that measured about four inches in diameter. We used smaller bamboo for each succeeding step. The cabins were functional but not insulated; they resembled the many houses or shacks we had seen in the countryside. We even whittled down some bamboo to use as nails. Only one-story high, we built the cabins up, off the ground to allow the rains to take over what would have been the first floor. Four or six men would sleep in what we hoped would be nice, waterproof shelters. The roofs were made of native grass. Since we did not have any caulking, we split bamboo to fit between each upright. While the cabins were not airtight, I am sure they would have been reasonably waterproof.

Because Headquarters dealt with administrative matters, we did not have much to do between January and April except to mark time. We played cards and ran for cover when the enemy bombed or strafed us. I do not recall any of our men being killed until April. We were not too far behind the lines, but we were far enough to just hear the big guns, not see them. The brass notified us whenever any of our planes took off from the two fields so we would be on the alert until their return since some Japanese planes might follow them home. We did see some Filipinos killed by bombs.

Even those of us who were not actually on the lines felt the effects when our rations were cut. Bud and I left camp, trying to find some civilians with food for sale. While he and I did not eat any iguanas or snakes, other men were lucky enough to kill this wild game. Some of the iguanas measured four or five feet in length and they had quite a bit of meat on them. Soldiers in the Quartermaster unit killed cavalry horses, mules, and carabao, but by the time portions were distributed to other units, the additional food made little difference. By the time the war was over for us early in April, we were on one-eighth ration.

We were running out of other essential items aside from food, such as medicine and ammunition. Water, while not plentiful, was sufficient, but it was chlorinated and in Lister Bags. We kept our canteens full and hoped we would not get sick from the water. When MacArthur left for Australia in the middle of March, we felt as if we were being left to be slaughtered. Many of the men were extremely upset at his departure while others did not think it made any difference who was in charge. We were still starving and running out of nearly everything.

The Japanese hit us again in the first week of April, this time hard. They had large numbers of fully equipped, fresh troops. They were sincere in their desire to finish us off. We had very little information available to us, regardless of what unit we were in. Communications were very poor. All we knew deep in the jungle was that there was a great amount of activity going on, and within a few days we were well aware of the fighting because of the noise level. As to our regiment's antiaircraft duties, we had more targets to fire at because of increased bombing runs by the Japanese. The enemy dropped more and more propaganda leaflets that suggested we surrender. This, of course, was out of the question. In fact, MacArthur had ordered his successor to fight to the finish. Apparently, Wainwright was going to comply. He and about ten thousand men, though, were on Corregidor and thus would not be affected by what happened on Bataan, at least not right away.

Just after our evening meal on April 8th, we received orders to destroy all of our big guns that could not be lowered to the point where they could fire point blank at the enemy. Using our 3-inch antiaircraft guns, our 37 mm guns, and .50-caliber machine guns, we were to form a last line of resistance, extending inland into the jungle, just above Cabcaben Field. Later we found out that we were to be the last line of resistance. Our group was assigned a position west of our Headquarters. We had a clear view of the valley we overlooked. Major Shurtz was the only officer with our group. I was the ranking non-com. We spent the entire night overlooking the valley. With the gradual coming of daylight, we still had not seen the enemy, or even anything that moved.

Come daylight, the Major told me that he was going to go ahead of the line to see if he could spot any resistance for us. He left me in charge. We waited patiently, without any sign of the Major, until about 10 am. We did see, in the distance, a Japanese tank coming down the trail with soldiers riding on the outside of it. A runner eventually arrived at our position to inform us that General Edward P. King had surrendered the entire Bataan forces. We were to return to our campsite for further orders. I stayed, however, to await the return of Major Shurtz. I remained at our post on the line until a runner came from camp to tell me that we were all to gather on Cabcaben Field by noon. Before leaving, I composed a short note and posted it in a conspicuous place in case the major returned. Then I followed the runner to camp.

# 14

# Surrender(ed)

Once back in camp, I could not find my knapsack. What disturbed me the most was that among the personal items I had lost was a Bible. I had received it as a Christmas gift from my parents when I was twelve years old. I learned of orders the men had received to stack in a pile all arms and possessions we could not carry. After a short, unsuccessful search for my knapsack, I finally had to take one from that pile. The knapsack had no name on it. It contained only a mess kit, utensils, and a few personal items. To safeguard as best I could some of my remaining belongings, I buried my college ring with a Masonic emblem inscribed on the ruby setting, a good pen and pencil set, and a few other items I did not want the Japanese to have. I used a glass jar and put it in a place that would be easy to find when I had the opportunity to return. As it turned out, I never did go back and even if I had, I would not know where to look if I had returned to that general area.

MacArthur ordered Generals Wainwright and King to fight to the last man. It should be noted that we did not surrender. General King surrendered us, the men on Bataan. He felt that in our condition (short of food, medicine, and ammunition), further fighting would only mean losing many more men. King believed that in spite of his orders, it was only a matter of a few days, during which time many more men would be killed, before we would all be wiped out. Under ordinary circumstances, it was probably the correct decision because no aid was available, at that time or even in the distant future. I am sure that if the men had voted on the issue, there would not have been a surrender. But we ordinary soldiers did not know the true situation. General King was right even though he was probably unaware of the Japanese Bushido training that we would face. This centuries-old doctrine dictated that the Japanese would commit suicide before they would ever allow themselves to be taken prisoner. That Bushido belief would be such an affliction on us.

The American and Filipino forces had been ordered to Cabcaben Field for the surrender. Bud and I joined other men who left the camp. We walked down to the road that led from Mariveles to Cabcaben. (Mariveles was on the southern tip of Bataan where only a few kilometers of water separated the peninsula from Corregidor.) Filipinos, also heading to Mariveles, crowded the road. All of these men were from the native Army and Constabulary. They were without weapons. As I mentioned earlier, Filipinos had very, very little training and they also were undisciplined. They had little heart for war, even to protect their own country. Most were without shoes, many with the footwear tied together around their neck. The Filipinos were more accustomed to going barefoot than to wear the heavy, Army-issue shoes.

Bucking the incoming traffic, it took us a little longer than it normally would have to reach Cabcaben Field. Once there, the area appeared to be almost full of Americans who sat on the ground, jammed together in rows. Japanese soldiers met us and herded us onto the field. Within a few minutes we were about three or four rows from the front of the large group that nearly filled the field. We faced Manila Bay and the road. At each corner of these several hundred men, Japanese guards stood watch, armed with a machine gun. Each time a man stood up to stretch his legs, the enemy soldiers would lower the muzzle of their gun and start to shout. What was being said did not make any sense to us since we did not know the language, although we well understood the language of the guns. After we sat for over an hour in the hot sun, a Japanese officer stood in front of us and yelled. No doubt he was delivering a speech. We continued to sit in the tropical sun as the guards shouted at us. No one seemed to know what to do with us.

We were amazed at our first sight of the enemy. The majority seemed to be short, clothed in good uniforms with strange caps, ones that we later wished we had. The caps were somewhat like today's golf or baseball cap, with at least three flaps attached to the cap to ward the sun off of their neck. The Japanese soldiers all carried rifles with fixed bayonets, which in many cases then made the weapons taller than the soldier. The officers we saw usually wore a sword; as the rank increased, so did the length of the sword.

What were our feelings? They were certainly mixed—anger, bewilderment, disgust, anxiety. We also recognized, with a twisted amusement, the irony that this could happen to us, the American Army. Soon other feelings surfaced—fear, a lack of confidence that we would be rescued, and a dread of the future. All of us were now caught in the web. Later, as we tried to figure out how we should act and react to our new situation, it felt as though we were stepping on eggs.

After another hour, because of the heat, we were all ready

to lie down. We were also running out of water. Suddenly, though, from a little north of Cabcaben Air Field, some field guns fired over our heads towards Corregidor. After several rounds, Corregidor replied. The first round fell short of hitting a target. The second one, however, hit one of the machine gun emplacements, eliminating a few of the Japanese guards. Seeing an opportunity to get out of the line of fire, we all started to get up and run, but a burst of fire from the remaining machine guns convinced us to remain in our seats. After a few more rounds were exchanged, including one from Corregidor that hit another machine gun group, we all, including some of the Japanese soldiers, started running from the field, up the road. The road proved more bearable in the heat of the day than the field had been since trees partially shaded the road.

Our walk became a dangerous one, though. If a Japanese saw a watch, a ring, or even a pair of glasses on one of us, the enemy soldier slapped the man around and grabbed whatever they wanted. These guards were frontline soldiers and they were not at all patient with the Americans. They would strike us with their rifle butt or act as though they were going to stick us with a bayonet. We soon recognized that we were not going to be treated with any respect. We could not gauge how we were to act. Sometimes a Japanese officer shouted at his men because the march south was being delayed due to the congestion on the road. The next minute an officer would strip an American of a possession he wanted.

Because of where Bud and I had been sitting on the Cabcaben Field, we were more or less in the vanguard of the group. No more than fifty men were in front of us. Looking behind us, all that Bud and I could see were Americans marching north and Japanese marching south. It was late in the afternoon and I had not eaten since the previous night. In addition to being hungry, I soon felt as though I was becoming dehydrated. Finally a large group of trucks came from the south, catching up with my group of about two hundred men. After quite a bit of jabbering, the Japanese made us climb into the vehicles, much to our relief.

As we rode north, Bud and I felt as though our luck was improving. The two of us stood in the front of the truck's bed, up against the cab. Japanese soldiers walking south hit and slapped the prisoners who were standing or sitting on the left side of the truck. Because of where Bud and I were, those same soldiers could not reach us. Looking ahead, I spotted a Japanese, who stood taller than most, walking toward us carrying a bottle of San Miguel beer. I had left my good wristwatch home in Clovis, carrying instead a one-dollar, Westclock pocket watch. Without thinking of the consequences, I pulled it out. As we passed by the Japanese, I grabbed his beer and held out my watch, which he quickly seized. I am not sure which of us was the happier one. The Japanese looked back at me and waved, so I guess he was not mad. As for me, I was grateful to get something to drink. I knocked the cap off of the bottle and shared the warm beer with Bud. Since we were both out of water, the beer tasted good. Just before dark, the guards ordered us off the truck. They herded us into an enclosure with a roof. A wire fence and guards surrounded it. We spent the night there, without food, although we were allowed to fill our canteens with water.

I would like to regress a week, before we were surrendered. By that time, we had been on Bataan for a little over three months. The physical condition of all the men was very poor. I had found some scales somewhere and was surprised to see that I had lost twenty-three pounds during our time on the peninsula. I weighed one hundred and seventy pounds. While I had not contracted malaria, I had suffered bouts of dysentery, diarrhea, and scurvy (vitamin deficiencies). Most of the men were in as bad a shape as I was in. Many were in much worse shape, especially those who had been on the front lines since they had not always been able to get their meals.

Both of the hospitals had been full at the time of the surrender. Two weeks before that day, I had visited the church at Hospital No. 2 where I felt disconcerted by the looks of the men in the wards. Very few of them were wounded. Nearly all of them were sick. Additionally, the hospital and the regimental doctors, along with the medical staff, did not have much in the way of medication. In fact, a man had to be admitted to a hospital in order to obtain medication, what little was available. In addition to these woes, the entire peninsula was running out of ammunition of all kinds. The shells we had for the 3-inch guns were 1918 vintage, and they could not reach the height the big, enemy bombers came in at. While we did not realize it at the time, we wore outdated helmets and uniforms. The "new" Army had better helmets and spiffier clothes.

What I am trying to say is that if we had had more food, there would not have been as much illness. Had we had more ammunition, we would not have had to ration our firing, and maybe we could have held out longer. Equally important, if we had been in better shape, the surrender and subsequent events would not have been as rough on the men.

Malaria especially took its toll since there was a limited supply of quinine. There were also not enough mosquito nets for every man. Malaria especially weakened the condition of the men on the front line; by the time of the last push by the Japanese, most units were down to half strength. How can you win a war under those conditions?

During the day and night proceeding the surrender, there was an enormous amount of loud activity. Orders had been given to blow up what little reserve we had of gasoline and ammunition. Weapons were to be destroyed. To make matters worse, a heavy earthquake in the mountains of Bataan occurred the night before the surrender. This, coupled with the fires from blowing up the dumps, created an unreal experience for us all.

One of the good things to come out of the surrender was that all of the nurses and many of the doctors were transported to Corregidor. A great number of able-bodied men also made it to that island.

As to our feelings about the surrender, I am sure that each man had his own thoughts and opinions. Certainly many felt disgusted with Uncle Sam. He got us into this position and then left us in it. There was also anger and bewilderment, but I do not remember feeling fear, terror, anxiety, or dread. There was also a feeling of excitement because of the unknown. Had we realized what was ahead of us, our feelings would have been very different.

Since we did not understand Japanese, and the guards did not speak English, in retrospect I guess we were lucky things were not worse than they were. The guards displayed a very superior attitude, and with the language barrier, they treated us very badly. It was quite nerve racking as we tried to deal with our needs or wants while at the same time complying with the demands of the guards.

On the morning of April 10$^{th}$, the Japanese gave each of us a ball of cooked rice. We were allowed to use what toilet facilities were available. The guards directed us to trucks and we headed north. Once again, the ride was a hassle with opposing traffic, Japanese soldiers marching towards Mariveles, and other trucks going south. When they had the opportunity, the enemy continued to shake us down, looking for valuables.

Every time we went through a little village, crowds of Filipinos lined the road. They waved or gave us a victory sign, although many were disappointed in the outcome of the conflict. As we drove through Angeles, Bud and I saw our bunk boy from Fort Stotsenberg. He waved at us and tried to give us some food, but the guards pushed him away. We reached San Fernando shortly before noon and were unloaded next to a string of railroad cars.

Japanese soldiers, whose other duties were to keep the local people from giving us food or water, heavily guarded us. The guards finally motioned us to get into the boxcars.

As we tried to limit the number of men in each car, enemy soldiers very rudely overruled us. The car Bud and I were in was so full that a person could not fall down; the closeness of the other men held him up. This was really the second part of hell. (The first part had been the beginning of what later became known as the Bataan Death March.) Men suffered from the effects of diarrhea or dysentery. They could not help themselves, and no one could help them. With the sun's heat beating down on the metal boxcars, the stench from the sick men was unbearable. The only good to come out of this experience was that the sick men could not fall down into their own droppings.

Finally we were unloaded in Capas. When the door opened, the guards quickly backed away, holding their nose and putting little masks over their face. As we unloaded, we had to drag several men out of the boxcar. They had fallen once they had the room to do so. In most cases, the fresh air revived them. A few deaths did result from the condition of the men and the train ride.

Our respite proved short-lived. The guards lined us up in a rag-tag order and began marching us. We did not know our destination and cared less what it was. We were so dreadfully in need of food and water. We were starving and, with few exceptions, we had no water at all. In my case, I had had only a small rice ball in the last forty-five hours. Some of the men were in better shape than I was in, but at the same time I was better off than many others. Bud had never been a heavily built man. With his weight loss, and with the sun beating down on us, he was in bad shape.

To give everyone credit, we all tried to help each other, especially those from the same unit and those who were with friends. We were a mixed up group. The two hundred or so soldiers came from at least fifteen different units. No man was on his own, however. If a man fell during the march, someone next to him would help him. The four-hour train ride had certainly drained many of the men.

The treatment on the march from Capas was brutal. To make us move faster, guards shouted at us and hit us with a rifle or sword. As I mentioned earlier, swords were a mark of rank. The longer the sword, the higher the rank. We found out on the march that someone of a higher rank could just as easily use his sword on a Japanese of lower rank as he would on us.

After a march of what we later learned was eight kilometers, we came to a big clearing. Guards instructed us to line up in some semblance of order. At this point we received our first formal shakedown. They searched us individually. While the Japanese had taken possessions from us before, we had never been thoroughly searched.

As this was happening, occasionally the enemy soldiers took one of our men out of the group and made him stand at attention some fifty feet away from the rest of us. As the search ended, a group of about ten had been pulled out of the ranks and separated from the larger group. Suddenly the guards shot and killed each of the ten men.

I was shocked because I did not know why they had been shot. Within a few minutes, word spread that these men had had in their possession something of Japanese origin. The enemy presumed that if one of us had such an item, we had acquired it after killing one of their soldiers. I was certainly glad that the only thing I had from a Japanese was a beer that Bud and I had quickly downed. Major Schultz from our Regiment had been one of the men killed in this incident. He apparently had some Japanese cigarettes. A kind-hearted guard had given it to him, a gift from one officer to another.

After this incident, the enemy lined us up again and marched us around a group of trees to our destination, Camp O'Donnell. The spider's net had become much large, with many more caught in the web. The spider had already taken at least ten.

# 15

# O'Donnell

After the enemy had finished their shakedown, and had shot Americans who possessed Japanese items, they led us into Camp O'Donnell. The majority of the men were just about gone, including me. I had been without a head covering for the past two days as the sun beat down on us. I was about to have a sunstroke. Quite a few others also did not have any head covering. All of us were in desperate need of water. We did not get any at this time, however. As we soon learned, the Japanese were either very unorganized or their own soldiers stood in formation for long periods of time to impress upon the men the importance of what was to follow.

Finally, after at least thirty minutes (it was probably closer to an hour), a Japanese soldier, in his native language, called us to attention. Of course, we had no idea of what the command was. But with a little coaching from the guards, who used their bayonet and rifle butt on us, we understood that we were to come to attention. What a ragged-type of attention it was, though.

After a few long minutes, a high-ranking Japanese officer came out of a building, climbed on a platform, and started to deliver a speech. As best we could understand from the interpreter, however, it was more of a harangue and a series of disconnected threats. To whittle down an extremely long speech, we were told that we were not "Prisoners of War" but "Captives." As such, we would not be given any benefits due POWs under the Geneva Convention protocol signed by most countries after World War I. We were their slaves, the officer explained. He also told us that we would never again see our homes. As you can well imagine, this proved very disconcerting to all of us. We laughed to ourselves about not returning home, but we later realized that his statement was closer to the truth than any of us could have imagined on that day at O'Donnell. The interpreter also informed us that we would now work for the "Greater East Asia Co-Prosperity Sphere." We were to do our utmost to cooperate.

What no one had explained to us was how the Japanese viewed prisoners of war. They did not believe in allowing themselves to be captured. They would kill themselves before such a disgrace would befall them. The Japanese had no compassion for anyone who allowed himself to be captured. Their Code of Bushido condemned such an occurrence. But we did not realize all of this that day. All we knew was that the enemy was not treating us as we felt they should. They gave us no food or water, for example, and mistreated our men. At this point, despair really set in. After this long speech, the Japanese officer dismissed us and we were allowed to sit down. Something had been said about this camp being our home. We did not understand every word that had been spoken to us, but bit-by-bit, we tried to put it all together. In most instances, the interpreters were not too good at their job. With few exceptions, each one bragged about attending a college somewhere in the United States, such as the University of Southern California, Harvard, or the University of California. Overall, their English left much to be desired. We had great difficulty understanding them.

Once we were dismissed, the first thing many of us did was to get into the water line. At this time, only one spigot dispensed water. It came out in a very slow stream, really little more than a trickle. I finally worked my way up to the front of the line where the guards allowed me to get some water, but it was only half of a canteen cup. I shared this with Bud. After resting a little, I got back in line again. The Japanese assigned us to barracks and the ranking American officer in the camp tried to get some type of organization established. I do not think we received any food that night.

We found the Japanese to be a strange people, especially when compared to us. Regardless of the race or color of Americans, or their national origin, the Japanese cannot be likened in any way to an American, not in language, religion, customs, dress, or fanaticism. The manner in which their military operated may have been, in some degree, similar to our Table of Organization with a class of officers, non-coms, etc. In most respects, however, we had great difficulty understanding the treatment of Japanese military men by their own Army or Navy.

The lowest soldier or sailor really took the brunt of the caste system. A person of higher rank could treat him like a dog. This continued with each successive step up the ladder. The man of lower military rank could be slapped or knocked down. He could also be hit with a rifle, a short sword, or a long saber. That lowly person could only submit and bow to the superior. This continued up through the highest ranks. There was quite a jump in the punishment a man of extremely high rank could decree for a lower ranking officer. Instead of being slapped or knocked around, the disgraced subordinate could be required to disembowel himself.

As for us, we were required to bow from the waist to any Japanese, regardless of his rank. I am sure you cannot believe an American would bow to any man. We might, if social rules require it, bow to a lady as a sign of respect to her standing or age, but to bow to a man, especially if he were shorter in stature, no, that would never happen. As prisoners of war, if we failed to bow, we were knocked to the ground. This happened several times until we understood the order to do so. I might interject that many a man bowed as required, but as he did so, he spoke in a low voice, commenting on the heritage of the Japanese to whom we were required to bow.

In these early days as prisoners, we saw that the Japanese soldiers were apparently as surprised as we were when the surrender took place. For us, it was a complete shock when we were surrendered. We had not been prepared for that turn of events. Our superiors had not indoctrinated us in any way except with the old fashioned instructions that you can read in any fictional book on war—give only your name, rank, and serial number. After a few months as prisoners, it did not seem necessary to withhold most of the information the Japanese asked us for. But we rarely told the whole truth.

One thing we quickly learned was that to the Japanese, if a soldier drove a truck, he was also a mechanic. Since nearly all Americans could drive, many jumped at the chance to drive a truck for our captors. Unfortunately, the trucks were usually in very poor shape. If the driver could not repair the vehicle, he would be beaten. If a man was a good mechanic, he ended up becoming a driver, one of the better jobs in camp.

When we first became prisoners, most of the men strongly resisted any attempt to understand the Japanese language. Initially, the gestures used with the order helped us to understand what was expected. For example, when we began what later became known as the Bataan Death March, the Japanese ordered us into columns of men, four abreast. The guards had to hit us with their rifles to get us to understand how they wanted us lined up. They enforced each succeeding order with their rifles, bayonets, or swords.

We were not ready to comply with most orders when the Japanese first took charge of us. Eventually, though, we all learned certain phrases. We knew the words that allowed us to count off in formation. We also learned the words that ordered us to come to attention as well as the ones that dismissed us, and the ones that ordered us to morning roll call, labor, and rest. Of course, the Japanese were in the same boat as the Americans and Filipinos. They did not understand our language or customs.

With few exceptions, all of us felt resentment at being required to learn the Japanese language. We did not want to conform and become subservient, to become, in essence, slaves of the winners. With a little experience, we soon learned that the more of their language we could understand, the easier it would be for us to outsmart the Japanese. We did not have to quickly jump in and do what we were ordered to do; instead, we could stretch out any work assigned to us by subterfuge. When under duress, an American can be cunning. This will be apparent as my story unfolds.

The entire experience of being surrendered to a culture as foreign to us as that of the Japanese became a learning experience of an extreme magnitude. What perplexed us so much was the inconsistency of the Japanese. In many instances, one guard would give you a cigarette while another one would knock you down for smoking. I believe that the discipline instilled in the Japanese by their culture created most of the problems. Some of the guards seemed to have empathy for us; they would give an American a cigarette and not fear the wrath of his ranking non-com. Another guard, however, was afraid of his shadow and anticipated being knocked down by his superior if he showed kindness or weakness by being nice to us.

It seemed that the guards shouted and were mad even when they relayed orders to us. Because of the number of men they guarded, they had to shout rather than speak in a normal tone. Often, two or more guards would issue the same order, but one of them might interject additional words, such as calling us *baka*, or crazy. In retrospect, I guess that whenever anyone raises his voice, a foreigner might think the person was angry.

As prisoners, we soon learned that failure to obey an order would, in most instances, result in some degree of brutality. The sooner one complied, the better. But think of what we were confronting as Americans—we were told to bow, and, without question, comply with an order, whether or not it made any sense. A person much shorter than us, a person possessed of an overbearing attitude, gave us such orders.

Those of us who were in this first group to arrive in O'Donnell did not really participate to any great degree in the Death March. We did walk a few miles and were assaulted by the frontline enemy troops as they proceeded south and we headed north. Considering our physical condition after months of war, the lack of food and water on our trip north was hard on us. In comparison to what happened to the rest of the men who endured the Death March, however, our journey to O'Donnell was a cakewalk.

We soon found out why the Japanese had rushed us to O'Donnell. We were to get it ready for the rest of the men. Originally, the camp was to have been an installation for the Filipinos inducted into their military service. In April of 1942, O'Donnell was only partially finished. The grounds had not been completely fenced and sanitary facilities were not in place. Only one water faucet was operational. Soon our officers created a Table of Organization. With specific duties assigned to the men, work began on the camp. I had not eaten for days. The night before we had been surrendered, I had a dinner, but on the actual day of the surrender, I went without breakfast, lunch, and dinner. The day after that, I ate nothing until the evening. Late in the morning on the day we arrived at O'Donnell, the Japanese finally served us breakfast. It resembled a rice gruel. Our only other meal that day was a small ration of steamed rice.

Twenty-four hours after we arrived, another group walked in. Like our detail, they numbered about two hundred men. They were to help us get the camp ready for the men arriving from Bataan. This second group had walked a little further than we had before the Japanese had picked them up in trucks returning from the front. The enemy treated them in the same way they had treated us. The second group also endured the terrible train trip north, the final eight-kilometer walk, and the shakedown as guards looked for Americans who possessed something of Japanese origin. Such men were promptly executed.

In respect to the first two hundred men who arrived at O'Donnell, the majority was from the 200th and 515th Regiments of the New Mexico National Guard because these units were near Cabcaben Airfield. We had all been sitting together on the field when the shelling had begun, and we had all run in the same direction to escape it.

At the time we had been surrendered, the Japanese had not realized the large number of military men who were on Bataan, nor had they been aware of how many civilians were on the peninsula. They also had not known that we were practically out of ammunition, medicine, and food. The Japanese had not been prepared to handle so many men who were in such poor physical condition. This ignorance, combined with bushido, their military code that trained them never to surrender, made the enemy see us as unworthy of assistance or care. I suspect that their attitude towards us helped to create the problems we encountered during our years as prisoners of war. Certainly, the Japanese showed no respect for us.

Of course, those of us already at Camp O'Donnell had no knowledge of what was happening to the remainder of our forces on Bataan. In the following week, we expected everyday to see more men arrive, but none came. We came to believe that they were being sent to other camps. Finally, eight days after we had first arrived at O'Donnell, a large number of men straggled in. They were in terrible physical condition.

# 16

# The Bataan Death March

Each day another group made its way into Camp O'Donnell. We hardly recognized any of our friends. They arrived as walking dead men—emaciated, dirty, ragged, seemingly sightless, living skeletons. For all intents and purposes, they were zombies. The Japanese had forced approximately 70,000 Americans and Filipinos to walk from Mariveles to San Fernando, a distance of about sixty-five miles. Remember that these men were already half starved. Many were sick with malaria, diarrhea, and dysentery. They now had to walk miles and miles in the hot tropical sun. Many had no headgear, food, or water. The horrors of this one-week journey became known as the Bataan Death March.

One could not conceive how anyone could live through such an experience. We had been in very poor condition upon our arrival. These men were even in a worse state. They had marched strictly on guts and determination. As we were to learn, the lack of water proved to be the greatest problem the men had faced on the march. Their thirst had been compounded by the lack of food and a brutality beyond belief by the Japanese. When a man fell down and could not get up, a fellow American, whether he knew the man or not, would stop and try to help him. A guard could come over to the two men and shoot or bayonet the weaker prisoner before he hit the standing American with that same rifle or bayonet. The desire to help each other extended to both officers and enlisted men. Rank disappeared during the march.

A person can do without food for quite a long time, but not without water. If a man broke ranks to get some precious water, in most instances he would be shot or stuck with a bayonet. Quite a few, who tried to get something to eat or to drink out of a caribou wallow, had their heads cut off. The slaughter of the prisoners was terrible and inhumane. To make matters worse, drinking the filthy water slaked one's thirst, but dysentery from the contaminated water followed, often resulting in death.

The Japanese treated the Filipinos, who they considered lower than the Americans, even worse. Natives along the road who tried to assist both the Americans and their fellow Filipinos were quite often shot. The enemy guards even bayoneted pregnant women.

It will never be known exactly how many men, Americans or Filipinos, were killed on this brutal march. Some became lucky enough to fade into the jungles or to find a hiding place in nearby homes. But in most cases, these prisoners were later found. After a beating, they were taken to the nearest prison camp. If Filipino natives were caught helping a prisoner, they were killed. Of the approximately 10,000 Americans on Bataan, it was estimated that about 8,500 made it to O'Donnell. Of the possible 60,000 Filipinos forces on Bataan, maybe 50,000 made it to O'Donnell. Think of the useless slaughter—bayoneted, shot, heads cut off, bodies ripped open—of so many men, unable to defend themselves.

Words alone cannot describe the Bataan Death March. Pictures would not be believed. Rumors could not be enough of the truth. The courageous men who were on the full Bataan Death March, whether they survived it or died en route, are true heroes. The ones who reached O'Donnell got there by the grace of God or with the help of their buddies. I do not feel I can be graphic enough to tell all of the stories we heard, stories I know must be true. Since I was fortunate to miss the worst of this March of Death, I cannot give a full account of it. Only those on this trip to hell would have sufficient knowledge to write such a book. I am positive, however, that they could not relive the truth, nor would the majority of people believe their story. I can, however, refer you to a book by Dorothy Cave, *Beyond Courage: One Regiment Against Japan, 1941-1945* (Yucca Tree Press 1992) that is the story of New Mexico's 200th Coast Artillery Regiment. Cave's book is based upon first-hand accounts from the beginning of the war through liberation in 1945.

Once at O'Donnell, the Japanese separated the Americans from the Filipinos with a road between two camps set up for the prisoners. The death rate continued to climb even after the men arrived.

# 17

# More O'Donnell

The first two groups of men that reached camp were truly a sad lot. Many were sick. They were all hungry and dehydrated. By the time the last prisoners in the march had arrived, the condition of men from these first groups had not improved very much. With just one water faucet for about four hundred prisoners, a constant line of men existed both day and night. The force from this faucet was barely a stream of water. I remember Bud and I talking about how lucky we had been to have grabbed that bottle of beer from the Japanese soldier. For all of us, our main, daily occupation was to get in line for water. The other main activity was to run to the ditches called toilets.

A little bit of organization followed the arrival of the first group at O'Donnell as we kept busy preparing the camp for more customers. The day after this first group had arrived, a barracks was designated as a hospital and latrines were dug. Officers also assigned some of the men to a kitchen crew, fencing, and other various work crews. These assignments really did not mean much. For the first few weeks, the great majority of the men were too sick to work. Half of the men given a heavy-duty job became ill the next day and then hospitalized. We could deal with the flies, but the maggots the flies grew into posed a constant problem. Any wounds unattended soon crawled with maggots, although the maggots could have a beneficial effect at times since they devoured dead skin and thus could help the healing process. In addition to malnutrition, dehydration, malaria, diarrhea, and other illnesses, several suffered from sunstroke. Since many men, including myself, did not have headgear, the brutal sun had taken its toll. While the sun had not taken me out, I was close to having sunstroke.

Other than being ill, the biggest problem we faced in eating was that, in most instances, the food was not what we were accustomed to. The Japanese gave us mostly rice, either boiled in a soupy gruel or steamed. We received no condiments with it. Our stomachs were not conditioned to such a diet. Even those who were in decent, physical shape did not actually enjoy this food. We ate it to survive, regardless of how tasteless it was.

We certainly had lost our freedom, but we did not lose our faith in the United States, in God, and in the great majority of the men in our camp. We also had not lost our dignity. As I mentioned before, buddies were still trying to take care of buddies. In nearly all instances, the Americans tried to help each other, regardless of whether or not they were in the same branch of the service, the same regiment, or whether they were friends or strangers. There were, of course, a few instances where someone would steal, especially food, clothing, and tobacco, from a fellow prisoner. And in any large group, there are always a few bad apples who are big time operators or who think that they are better than others. These individuals would do anything to take care of themselves.

One such SOB during the war even had the gall to later write a book in which he bragged about how he had outwitted his fellow Americans during their trials and tribulations. Shortly after our arrival in O'Donnell, when men lined up fifty deep to obtain a little water from the single faucet, this man claimed that he had rushed to the front of the line. After telling everyone he was from the hospital and had been sent to get water for the dying men, he proceeded to fill up a bucket that he supposedly took back to his buddies. Meanwhile, all of us got only a half-cup of water once we reached the spigot. This individual also claimed that he had approached the Navy in Mariveles, before the surrender, and procured a truckload of food for a non-existent Navy group. He also asserted in his book that he went back to Japan after the war as the only enlisted man called to be a witness against the Japanese. He claimed to have testified about their treatment of Americans and the atrocities committed by the guards. This man, however, was one of the great exceptions in respect to the manner in which Americans conducted themselves.

Within the camp, our barracks were Nipa huts with a central, raised walkway. Eighteen inches above the walkway on each side was a platform made out of bamboo strips. About four feet above the first platform was another one. Each platform was about seven feet deep. Each barracks contained one hundred men, twenty-five on each level on each side. This was our home. Each morning when we got up, we reached over to see if our neighbor was still alive.

How sad it was to watch men die from starvation. Many would simply lie down and give up. I remember one pair of brothers from Clovis, Dean and Junior Chalk. One brother took care of the other, trying to get him to eat what little food we were given. That brother saved the food when his sibling refused it, hoping he would eat it later. The first brother died on May 29, 1942. The surviving brother just gave up six days later. Many, many other men did the same. Lacking any hope, they just laid down and died. Sick, hungry, but unable to eat, some men traded their small portion of food for a cigarette. The tobacco industry would have been proud to see so many men die of starvation caused by trading food rations for tobacco. In the beginning, only a few had to be buried, but later this number increased dramatically. The death toll seemed to be greater each day; at one point it reached over one hundred men a day.

The largest work detail in camp, and also one of the first ones, was the burial detail. Every morning more men would be found dead, both in the barracks and in the so-called hospital. The high water table created a problem, though. Underground water was so close to the surface that a decent burial could not be done. It was not uncommon for one person to hold a body down with a shovel while another man covered the body with dirt.

Some work details labored outside of the camp. Every few days the Japanese asked for volunteers. Such opportunities were met with trepidation—would a prisoner be better off out of this stinking hellhole or might the odds of survival decrease even more, separated as volunteers would be from most of the other Americans? We also never knew what kind of work detail we were volunteering for. In many instances, men agreed to leave camp with hope that more food would be available to them or that maybe they could find some medicine.

After about a month in camp, I had concluded that it would be better to volunteer for a work detail rather than to remain in camp. I disliked the thought of leaving Bud and other friends, but Bud had recovered a bit. Although he did not seem to be in danger of dying, he was still too weak to work. On May 14th, after I had been in camp for just over a month, I volunteered for a work detail, not knowing exactly what labor would be involved. It turned out I was one in a small group of men. There were about fourteen of us. The Japanese took us back to Bataan by truck. Once we had driven several kilometers into the peninsula, the guards put us in a little schoolhouse near Lubao. We were a salvage work group. One day we loaded boxes of ammunition onto trucks, the next day food. Each day we loaded different items onto the vehicles.

It happened to be a good work detail. We had two trucks to carry the fourteen Americans and six Japanese. All of us slept in the schoolhouse. We Americans ate what the Japanese cooked and they treated us halfway decently. Some slapping and wild antics occurred on the part of the guards when we did not understand them, but they never really beat us. We worked as hard as we could without allowing our labor to benefit the Japanese cause. Often, we made the guards understand that we were too weak to load some of the heavy ammunition so that they would help us. We also made sure that it took us much longer to load a truck than the Japanese thought it would take. We had to work as hard as our physical condition allowed us to, but we were given a little freedom and could scrounge for food. I noticed that the Americans on this work detail seemed to have a better attitude—they were going to survive.

To my despair, within two weeks I came down with a good case of malaria. The bad part of this ailment is that a person loses his appetite. I had no desire for food; in fact, the smell of food repelled me. At first, the Japanese left me alone in the schoolhouse while everyone else worked, but eventually a guard took me back to O'Donnell where they traded me for a whole person. I arrived back at the camp on May 26, 1942, too sick to know what was happening. I have no recollection of that day. I did realize, when I became lucid after the fever and chills, that much of the camp had been evacuated. Rumor had it that the men had been sent to another camp called Cabanatuan. The Japanese evacuated O'Donnell because of the tremendous loss of life that had been occurring there. Apparently, they thought that a new camp would stop the Americans from dying off on them. These deaths had been caused by the illnesses and malnutrition during our months on Bataan, the additional toll that the Death March had taken on the men, and the conditions at O'Donnell itself.

On June 4$^{th}$ I was loaded up with many other sick prisoners and transported to the new camp. I remember that day. While on the work detail at Lubao, I had found a little, single cot mattress and it had been returned with me to O'Donnell. On June 4$^{th}$, Colonel Luikart, my former commanding officer, rolled up my mattress and loaded it along with me onto the truck. Luikart rode on the same truck and when we arrived at Cabanatuan, he helped me unload and settle into a barracks.

# 18

# Cabanatuan

The first few days in the new camp were a blur to me. I was ill with malaria, suffering two days of fever and then a following day of chills. I did not eat. Because of my illness, I have very little recollection of my whereabouts. I do not even recall who looked after me, got me food (for which I had no appetite), brought me water, helped me to the slit trench, or took me to the camp doctor. I do know that on June 11th I was sent to the hospital.

The camp had a very large hospital compound. The main road into Cabanatuan bisected the camp. All of the prisoners were on one side. The Japanese facilities were across the road; some American truck drivers also had accommodations on this side of the camp since they worked for the Japanese. The hospital was in the Japanese section of Cabanatuan. Aside from it, the medical compound included barracks for the American doctors and a dental clinic. Our doctors were spread too thinly to visit each patient either daily or weekly. They depended on the information from the corpsmen. These corpsmen, acting under orders from the doctors, issued medication. The amount of medicine available, however, could have been kept in a small box. American and Filipino forces had suffered from a constant shortage of quinine and other medicines even before the surrender. While our medics vainly tried to do right by the sick and injured, they simply did not have sufficient medicine to get everyone back on their feet.

For the camp area as a whole, barbwire was the only fence around the enclosure. Guard towers had been erected at strategic intervals and at each corner of the camp. Barbwire also separated the prisoners' barracks, the kitchen, the American camp headquarters, and the hospital from the central road. Doctors in the hospital attempted to assign the patients with the same diagnosis to the same ward or barracks. One ward at the end of the hospital compound was numbered "0." As illnesses worsened, another zero ward was added, identified as "00." It was also fenced off from the hospital by barbwire. The zero and double zero wards, as these two separate buildings were called, were for the men who would probably die within the next twenty-four hours. After these wards, the other barracks were numbered beginning with "1."

By the time I had arrived at Cabanatuan, Corregidor had finally been surrendered. Since my knowledge of what happened on that island is based upon hearsay, I will not try to describe the problems our men experienced there—the enemy shelling, bombing, and strafing. I mention Corregidor because many prisoners from there arrived at Cabanatuan. At first, Cabanatuan consisted of two camps, Cabanatuan Camp One and Cabanatuan Camp Two. But within a short time, the enemy closed one camp as some prisoners were taken out on work details and others were taken to Japan.

I also mention the men from Corregidor to explain that

differences existed among the prisoners in respect to their physical condition. Generally speaking, those taken from the island were in much better shape than the men from Bataan. The men on Corregidor had endured another month of war with its terrible shelling and bombings. But they apparently had some advantages that were not available to those of us on the peninsula, such as better hospitalization, more medicine, and, I suspect, more food. If a man on Corregidor had not been wounded, he was in better condition and also had more money. At Cabanatuan, money proved to be a useful and valuable item, but it was very scarce.

Shortly after Corregidor had been surrendered, with very few exceptions the Japanese segregated the highest ranking officers, lieutenant colonels and up, from the rest of the troops. The field grade officers were kept in different camps. Soon afterward, the Japanese sent American officers to Formosa and later to Japan, Korea, and Mukden. The few field grade officers left in the Philippines stayed there mainly to act as camp commanders for the larger camps.

As at O'Donnell, I do not believe any of the prisoners ever completely understood the Japanese. One guard would give one of us a cigarette, the next guard would knock the American down for smoking in his presence. I was greatly surprised when the Japanese guards allowed me to salvage the mattress when I was on that work detail. I was even more surprised when they allowed me to take it back to O'Donnell and then to Cabanatuan.

Also mystifying was the manner in which prisoners were assigned to various camps on Luzon. In the old city of Manila, Bilibid had been a prison from the days of the Spanish American War. Now it seemed to serve as a relay prison as the Japanese moved our men from one part of Luzon to another area, or from one camp to another. Bilibid became infamous, but on the positive side, it had a hospital for men who needed better care than they could have gotten elsewhere. I am not personally knowledge about Bilibid because I was never given the chance to visit it nor was I ever forced into its confines.

As I mentioned earlier, on June 11th I was sent to the hospital with a bad case of malaria. Although its severity can vary, that illness seems to impact each person about the same way. In my case, I had a high fever for usually two days, sometimes three. Severe chills followed the fever. During either the fever or the chills, a person loses his desire for food. Sometimes a prisoner would be too sick to go for his food allotment. In that situation, another man would get it and bring it to the ill prisoner who usually had the good sense to save the food until he felt better. In my case, I seemed to feel better in the late afternoon, although I still had no desire to do anything since I was exhausted and usually had a terrible headache.

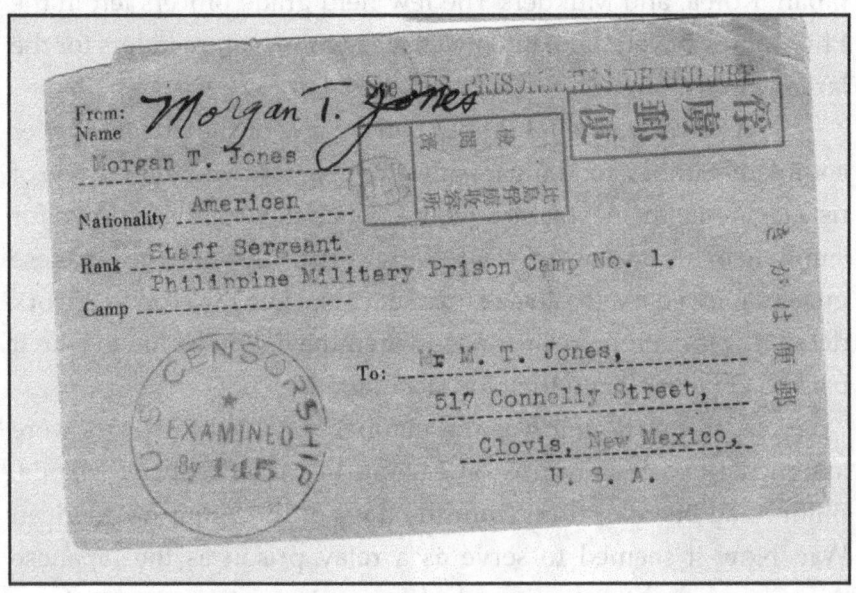

As POWs, we were allowed to write our families using only this type of postcard. I sent this one from Cabanatuan.

> IMPERIAL JAPANESE ARMY
>
> 1. I am interned at ___The Philippine Military Prison Camp___
>    ___No. 1.___
> 2. My health is — ~~excellent~~; good ~~; fair; poor~~.
> 3. I am — uninjured; ~~sick in hospital; under treatment; not under treatment~~.
> 4. I am — ~~improving; not improving; better~~; well.
> 5. Please see that _____
>    _____ is taken care of.
> 6. (Re: Family); ___Love to everyone.___
>    _____
> 7. Please give my best regards to ___all.___

**Note how I was very limited in the information I could send my parents.**

My two days of fever and one day of chills would be followed by a few days of recovery. Then the routine would start all over. (Many men with high fevers, however, would go completely out of their head and would have to be restrained for a short time.) When my body temperature rose, I remember wishing I could obtain an ice-cold glass of orange juice. As victims of malaria became more rational, such dreams were common. Later, after the war was over and I was back home, I would anticipate having a recurrence of malaria just so I could enjoy that ice-cold orange juice. The absurdity of this dream was that, in normal situations, I did not like orange juice.

Even in such periods, I contemplated eventual freedom, and I think most men had such dreams. Rumors of freedom were everywhere, and they were believed. One had only to listen to them to be convinced. Around the holidays, whether they were Japanese or American days of celebration, rumors gained even more credence. As a Japanese holiday approached, the rumor had the guards increasing our food allowance. A new camp commander also meant, we thought, more food. Very few of these rumors ever came to fruition.

We lived in barracks that were about the same as the ones at O'Donnell. They were standard military issue. Each building accommodated about one hundred men. A prisoner's desire in respect to assignments within the barracks (upper or lower bunk, for example) depended on what was available at a particular time and who was in charge. I usually preferred the top bunk since no liquids could be spilled on me and no one suffering from diarrhea could be above me. I had to climb three or four ladders to get to the top bunk. With my mattress, space proved to be a problem since the mattress was a little wider then the space assigned to each man. (When I was sent to the hospital, I left my mattress with friends who protected it.) The bottom of each bunk was supported with slats of thin bamboo, with small spaces between each strip. Because of the emaciated condition of most of the men, these bunks were not the most comfortable sleeping accommodations.

Outside, if it was not raining, it was usually too hot to sit in the sun. The only shade available was that provided by the barrack buildings. When the sun went down, those agreeable to conversation gathered on the ground outside of the barrack to tell tall tale stories which were supposedly true but which were usually greatly exaggerated. In one barrack I was assigned to, we had a Polack who bragged about Detroit. Whatever topic we discussed, there was a Polack who lived in Detroit who had a bigger store, automobile, diamond, café, or Olympic record. I finally had all I could take and tried to make a bet with him that if he could find a Polack holding a record on anything, I would find a Jones who was just as good. But he was silent when I proposed that.

Officers and enlisted men were quartered separately. Officers' barracks were not as crowded as the ones for enlisted men. Officers also did not have to work or go on work details with the exception of an American officer who had to accompany a work detail that left the camp; that officer would be in charge of the group. Usually, one officer was assigned to fifty or more men, although the ratio depended on the size of the work detail, its location, and the difficulty of the labor. The American Camp Commander seldom received any information on these work details. Bob Stephens, my next-door neighbor in civilian life, was picked for a very large work group. We originally did not know his destination. We found out much later that this group of one thousand or more men went to Mindanao, the largest, most southern island in the Philippines. I do not think I saw Bob again until the war was over.

Cabanatuan was another O'Donnell, except for its size. It was much larger. The American Camp Commander had a much bigger job with many, many more prisoners, no sanitary facilities, and the approaching rainy season. Another Table of Organization needed to be set up. In other words, we had to get straddle ditches dug, walkways prepared, and kitchen crews assembled. Officers had to be assigned to the kitchens, to handle supplies, to set up sanitation facilities, to serve as interior guards, and to other work details inside of the camp.

Because of the O'Donnell experience, it proved to be a little easier to get organized at this second camp. It was not until the end, or near the end, of the rainy season, however, that adequate toilet facilities, similar to outhouses, were finally prepared. Prior to that, the basic straddle trench had to suffice. The food was not much better than what we had eaten at O'Donnell. We also had no more medication at Cabanatuan than we had had at O'Donnell, but at least now the men were becoming more accustomed to our life and they learned to exist on what was available.

One of the first orders we received from the Japanese was that each unit had to split into groups of ten men. Should one of the ten escape, the remaining nine would be executed. This worried everyone. Escaping was not much of a problem. On a dark night, especially if it was raining, all a man had to do was simply slip under the barbwire and melt into the jungle. The situation the vast majority of the escapees would have faced, though, would have been what to do afterwards. We had no money, we faced a language problem with the native population, and we did not know what direction to go, since we were seldom aware of what was beyond the horizon. Was it the jungle, a town, or a Japanese camp? Could a prisoner find a Filipino family who would hide him and feed him? Certainly, one would not want to involve an innocent family and create problems for its members.

One solution to our dilemma for a number of men who had money was to escape during the night, walk to the nearest *barrio* or village, buy some food there, and then slip back into camp. Some were able to do this for several months until the Japanese found out about this ruse. The Japanese promptly posted orders that any man caught leaving Cabanatuan and returning would be executed. Within the week, a rumor spread that some men had been caught slipping back into camp. In a few days, several guards took a group of four or five prisoners to a field about fifty yards from the wire fence on the hospital side. There the Japanese forced the men to dig a big hole and then kneel in front of it. The guards, standing behind them, shot them in the head. The ones who did not fall into the grave were pushed in. Another detail of prisoners assembled to cover the grave with dirt. When this happened, I was in the hospital and saw the entire event. Actually, all of the ambulatory prisoners were required to watch the execution. I did not know who these executed prisoners were or where they were from. I did have considerable empathy for their souls and for their families.

The Japanese did not treat the Filipinos any better than the Americans. As for the Filipino prisoners from Bataan, many more of them died from their treatment at the hands of the Japanese, or from lack of food, than the Americans. The Filipinos in most instances, however, were only imprisoned for a few months. They were set free to go back to their families if they could locate them.

Civilian Filipinos were occasionally found guilty of some minor infraction, such as not bowing to a guard. The Japanese tortured them horribly. A good number of times the Filipinos were strung up on the posts at the entrance to Camp Cabanatuan. Every Filipino passing by was required to beat on these individuals or hit them with sticks. This continued until the Filipino died. In several instances, the Japanese beat the native unconscious, strung him or her up, cut their head off, and then left the body on the post for several days. Usually the Japanese would rape the women when they thought the Filipina had committed an infraction. Aside from all of this, every Filipino who passed the guards had to bow to them.

Several times the Japanese also strung Americans up on poles outside of the main gate. They had apparently angered the guards in some manner, and eventually paid for it with their lives. The Japanese forced the Filipinos to beat on the Americans every time the natives passed the gate. After a day or two, if the Americans had not died, guards bayoneted them.

After I had spent a little over two months on the hospital side of the camp, I went into remission from the malaria and returned to duty. The more able bodied prisoners had been sent away from the camp on more labor-intensive work, but there were a number of so-called "local duty work details," so we did not sit around for very long. One daily job consisted of going out to get firewood for the kitchens, another was to work in the garden. The Japanese had

had the Americans plant a huge vegetable garden so we could help to feed ourselves. I drew this garden work detail quite a few times once I had recovered from malaria. I found such work to be very hard since it was an all-day job in the hot sun. We were not allowed to sit down. The only way we could water the garden was to carry, sometimes for at least fifty or more yards, wooden-handled, five-gallon, tin cans. We carried two cans on each trip. This proved to be a major chore for us since most of the men were weak. As a rule, the men who worked in the garden suffered particularly harsh treatment at the hands of the guards. The Japanese carried short sticks or clubs. After the guards used them on some of the prisoners, it was not unusual for the workers to carry two or three unconscious men back to camp everyday. Sadly, the Japanese kept the beets from the garden. We got the tops. The guards always kept the choice vegetables. We got what was left. We received the raw end of the deal every time. If a caribou was killed, the Japanese took the meat and we received the blood pudding. Why should we complain? We should have been accustomed to such treatment.

After the rainy season, the new toilets not only proved to be a great improvement on the straddle trenches in respect to our comfort, but also in respect to our health. A huge number of men suffered from very bad cases of diarrhea and dysentery. When it rained, it required complete attention to detail when one used the straddle trenches to insure that we did not slide into the mess. Especially at night, using the trenches was extremely dangerous. It was not uncommon at night to hear a man calling for help. Many a man slid into these sanitation facilities even in the daytime, though.

Even worse was the number of men who, when they needed to relieve themselves, were so weak and ill that they could not make it to the facility or make it back to the barracks. They laid in the mud, rain, and human filth all night until someone fell over them or when daylight revealed their body. With our twisted sense of humor, there was a way, though, that a man could get partly cleaned up.

When it rained, at either end of the dry season, the rain was warm. In such clement weather, a prisoner, with his clothes on, could take an outdoor shower to clean his garments. After doing that, a man could disrobe, take a shower in the nude, and thus clean himself up, too. It proved to be quite an experience to live in a bamboo and nipa shack when a typhoon hit. It amazed us that the huts could withstand the typhoons. Such weather meant a lot of wind and freezing cold. Once wet, few men had a change of clothing. What you slept in was what you wore all day, every week, until it rained and you could wash the clothing. As friends passed away, you could increase your wardrobe to two outfits. One could be worn and another washed. If a man had only one set, there was always the "g" string, the one article of clothing issued to us by the Japanese.

The death rate in Cabanatuan decreased slightly as sanitary conditions improved and as Americans became more accustomed to the diet, or lack of it. Actually, the food had much to do with the numerous deaths. We found it extremely difficult to stomach the bland diet of rice. The morning meal, called *lugao*, consisted of very soft, liquid rice. If we did not add some condiment to it, the food remained tasteless. We also drank rice coffee in the mornings. This was made from raw rice that was burned and then used as coffee grounds.

Lunch and dinner, the other two meals, regardless of what they were called, consisted of steamed rice and some type of soup. The Japanese gave us some greens that we called "whistle wood" because they were hollow and hard to eat. At times we also received *camotes*, a sort of tasteless yam. Other food items the Japanese gave us were squash, turnips, beets (especially the greens of these last two vegetables), corn, eggplant, tomatoes, gourds, green beans, mongo beans, little green beans, black beans, limes, oranges, mangoes, papaya, and chayotes. Seldom, though, did we get more than one type of vegetable with a meal. We also ate pomelo; it appeared to be like a grapefruit, easily peeled into sections, but each part was very dry, not juicy as was a real grapefruit. All of these came from our garden. We were also given food items such as eggs, chicken, caribou, fish, pork, Vienna sausage, cabbage, peanuts, garlic, onions, cucumbers, and various other vegetables. The Japanese gave us condiments as well.

Yes, we had fruit and vegetables, but one must understand that the Japanese issued a limited quantity of these foods to each kitchen. For instance, one day we received eleven eggs for two hundred men and, with the same meal, one chicken. The eggs were hard boiled, then diced, and dumped into the soup along with the chicken. It was the same for the fruits and vegetables. All were diced and put into the soup. Sometimes we would get such a large quantity of one type of vegetable that we could identify it. We especially received plenty of beet tops. From the caribou came blood pudding. The cooks boiled and sliced it, serving it to us as if it were a piece of cake. Condiments such as salt, pepper, garlic, cinnamon, and sugar helped with the taste of the soup. There is no way, though, to disguise the taste of beet tops to make them more palatable. When a person is hungry, he will always eat anything given to him, and we were hungry. We would bitch about the food, but we would eat anything.

Ingenuity is the middle name of most Americans, and we drew on this characteristic in the camp. If the supply of food was sufficient, the kitchen crew serving the rice would fill up the mess kit. It did not take too long before some of the men found a way to enlarge its volume. They placed the kit in soft dirt and then gently pounded out the inside bottom with a blunt object. Slowly but surely, the mess kit expanded to such a degree that it now held twice the usual volume of food. These men got away with this a few times before the kitchen crew caught on, probably because someone complained about the inequity.

The Red Cross packages, that we started to received on Christmas Day, 1942, really helped us turn the corner on the multiple deaths that occurred daily. It was not just the food they contained. It was the thought that someone had not forgotten us or had not written us off as out of the world. The disposition of the Red Cross packages differed at each camp. Depending on the whims of the Japanese Camp Commander, what a prisoner received and when he received it varied. At times, a man could be given an entire package, one that the Japanese had not touched. Other times, however, men received packages where the Japanese had removed some of the contents. Sometimes, the kitchens opened and distributed the packages instead of serving us the usual fare. I was in the hospital on December 25, 1942, and the package I received could not have been more appreciated. It was from the British Red Cross. On January 1, 1943 I was given an American Red Cross package. We really were in hog heaven with all of this food.

People have questioned me several times as to the contents of these packages. Each one was a little different, but they usually held oleo, beef steak stew, barley candy, cheese, biscuits, soap, tomatoes, condensed milk, fig pudding, a chocolate bar, and tea. These packages contained from eight to ten pounds of food and smokes and one hundred pounds of hope and goodwill. The American package I received on New Year's Day included evaporated milk, biscuits, cheese, cocoa, pilchards, corned beef, a chocolate bar, sugar, soup, prunes, coffee, cigarettes, tobacco, and oleo. On January 23, 1943 we received a Canadian Red Cross package. It had salmon, corned beef, sardines, tea, sugar, cheese, biscuits, powdered milk, butter, chocolate, and jam.

Immediately the death rate started to drop. We now had

American-types of food, and condiments we could mix with the rice. This helped everyone to eat better. Some of the items, such as the fish, mixed very well with the rice. As I mentioned earlier, equally as important was the hope that these packages gave us. Even though the packages did not have our individual names on them, we knew we had not been forgotten.

I had returned to the hospital on November 11, 1942 with malaria, beriberi, edema, and vitamin deficiencies. In the hospital, rumors did not circulate as fast as on the duty side of the camp. Before the men received them in the regular barracks, I am sure there had been rumors that the Red Cross packages had arrived in camp, but their disbursal was a big shock to those of us in the hospital.

By the end of 1942, none of us had received any mail or packages from home. We did not know if anyone knew if we were alive or dead. We also worried about what our loved ones were going through. I know it was much worse for the married prisoners who had families than it was for those of us who were single, such as myself. I knew I was alive. Even though I was sick, I also knew I would recover. I was happy that my parents did not know that I was ill. I hoped they knew I was alive. Little did we realize how our loved ones suffered during our captivity.

Another problem we faced aside from day-to-day living was watching our friends die. To a degree, we became immune to this situation. I know that what I just wrote seems to be a hard-hearted statement. But when you see friends, and strangers, die, and watch up to one hundred men buried in one day, you do become hardened. Seeing men die like that, you get to the point where it does not mean much to you. If you analyze it, it is a matter of survival. Of course, there were feelings involved with very close friends. As it happened, none of my close friends died when we were in the same camp. Only later did I hear that some good friends did not make it, and then it was too late to have deep feelings. While you grieved for them, and even worried about telling their families the details of their death, you still had to worry about yourself. I really do not remember if I worried about dying. In most instances, I believe we were too concerned about getting more food or avoiding a beating from a guard for some so-called infraction.

I received word recently that one of my good friends, Lester Morrison, had died from cancer. I knew he had been fighting it for several years, but he had seemed to be winning. His death was a much bigger shock to me and hurt me more than if he had passed away in Cabanatuan. Lester and I had spent two years of hell together, fighting it everyday, both in the Philippines and in Japan. While he did live fifty years afterwards, it was very hard to lose him.

In the camp, we just existed, trying to get by day to day. I do not think that we worried about tomorrow. We had enough problems each day. There were times when we wondered when it was all going to end. I do not think I ever thought about not making it. I am sure that if we who survived had ever felt that we were not going to make it, we would have died. I am sure this is what happened to the ones who gave up. Many were too sick to live, but quite a few of those men came home. Many were too sick to live and they didn't.

Bud was one of the men who was too sick to live, but he did. He stayed in the double zero ward for a long time; it turned out his hospitalization occurred at the same time as mine. The men in the zero and double zero wards could have company from the duty side but not from the rest of the hospital. In spite of this rule, I visited Bud nearly everyday if I did not have a fever or chills. I walked down to the fence between his ward and the rest of the hospital. If I did not see Bud, I asked someone to tell him I was there. Usually he dragged himself out, but sometimes Bud did not feel strong enough to leave his bunk. If that happened, I returned the next day.

Another friend, Jack Aldrich, was in the zero ward. He had a brother, Bob, on the duty side of the camp. They were both from Clovis and in the 2nd Battalion Headquarters Battery. Jack was in very bad shape. One day when Bob went to visit his brother, I was also there to see Bud. When I saw Bob, he told me that Jack needed a blanket and asked me if I knew where he could get one. I got one for Jack and gave it to his brother. Jack recovered, and by chance, we spent the last two years of the war together in two camps. I do not remember giving Jack the blanket, but he told me this story several years ago, after the war. Jack remembered what I had done for him because he told me the blanket helped him to survive.

I am sure that the most precious item for us during our imprisonment was water. One can exist for many weeks without food, but lack of water can make a human being into an animal. Except for one camp, from the time the American and Filipino forces moved into Bataan through the time I spent in my last camp in Japan, we were always short of water. The men on the Bataan Death March probably survived on the least amount of water. As I explained earlier, in O'Donnell we lined up continually for water from, at first, just one faucet until the Japanese opened up another one.

In Cabanatuan, water was still precious but not like it had been up to that time. You learned to keep your canteen full of water, and refill it whenever it started to get low. You also always carried a spoon in your pocket, regardless of where you were or where you were going. You did this in case you had an opportunity to find something to eat.

There were other sacred objects. Aside from water, men would trade anything— their next meal, cigarettes, tomorrow's food, or clothing off of their backs. Many of the men traded their food for smokes. The majority of those who did that eventually died from lack of food. It is too bad that it took fifty years to find out that cigarettes are addictive. We knew that in 1942.

I do not know what Jim Hamilton, my friend from Clovis did for smokes, or how he handled imprisonment. I do not recall ever being in the same camp with him. Many events from those years are so clear, yet some situations or people are complete blanks. I do not know where some men were or what happened to them. It is as if, for me, they did not exist during that time. For many years after the war, most of us tried to forget being a prisoner of war. It did not help.

Situations could change in each camp depending on the whims of the commandant, the vagaries of war, and circumstances within the camp. We always felt that changes on the war fronts and battlefields impacted the amount or type of food we received and the liberties the Japanese gave us. We especially believed this when the treatment became worse.

Helping us through all of this were the chaplains. As with the medical corps, they continued their previous duties even though they were now prisoners. I am sure that the chaplains gave considerable strength to many men of all faiths. I recall talking with Chaplain Taylor on one of my extended visits in the hospital. My question to him no doubt resulted from my reading the Bible, especially the New Testament and Psalms. Many chapters in Psalms end with the word "Selah" and I wondered about its meaning. He replied, as I remember it, that "Selah" was used in place of "Amen."

The Chaplains represented the major various American religions, Catholicism, Protestantism, and Judaism. Each prisoner could thus see a chaplain of his faith. All of these men were extremely busy. People called upon them all day and night due to the initial high death rate in the camps. I am sure that as the deaths declined, so did the business of the chaplains. They were still a needed strength for the men and always made themselves available.

Similarly, the medical doctors were also very busy as their services were required both day and night. Doctors were available on both the duty side and on the hospital side. Sick call was held every morning on the duty side, with a good daily turnout. It was not unusual for a doctor to receive a beating from the Japanese when he marked a man as too sick to work, thus excusing him from duty. The Japanese became extremely critical of the doctors for reporting so many men as ill, despite the refusal of our captors to supply medication to prevent so much sickness. At times, in fact at most times, the Japanese made men work who were too sick to do so; many could hardly stand up or walk to work. This occurred in every camp I visited. The Japanese beat many a doctor because he would not cooperate and give his approval for a sick man to report for work. Sometimes the doctor would win, but usually the Japanese did. The medical men also received brutal treatment when they attempted to obtain more medication and bandages.

During one inspection, Japanese medical officers traveled through an area of the hospital where there were a number of diarrhea and dysentery cases. The path to the slit trench was a mess since many of the men were not able to hold it until they reached the trench. The Japanese did not like what they saw and ordered the doctors to tell the sick men that such unsanitary conditions would not be allowed. The doctors tried to impress on the visitors the need for medicine to eliminate this problem. The Japanese, however, thought that just their orders could stop it.

The medical corpsmen were also unsung heroes. They never received credit for the extremely dirty tasks required of them. They worked with the doctors on the duty side and especially on the hospital side. Along with the physicians, the corpsmen had to be extremely hard on the patients. It was not uncommon, in fact it was necessary, for the corpsmen to force a patient to get up and exercise, go for his meals, or go outside of the barracks. Because so many men felt so sorry for themselves, the best medicine the medical staff could give a patient was to be overly harsh with him. If a casual visitor, not knowing the history of such a patient, had witnessed some of this stern treatment, he would probably be critical of the doctor or corpsman. The medical staff should receive more credit for their efforts.

I started out on this diatribe to mention how it was impossible to understand the Japanese. Even little things, such as the American officers' attempts to get additional food or medicine, at times made the Japanese mad; as punishment, they would deny us something. Overall, there was no logic or pattern to the way they acted. If a prisoner escaped from camp, or they caught him trying to escape, the Japanese cancelled privileges, such as religious services, for all of us. At other times, everything would seem normal and then suddenly the Saturday night entertainment programs put on by inmates would be cancelled without any apparent provocation. Perhaps the Americans had won a major battle in the war. One good example of how our treatment could change concerned the battle between American and Japanese forces on the small, South Pacific island of Bougainvillea. Conditions in our camp had worsened. We heard that Americans had landed on Bougainvillea. None of us had ever heard of the place. Hell, we could not even spell it and still can't. We assumed it was an island, but we did not know where it was located. Conditions continued to be bad in the camp. Then we heard that the Americans had been pushed back into the ocean, with few Japanese casualties. The next news we received was that the Japanese had abandoned the island since it was not of any military importance. We still did not know where Bougainvillea was. In camp, conditions eventually loosened up a bit.

Sometimes a person in the compound located a map to

pinpoint the location of such battles. Our hosts had been very good at keeping any type of maps from us, but sometimes books had maps in them. In most cases, however, the Pacific islands were so obscure that they were not on the maps. Locating an island, though, was not necessarily good news. It could prove more disheartening than not knowing an island's location since the action was happening further south than where we wanted it to be. Of course, we expected to hear that American troops were landing on the island just south of us.

We received such news from different sources. Prisoners on outside work details, such as the truck drivers, gave us the most news. Many times we listened selectively to the news. Clandestine radios delivered the most aggravating news. They told us about the progress of the war in the Pacific and the European theaters. As in the Pacific, sometimes the places in Europe were also unknown to us. The news that Americans had landed in Africa really blew our minds. What were they doing there? Why fight in Africa?

Americans are scavengers, and as such, some of the men had assembled the radios from various parts. That ingenuity was also apparent as some of the prisoners found a way to make money in the camp. Men who had been barbers in civilian life had carefully saved their scissors and combs. At Cabanatuan, they gave haircuts for a few pesos. Many of us got most of our hair cut off and then shaved our heads. This eliminated one more area where the lice and bedbugs could play. Ironically, those creatures helped us pass the time in the camp. It could be an all day recreation to debug ourselves. We would take off all of our clothes except for the "g" string and put the clothes out in the sun to air. Then we patiently killed each bedbug individually. But it proved impossible to kill all of the varmints since their eggs continued to hatch.

One time I gave Bud a haircut. Although it was a labor of love, it turned out to be a bad haircut. Bud graduated from zero ward when I was hospitalized. He badly needed a haircut. I borrowed some scissors from a friend and went to work on Bud. He cautioned me about a wen he had on his head. A wen is a cyst. I did not know Bud had such a thing, but as I carefully cut his hair, I felt this small lump. He had had this growth for years, but he kept his hair long enough to hide it.

Bud and I made one score in Cabanatuan. Tom Bowman, Bud's good friend who I also knew, had been a Mess Sgt. in $2^{nd}$ Battalion Headquarters Battery while we were at Fort Bliss; he had worked right below our Mess Hall. At Cabanatuan, Tom had one of the better jobs. He secured a permanent position as a truck driver. He and other drivers lived in a couple of small huts near the guards' barracks. They had to be near the Japanese since the truck drivers were on call both day and night. This meant that they lived between the fences where the prisoners were on one side and the hospital on the other. Tom and the others apparently had plenty of freedom, even when they worked. For example, they bought items from the Filipinos when they drove to the villages.

One evening, Bud and I were talking across the fence with Tom. He asked us if we would like to buy a 50-kilo sack of sugar for about fifty pesos. We jumped at the opportunity even though we did not have the money. Bud and I felt sure, however, that we could raise it. We therefore made arrangements to meet Tom the next night at midnight to purchase the sugar. Bud and I contacted some of our friends who were officers, but at that time they did not have much money. After several hours, we managed to borrow the cash from a candy maker in exchange for half of the sugar sack. That night, we met Tom at the fence and exchanged the money for the sugar. It was the last time we ever saw Tom. Between Bud and I, we got the 50 kilos of sugar onto my back, with Bud helping to lift it a little while I carried it. Hauling that sack, which weighed approximately 110 pounds, proved to be a big burden in my weakened condition.

My knees buckled several times, but we made it to the top end of the camp to pay back our debt without stopping. I am not sure we could have lifted the sack up to my shoulders again if we had paused to rest. A full cup of sugar was going for one peso at that time. Bud and I sold some to the officers. We used the money and the rest of the sugar to live on. That exchange with Tom had really helped Bud and I, and we were indebted to him. I understand that Tom was on one of the prison ships sunk en route to Japan.

I recall wandering through some of the other areas of the camp where I saw all of the candy makers, who knew me after we got that 50-kilo sack of sugar. They made candy by melting the sugar and adding peanuts or coconut shavings. The candy makers used toothpaste as a filler. I do not know what other ingredients they put in it. Ironically, I did not have the money to spend on the candy. Bud and I did taste the candy one time, but it was not to our liking. On that tour of the top end, the business acumen of the Americans became very evident. Their activities seemed to be more evident as I went on up the slight hill to the top end of the camp. (At Cabanatuan, I had been assigned to the lower part of the camp, the area nearest the front gate.) I guess those at the top end, because they lived further away from our captors than the rest of us, felt that they had a little more freedom.

Regardless of where we lived, as prisoners we enjoyed very little entertainment in the camp. What we were allowed always depended upon the feelings of the Japanese Commandant of the camp. From the Philippine Red Cross, we received balls and gloves for baseball. We did not have a field, although we did have sufficient room for a baseball diamond. Without energy or strength, we could not have had a baseball game. Even if we had had one, very few of us would have had the strength to run if we had hit the ball. All we could do with the equipment was to play catch, yet we could not even do that for extended periods of time.

At times, the chaplains were permitted to hold religious services, while at other times they were forbidden to do so. The chapel was available to us at the whim of the Japanese Camp Commandant. Many men brought books, which we passed among us, to the church services. At times, books furnished by the Philippine Red Cross were also available.

In civilian life, many of us had led a very sheltered life and we had not been aware of many things that had happened around us. It was the same in prison life. In a camp with several thousand men, most of us remained with our friends in our own little area. While I was in Cabanatuan, I did not know where the library was and I do not remember ever having a book to read in camp, aside from my Bible, of course.

Sometimes educational classes were held, but always with the consent of the Japanese. A number of Mexican Americans prisoners, such as those from New Mexico, gave Spanish lessons. Some men also taught classes in math and hygiene. At night, someone gave astronomy lessons. The Big Dipper in the Northern hemisphere was pointed out to us, as was the Southern Cross in the Southern hemisphere. They were beautiful constellations. These were some of the efforts to not only keep us occupied, but also to educate us.

After we had been in Cabanatuan for about a year, five or six prisoners got together and made up a little band. It was a very good group. The band, led by the trumpet player, played one of the best arrangements of the song "Avalon" that I have ever heard. I hope all of them made it back home after the war because they gave so much to the men. On Saturday nights, another group with somewhat less talent put on plays. At times, the Japanese attended these concerts and plays. Our captors seemed to enjoy these productions as much as we did.

The men passed most of their time, however, in small groups

just talking with each other. They wishfully thought about how they were going to celebrate Christmases after the war and what kind of house they were going to build. I am sure that many of these dreams came true. When a group of Clovis men got together, we reminisced about happenings in our town, who did what and why. One of the big discussions Bud and I had was when we tried to remember what kind of store, and who ran it, was on each block on Main Street. We started with the railroad freight office at the foot of Main Street and went all the way to Eighth Street, which was the end of the business district. After we covered that several times, we started from Main Street again, but this time we went east on First Street, then west on Seventh Street, covering the businesses that existed at that time. When Bud and I got stuck, or when we argued as to who was correct on some building, we sought out other Clovisites to ask them their opinion. We finally got to the point where we knew the owners and occupants of each business building. Sometimes it was a surprise as to who the owners were.

All of the men also talked about food. It would be impossible for me to cover all of the items discussed, some of which I had never heard of. Most of the food talk centered on desserts that the men planned to bake when they got home. Some of the lavish dinners dreamed up normally would have been too much food for one person. But we did not want anyone to go hungry when we got home. With the advent of the Red Cross boxes, we felt better. As such, we were not in as much danger that the spider would ensnare us in its web.

# 19

## Cabanatuan – Odds And Ends

You could always find someone taking care of a bunkmate, a buddy, or a dying person. Everyone tended to stay with friends. If that became impossible as the Japanese sent prisoners from one camp to another, or if friends ended up in the hospital, it was very easy to make new friends. Men could become such good friends that their relationships lasted through the years, even into peacetime.

I recorded information on my friends in a little notebook I had picked up when I was on the work detail in Lubao. As I mentioned earlier, we stayed in a schoolhouse and that is where I found the notebook. Whenever I had some kind of a pencil, I wrote down information in it. At times a pencil got lost or worn out, but one was usually available from a friend. I recorded the addresses of the friends I made in prison. I have to admit, though, that after the war I never tried to locate many of these men. No doubt they were as busy I as was in those years—finding a job, moving from town to town because of work, or perhaps lack of work, getting married, and, most importantly, raising a family. For example, like me, Lester Morrison returned to Clovis at the end of the war. In a year or two, however, he moved away. For years we did not know where each other lived. Finally in 1988 or 1989, I found his name in a Fresno, California telephone book. I contacted him and we kept in touch until he passed away in 1996. This was typical for most of my friends. The movements of our parents made it even more difficult for those of us who came home to keep in contact with each other. In my case, during the war the railroad had promoted my father, transferring him from Clovis, New Mexico to Amarillo, Texas. After I came home, I first lived in Amarillo, but within three months I had returned to my old job with the railroad back in Clovis. With all of these coming and goings, accompanied by the start of a new life once I married, the notebook was stored, forgotten.

In the notebook, I wrote down our thoughts about food, my weight changes, dates of important events, and the different camps the Japanese sent me to. I also included the prisoner of war numbers assigned to me in each camp. In some camps, we were required to wear tags with these numbers on them. By the end of the war, the Japanese had given me six different numbers.

I began my notebook by using the inside front cover and back cover for a calendar. I entered important dates relating to my service record and inoculations by first the American Army and then ones from the Japanese. They loved to give shots and apparently were afraid of smallpox. Each time the Japanese vaccinated us, they gave us four shots. None of the smallpox ones ever took on me since I already had a huge vaccination scar from before the war.

Notebook pages also list the various ailments and sicknesses I had, the personal property I had lost at the surrender, and even the amount of money the Japanese Army or Navy paid for my labors as a prisoner. That sum totaled $70.75 in Philippine money. One entry for September 1944 shows that I made thirteen pesos. I must have put in a lot of overtime that month since the usual pay was from two to four pesos a month. Like others, I spent that money by buying food.

The notebook includes a list of the original fifty-four Clovis men in Battery E as well as the original, Clovis men in Headquarters Battery, $2^{nd}$ Battalion. Next to their name, I wrote down what happened to them, and, if they died, the cause of death for those I knew about during my years as a prisoner. I also have pages that cover my weight, a list of the contents in the Red Cross packages and when we received them, as well as a list of correspondence and packages received from home. I also wrote some miscellaneous notes as to books I read or wanted to read. Aside from the contents of the Red Cross packages, I devoted a page to the different foods the Japanese gave us, but I did not put down the amount, as some were too little to weigh. Food occupied several more pages as I wrote down items I wished I had. I even recorded meals I anticipated upon my return home, with an entire page detailing the first meal I intended to have.

I wrote down, too, bets or wagers I made with numerous friends. I never collected on any of these due to my inability to find out the results of the bets or due to the deaths of the men themselves. Most of the wagers covered sporting events held in the States and various aspects of the war. One bet I won was that the Japanese would hold out more than ninety days after Germany surrendered. I won, but it was close.

I also entered in my notebook a few poems written by friends, but the penultimate inclusions were several pages of Japanese words, with the English, Spanish, and Italian equivalents. The notebook has one page torn in half with my name, written in

English, underscored by the Japanese equivalent. I gave the other half of the page to a Japanese guard with whom I had become friends. His sheet had his name in Japanese and I had also printed his name in English, along with my name. Throughout the years I kept the notebook, I had been very careful in using it since I did not know how many years I would need to write in it. As it turned out, I had the calendar figured too closely—I still had room for six more months.

The notebook, like my other possessions, including the mattress, would be left with whoever bunked next to me if I had to be sent back to the hospital because of a good case of malaria. My personal belongings were always there when I returned to duty. If your close buddy or bunkmate passed away, you inherited his possessions, unless he had a better friend on the other side of camp or out on a work detail. If that happened, you held onto those possessions until the friend could claim them. Anytime you could identify something as yours, it would usually be returned to you without a fuss or problem. Sometimes, though, jealousy for personal possessions came to the forefront.

Fights between men, for any reason, were rare. If one did occur, though, in most cases the stronger person prevailed, if either prisoner was actually strong enough to fight. Barracks leaders or officers, unless these men were involved in the confrontation, tried to break the fight up before it got too far. The best reason to do so was to prelude the guards from seeing or hearing it. The Japanese felt that if we were feeling good enough to fight, they must have been feeding us too much. Also, their discipline was much harsher than our own in such instances.

The weeks I had spent being sick proved to be a long, monotonous time for me. Thanks to the Red Cross packages and medicine furnished by both the Philippine and American Red Cross, I finally recovered enough from my malaria and beriberi so that I could return to the duty side on May 2, 1943. It sure felt good to feel well enough to walk around, even though it was just in the big camp garden when I worked for a time. I ended up with more food once I was released. Men on the hospital side received smaller rations than the duty side because the Japanese felt that workers needed more food so they would have energy to work. They did not believe that sick men needed more food to get well, and in reality, most of the time many in the hospital were not interested in food. The Red Cross packages contained raisins, sugar, and other fruit. With these ingredients, someone always tried to make a potent drink. When I was hospitalized, I contributed some ingredients from my Red Cross box and, as such, I received some of the drink. It wasn't bad, and the drink fortified our weak diet.

Unlike food, the hospital side did have a little more medicine than the duty side. The doctors on the duty side held sick call daily and dispensed what little medicine they had. Many substitutes were experimented with when medicine was not available. The medics advised those whose bodies did not manufacture enough iron to find common nails, immerse them in water until they rusted, and then drink the water. The men were to do this several times. One has to be ingenious and adaptive in such occasions. The kitchens saved citrus peelings for the doctors who in turn gave them to patients with scurvy.

With the exception of rice, which we never received enough of anyway, the other food items the Japanese gave us were insufficient to maintain our weight and strength. Remember that we had been on one-fourth rations or less when our imprisonment began. Once in camp, we had to adjust to an entirely different type of diet, and even less rations. All of this had a bearing on our lives.

Soon after I returned to the duty side, I got a job in one of the kitchens. In prison camp, these were the near choice jobs. (Driving a truck was an even better one.) While the officer and non-coms in charge of the kitchen tried to be fair and honest to all, it was impossible not to get a little more to eat if you worked in the kitchen. Lester Morrison told me about that job. As it turned out, a man I had known for many years, Major McCollum, was in charge of the kitchen. He was with the Carlsbad, New Mexico unit of the New Mexico National Guard. McCollum had worked in the potash mines outside of Carlsbad but years before that job he had worked for the Santa Fe Railroad in Clovis. That is where I had met him and his wife. At Cabanatuan, when I went to see the major about the kitchen position, I guess he took one look at me and decided I needed a little more food than I was getting, so he put me to work. McCollum probably wanted to help me because of our railroad ties and also because he knew my father well. (Incidentally, the major became one prisoner I was able to stay connected to through the years since in the 1960s and 1970s we both worked in Los Angeles, California. Periodically, we met for lunch during those decades.)

The work crew lived in the back of the kitchen. Such a close location helped us get up early enough to ensure that breakfast would be ready at the appointed hour. As the population of the camp increased or decreased, the number of kitchens changed. Each one served about the same number of men, usually about two hundred. Once in a while the Japanese issued us vegetables. The kitchen crew peeled and diced these to make them stretch as far as possible. Then we threw the vegetables in water, adding a little salt. (Salt was usually the only condiment available.) Pineapples were given to us quite a few times, but as I noted earlier, rice was our basic staple. It was almost always polished rice; unpolished would have been better for us since it had more vitamins and minerals.

We cooked the rice and soup in vats similar to woks. These were about four feet across. To make the morning coffee, raw rice would be scorched or burned and the grounds or grains boiled. The coffee was hot. We used stoves that were concrete fireboxes with a single large hole at the top in which to set the vats; small doors fed the fires. The kitchen crew poured the rice into the vats, added water, and then allowed the rice, covered with a wooden lid, to steam. After this was done, three or four men stood on the concrete firebox to lift the vat off of the fire and put it aside to cool. Worms in the rice added to our protein, but by the time they were boiled in the rice, the worms were just little shreds. The prisoners would file through with their mess kits and canteen cups as the kitchen crew dished out the rice, vegetables, and a cup of soup. As I mentioned earlier, the men handing out the rice had to be very scrupulous in doing that, especially to a friend, although it proved to be exceedingly hard to be consistent without actually counting each grain.

After about a year in the camps, the Japanese paid the men "generously," whether they labored on a kitchen crew or on another type of work detail. Privates received .10 centavos a day and non-coms .15 centavos. With few exceptions, officers did not have to work. Some were sent out, however, on work details to oversee projects and to try to keep the Japanese from overworking or being brutal to the men. If officers worked, the Japanese paid them quite a bit more based upon their grade. With this largess, we could buy items. In a joint operation, the Japanese and the Americans set up commissaries where we could buy things. They carried merchandise based upon items the men desired and what the Japanese allowed, such as tobacco, coconuts, bananas, and sugar. The commissary also carried little hot peppers. They were really hot. The peppers were smaller than a little fingernail, but size had nothing to do with the taste.

While the men always talked about food, what they discussed depended upon the time of the year. In the hot, dry season, salads and fruit became the focus. As the Thanksgiving and Christmas holidays approached, we spoke about turkey and dressing. In the cold, rainy season, our topics became stove-hot and spicy food. I personally occupied myself with thoughts of desserts such as pies and cakes, especially anything with chocolate in it. Those of us who worked in the kitchen even talked about the food we were going to get when we got home. We were also hungry even if we ended up with food the other men did not get. One of the side benefits of kitchen work was eating the burned rice on the bottom of the vats. Doctors used the more burned rice to assist them in treating diarrhea. For those of us on the kitchen crew, after cooking a meal, we cleaned up and got ready for the next meal. It could be hard work and it did make for a long day. Illness sometimes took me off of kitchen duty. Apparently, once a person has malaria, it is always in his system, although I have never had a relapse since I returned to the duty side of the camp in May 1943. For many years after the war, blood banks would not take my donation. I have AB positive blood, a rather rare type. Once the Los Angeles Blood Bank called me, asking me to give, and I did. When the staff there found out about my malaria, however, they stopped calling. I have no desire for a relapse of my malaria, even though now, after the war, I would have the opportunity to see if the orange juice I dreamed about as a prisoner suffering from malaria tasted as good as I thought it would be.

Aside from malaria, edema and beriberi were two other problems that sent me to the hospital at Cabanatuan. Nutritional deficiencies caused both of these afflictions. Edema was a swelling of the joints, especially the legs and feet. Dry beriberi also affects extremities; the pain felt as though needles were being stuck in my toes and feet. Some men had such bad cases of beriberi that they could hardly put their feet on the ground. If either the dry or wet beriberi (which affects the cardiovascular system) was bad enough, the prisoner could become bedridden. Fortunately, Red Cross packages helped me with my vitamin deficiencies. I am sure that aside from the doctors, no one was aware that medical problems such as those that plagued others and me were caused by our poor nutrition. Scurvy also was a problem, but after about a year we started getting limes and pineapples, which eliminated the scurvy.

I know I have mentioned this before, but I cannot express my appreciation enough for those Red Cross packages, regardless of which country sent them. At one point, the prisoners heard of a relief ship, I think it was the *Gripsholm*, heading for the Philippines and the possibility of a prisoner exchange. While that exchange did not happen, I believe the ship we anticipated ended up bringing Red Cross packages. As the war progressed, the Japanese transferred me to other camps, and each one differed as to how many packages a prisoner received and how they were dispersed. In some camps, the Japanese gave us complete packages while in others they took what they wanted out of them. Of course, we blamed the Japanese for any problems that occurred in the distribution of any clothing, food, or medicine meant for us. Many Filipinos tried to help get items to us, but in most cases the Japanese refused to allow any aid to the prisoners. Any aid a person received was a big plus and certainly helped people survive.

Black markets existed in some of the camps. Goods could be obtained through Americans who had been civilians working in the islands before the war began. Some of these men were held at Cabanatuan along with those of us who had been in the military. These civilians were able to make contacts outside and inside of many camps. After I had arrived in the Philippines, I contacted one American couple in Manila who were related to some friends of my family in Clovis. My parents had written me, asking that I visit the couple. Before the war broke out, I had called them and I gave them news about the woman's sister, who I knew quite well. The woman had heard about me from her sister and was happy I had contacted her. Once the war began, I had no idea what happened to this couple, but while at Cabanatuan, I sent the woman a letter through Tom Bowman, the truck driver I knew. I do not know if he passed it on or not. (Rumor had it that a letter given to most Filipinos would be stamped and forwarded to the address on the envelope.) As it turned out, I never heard from the couple. By the time I was repatriated, the woman's sister and her husband had passed away, so I never learned what happened to them.

Aside from some of the civilian prisoners, a number of the military men who had been based in the islands for several years had made many contacts during that time. They were able to get messages out of camp and were thus able to receive aid as a result of the messages. A number of Filipinos and other nationalities that had some freedom in the islands were able to get aid to their imprisoned friends or relatives. Money and medicine were the two most valued items. Both could help men survive. The cash could be used to buy medicine and additional food. In some instances, money could be used to bribe a guard if a man got into trouble, or assist in getting something in or out of camp. Medicine was as good as money and, if one was sick, better than cash. It could also be converted to money.

As this underground trading system developed, the brutality of the guards did not change. One escape occurred and as a result, the nine men left in the group were killed. In another incident, the Japanese mounted several prisoners on the posts at the camp's entrance. Filipinos passing by were required to beat on the men until they finally died. I am not aware of the guards torturing to death any of the men from New Mexico, but a number of the 200th and the 515th were badly beaten on work details.

I did have one instance of good luck at Cabanatuan. I mentioned earlier that upon the surrender, we were ordered to return to Cabcaben Field. But as I proceeded to do so, I could not find my field pack, or knapsack, which contained personal effects, especially my Bible. I finally got it back at Cabanatuan, with a bit of history tied up with its return. The Bible, given to me by my parents, has my name printed in gold on the cover. When I recovered the Bible, I penned the following inscription on one of its pages:

"Lost April 7, 1942, night before we were surrendered on Bataan. Recovered September 23, 1942, in Cabanatuan concentration camp. Robert Paul Wilson found the Bible on Bataan. Wilson died July 5, 1942, in Cabanatuan. Wilson was from Sweetwater, Tennessee. Mallard McCullough the next person to have the Bible died later. Jim Haynes the next holder of the Bible was in the hospital when I heard of the location of the Bible. It was being held by A.M. Walker on the duty side. John E. Reynolds discovered the Bible with my name on it. I had returned from the hospital side a month before it was recovered. Reynolds was from Clovis and we were in the same Battery originally and he advised me of the location of the Bible."

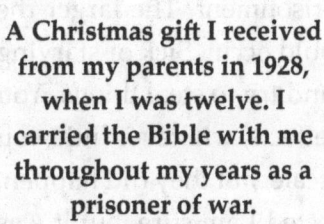

A Christmas gift I received from my parents in 1928, when I was twelve. I carried the Bible with me throughout my years as a prisoner of war.

Most of those who came into possession of my Bible did not survive. I was not acquainted with Wilson, McCullough, or Haynes. John Reynolds later died. Since that time, as a result of recovering my Bible, I have read it or successors everyday or night whenever I could. I know that sometimes while I was in prison, I was not well enough to read it. Today, the physical condition of this Bible is deplorable. Prison experiences were hard on both the Bible and me.

Aside from this Bible, I also had a copy of the New Testament with me in the camps. I had acquired it at Fort Bliss in January of 1941. It is what some call a Soldier's Bible, distributed to those in the military by the American Bible Society. It is small in size, made to fit in the uniform pocket over one's heart. Since I had lost my field pack at Bataan, the New Testament could not have been in that at the time of the surrender. I must have carried the New Testament in my pocket. I certainly read the book a considerable number of times during the war, underlining passages and making notations on its pages. The strangest entry, made in the Philippines on November 21, 1941, reads, "Private First Class Buren D Johnston, Barracks 14 hospital area to get my watch #2744051, pen and other valuables (Bible etc.) in case of my death." I had trained Buren to become my successor as the Company Bugler at Fort Bliss in 1941; he was a good bugler so I had trained him well. When I wrote that bequest a few weeks before the war began, we were on full alert and expecting something to happen. I have no recollection of where or how I obtained the watch.

I could have lost my Bible, New Testament, and other possessions at any time during my imprisonment. The larger the camp I was in, the more bad incidents would occur. Sick or starving men could lose their perspective on life and try to steal things. You had to watch and protect your personal effects, whatever little you had. Such thefts did not occur on a large scale, but they did happen.

I saw another problem, not unexpected I am sure, but it was

a surprise to me because I was still a civilian in my mind. The problem was the jealousy among the officers, especially between West Pointers, Regular Army, National Guardsmen, and those who came up through the ranks. Each seemed to feel that they were better officers than the others, regardless as to how they had become officers. I saw them as just like enlisted men, some good, some bad, and some not worth shooting because of the expenditure of time and ammunition. Many officers were very democratic but some felt they were blessed with a golden spoon in their mouth. It appeared to me that some had actually been born with a lead spoon up their anus.

One of the most telling quotations I have ever read appeared on page 199 of a book I read within the last few years, and I quote the end of the officer's mentality:

> "...but again, we had to contend with the fact that we were officers and the others were not. That showed up in the subtle, underlying resentment that enlisted men naturally tend to exhibit towards Commissioned Officers. It also keyed to our being better educated and having different cultural tastes and backgrounds..."

The officer who wrote this was hospitalized at Bilibid. Hopefully he lived to regret his feelings at that time. He may have deserved his supercilious position. He would have been surprised to know that many enlisted men held some officers in high regards and would obey their every command. I have no idea now as to this officer's identity. I believe I would consider exposing his name, if I were less of a gentleman even though I was not a commissioned officer. Since I was a college graduate, if I had waited to join the military and not enlisted before the war began, I could have been an officer, or if the surrender had been delayed just a few weeks, my promotion to $2^{nd}$ lieutenant would have come through and I would have had another chance to be a commissioned gentleman.

But I have no regrets. I am proud of my actions during all of my imprisonment.

I was assigned to various work details. Each one was different. The Nichols Field detail was one of the most extreme in all aspects. Nichols Field was an airfield more or less within the city of Manila, at its outskirts. The Japanese Navy, which had taken it over, requisitioned prisoners to maintain the field and to upgrade it. The information we heard at Cabanatuan indicated that the brutality at Nichols Field was worse than any other place. There were more beatings, less food, the labor was harder, less water was available to the men, imprisonment within prison occurred there, and there was various types of torture. The water treatment was one of these. It consisted of forcing water down a prisoner's throat and into his stomach. The Japanese then dropped heavy weights on the American or jumped on his stomach. Other forms of tortures forced a prisoner to stand for long hours in the hot sun without moving; if he did move, guards beat him and made him stand even longer. A man could also be forced to squat for long periods of time with a rod, pole, or sword under his knees. Prisoners were also put into cages that were too small to lie down in or stand up in. Withholding food or water became another form of torture. Americans had to be on their best behavior, work the hardest, and complain the least. The Japanese still treated them as dogs most of the time.

The port detail in Manila could be very beneficial for the prisoner, but it also could turn into a bad time for him. Apparently more opportunities to steal food, medicine, and other items occurred at the port. But if the guards caught a prisoner doing any of this, atrocities and punishment followed. The Japanese sent many men to Mindanao where the treatment was both good and bad. It was a rather large camp and some of the prisoners escaped, but most returned to Cabanatuan after the Japanese no longer required their labor at Mindanao.

Bilibid seemed to be a way station in the transfer of prisoners. While the Japanese took most details directly to the work camps, as men became sick or injured they were usually returned to Bilibid. Once at Bilibid, prisoners could be sent to the sites of other work details, to Cabanatuan, or in some cases the men stayed at Bilibid.

Regardless of where we were, worms became one of our biggest medical problems. No doubt we got them from our food or from the filth caused by the lack of sanitary conditions. We really could not afford to retain the worms since they received more of the nutritional value from our meager diet than we did. The method by which we got rid of them was, for many, worse than having the worms. Our medics used Ipecac to help us deal with this problem, and they used a considerable amount of this medicine. Ipecac is taken orally, after which we were admonished to lie down, motionless, to allow the Ipecac to work its way through our system, which discharged the worms. If, however, a prisoner moved too much after taking the medicine, he vomited up the Ipecac and, sometimes, the worms as well. This was very unpleasant. A medic administered additional doses of the Ipecac until the worms were eliminated.

We also had to contend with the flies. They were sometimes so bad at Cabanatuan that a bounty was paid for their extermination. We even held contests as to who could kill or capture the most flies. If conditions were right, the larva of the flies turned into maggots. With our very elementary sanitation system, especially initially, the maggots were numerous. The very sick, particularly those with cuts, abrasions, or wounds that had not been properly cared for, suffered from an infestation of maggots. Once those pests settled in, they were difficult to get rid of. As time passed, and we learned from our experiences, one by one most of these problems were eradicated.

Coupled with our lack of experience, other factors contributed to situations getting out of control. Due to the physical condition of a great number of the men when the camps were set up, we allowed problems to exacerbate. Additionally, the lack of organization, doctors, medicine, and decent sanitation conditions made things worse. The surrender had happened so fast, then the imprisonment. The necessity to take charge of the resulting chaos without the resources to do what was necessary proved overwhelming. We could be tempted to blame all of this on many ranking individuals, both military and political. But what's done was done, and it will not help to blame anyone for our predicament.

In spite of our problems, we scavenged some items that we used to bring some light moments to our lives. Name any object and I think you could find it in a prison camp, especially a big one like Cabanatuan. I mentioned before musical instruments that the men had. One man found an old bellows blower similar to the type blacksmiths used to fan the fire; I have no idea what he used it for. From other scavenged items, we had at least one radio in several camps. In 1943 when I worked in the Cabanatuan kitchen, a friend and I set up a five-hole miniature golf course. I had found some men with two or three clubs and three or four balls, so we designed this little golf course for recreation.

We all enjoyed other forms of entertainment, too. I mentioned earlier the plays that the prisoners put on. Some of the skits required females for the roles, and sure enough the men located some women's clothing. The Philippines Red Cross furnished us with books and games, such as checkers and playing cards. Some prisoners brought their own cards and dice into camp. The cards were as dog-eared as they could be; they probably had been marked at one time to give their owners an edge in the game.

For me personally, the time I spent working in the Cabanatuan kitchen was possibly the best months I spent at that camp. Having recovered from malaria, I was not sick. It was the dry season and the weather was good. Showers had been erected and hooked up to water. I appreciated that after a hot day in the kitchen. The kitchen work proved hard, the hours long, and the pay low, but the comradeship was good. We also had slightly more food. Sometimes I located a scale to weigh myself on. I tried to keep a record in my notebook of my weight. But the accuracy of the scales was in question since they were not tested and certified periodically as scales are in the United States. According to the doctor who examined me when I entered the National Guard, I had then weighed 193 pounds. The next record, from my notebook when I was hospitalized at Cabanatuan, lists my weight at 120 pounds. In March of 1943, I weighed 167 pounds, and after working in the kitchen, I gained a little over ten pounds.

Telegram received by my parents in March 1943 informing them that I was a prisoner of war. It had been one year and three months since they had last heard from me.

I was assigned to the kitchen for a little over four months. By the end of that time, several groups of men had left camp on work details and so our kitchen was closed. Along with the others from the kitchen, I was transferred to Group II (we had been in Group I). I then worked in camp on an unloading detail and then in the garden until October 12, 1943. On that day, the Japanese assembled a work detail of eight hundred men. Lester Morrison, Jack Aldrich, and I were in that group. I do not recall for sure, but I think we volunteered because the camp was disintegrating. With the departure of eight hundred prisoners, Cabanatuan would be much smaller, and as I observed earlier, sometimes smaller was good and sometimes it was not. For me, it seemed like it was a good time to take a chance on better living conditions by volunteering for the work detail.

The Japanese loaded us onto trucks and off we went. Rumor was rife as to our destination. At one point, because of the direction the convoy headed it, it appeared that we were on the way to Nichols Field. That possibility filled us with dread. How lucky could we be to have avoided Nichols Field? The spider was still drawing men into its deadly web, but not like it had in 1942 when so many had died.

# 20

## Las Pinas

Upon arrival at our destination, we had the usual problem of getting an accurate prisoner count. When we finally stopped in front of a large compound, we were told to line up and have *tenko* or *bango* (either word meant a roll count). It never came out correct the first time, either by accident or on purpose. The Japanese had to count us again. That day there was a drizzling rain, not a heavy one, but annoying enough to completely soak us by the time the guards were satisfied we were all there.

On such relocations, the Japanese divided us into groups of fifty men each. After the count was done, the guards marched our group into the compound. We were the fourth set of fifty men and were assigned to Room 4 in the first barracks. We learned that this camp was called Las Pinas, spelled with an accent mark above the "n" because it was a Spanish name.

A description of the camp would begin with a small courtyard immediately inside of the gates. In the first building, up a short set of steps, were the camp headquarters and a room for the American officers on one side of a hallway. The hospital quarters were on the other side of the wall. Another small courtyard was located between the first and second buildings, then another building. All of the buildings had the same layout—two rooms were on each side of a center hallway reached by a short flight of steps. The Japanese housed two hundred men in the four rooms located in each barracks. In total, there were sixteen rooms for eight hundred men.

The layout of each room was the same. Upon entering it, there was a small area where we were to remove our shoes. Our home was on an elevated platform that acted as our bedroom and dining room. The Japanese allowed us to pick our own individual bedroom. The allotted space across the platform was for ten men, with rows of five. I became lucky and got the fifth or back row, which meant I was next to the back and side walls. Each room had a row of windows along the back. These could be pushed open and kept open with a prop. We could also close and battened them down for the rains that were sure to come. Each barracks of four rooms had a wide, covered porch in front of the rooms. Again, as with the first row of buildings, we went up a few steps to reach the level of the building and one could continue through the center hallway down to the next courtyard. All of the buildings had tin roofs. We had a few typhoons during our stay in Las Pinas. Unless you have been in a typhoon, you cannot believe how hard it can rain and how hard the wind can blow. Even with tin roofs, at times we were afraid that the wind would blow the roof off of the buildings.

The entire complex was made of wood. To the right of these four barracks, next to the front barracks, was a small building that later would be used as a commissary and library. Toward the back of the camp was a long shower building and latrine, and after that the kitchen. All of this was located on one side of the barracks. A high wooden fence completely surrounded the compound.

We were pleased with our accommodations compared with many we had been accustomed to in the past. From the standpoint of comfort, Las Pinas probably had the best barracks we had lived in. The buildings had much better shelter from the wind and rain, open windows, and the barracks were not too confining. The ranking non-com was in charge of the room, with an officer for each two rooms. One of the best features of this new camp was the availability of water. There was plenty of it. We were leery, though, of what was to follow, what kind of work we would have to do, who would be in charge of it, and how the food would be.

Were we going to be lucky, or would we be assigned to a mean work detail? Quite often, a very small work detail was the best because you became better acquainted with the guards and thus closer to them. At first, the Japanese would usually be mean and rough, but after a few days, if the prisoners behaved, the guards softened up. In camps bigger than Las Pinas, there would be more guards and supervisors; prisoners would be assigned bigger jobs, and the Japanese would be in a bigger hurry to finish them up. After a few days of getting settled and organized, assigning kitchen and latrine duties, the guards finally marched us off to our new positions. We were to become engineers of many types— architectural, civil, geological, mining, railroad, and sanitary.

In reality, our job was to construct an airfield out of a rice field. We had to knock down the rice paddy dams, level the high and low spots, and then construct drainage ditches and revetments to protect the planes. All of this work would allow the Japanese Navy to train pilots to expand their war effort. As I mentioned earlier, we were working for "The Greater East Asia Co-Prosperity Sphere." That had been one of the first announcements to us upon our arrival at O'Donnell. We were all to increase the prosperity of East Asia, with the help of the Japanese. Certainly, we had to assist our "employers" and not work against such a worthy undertaking. We were to be diligent and work hard to reach the Japanese goals. The pay was quite poor, the food insufficient, but we could count on steady work and we did not have to worry about being laid off.

At Las Pinas, we soon learned that building the airfield would be, in some respects, a very bad work detail even though the Japanese usually did not bother us from the time we returned from work until we left again the next morning. Of course, this unmolested period only lasted about ten hours since we had rather long workdays.

Whether it was the rainy or the dry season, our days were about the same. We were up at dawn, enjoyed *tenko* or morning roll call to be sure everyone was still in camp, went through the chow line, washed our mess kit, donned work clothes, assembled in front of the camp, counted off, and then walked about two or three miles to the work site. We labored until nearly dark and walked back to camp. Upon our arrival there, we endured another prisoner count to see if anyone had stayed at the work site to continue laboring for "The Greater East Asia Co-Prosperity Sphere." If all of us had returned to camp, the guards released us to our barracks. We showered, ate, rested, and visited a little bit with each other. Then it was lights out. Come daylight, we repeated this routine.

Las Pinas was located on the outskirts of Manila. I have heard that the Manila International Airport stands on part of the airfield we constructed. I do not know whether this is true or not. I do know that my time on this detail was the hardest I have ever worked in my life. The men with me have said the same thing. Once we arrived at the work site, the Japanese segregated us into groups of fifty men; the groups were not necessarily the same fifty that lived together in the barracks.

After demolishing the rice paddy dams, for our first project we knocked down the high spots, filled in the low spots, and leveled the area. We accomplished this by becoming construction engineers. We laid a railroad track from several hills to a big depression several hundred feet long. Of course, the length of the track depended on the distance from each hill to the hole. The Japanese furnished us with little, narrow gauge carts on flanged wheels that fit the narrow gauge railroad we had laid. These cars were flatbeds about six feet long and about forty-eight inches wide, with an open box sitting on the flatbed. The box was a few inches smaller than the flat. The box was wide at the bottom but a little narrower at the top. It had two handles that stuck out at each end. Now we became railroad engineers.

When we did this, we worked in groups of two partners, or four men per group. At the hill, we all dug and shoveled the dirt into the cart. Two men then pushed the cart down to the hole where they dumped the contents by lifting the box off of the flatbed. Then they upset the flatbed to remove all of the contents after which they returned to the starting point. While these two men were pushing the cart down to the low spot, the remaining two men dug out more dirt and were ready to fill the cart again when it returned.

On this project we worked in groups of four men per cart, so with ten carts, forty of us worked together. While one group worked on one hill, the others would be scattered all over the area doing the same thing. In each location, the men filling the carts had to finish loading their carts at the same time. Should one or two groups of four not finish at the same time as the other nine or eight carts, retribution was sure to follow.

Guards accompanied us to and from the field. While we worked, they surrounded the field, watching to see that no one decided to visit the town. Connie Mas, in charge of fifty men, was the supervisor I worked under. I was never sure if he was a civilian or if he was in the Navy. He wore a Navy hat but dressed in civilian clothes. After a few weeks, the Japanese brought in a junior supervisor to assist the head supervisor. (I use the word "junior" because he was a young man from Taiwan, more like a teenager than an adult.) The two supervisors kept us very busy. Connie usually stationed himself where he could easily see the entire group. The young kid kept busy walking up and down the line, urging each man on with a stick applied to whatever part of the prisoner's body that the junior supervisor could easily hit, the arm, leg, back, or head. If we still did not move fast enough even with this "encouragement," Connie intervened. Using a bigger stick, he tried to create more of a desire in us to cooperate. Neither was afraid to use beatings as a form of persuasion.

At times, the kid would play with us and be a little easier on us, but at other times he acted just the opposite. On one occasion he gave me a swat without cause. As he walked away from me, I picked up a clod of dirt and threw it at him. I missed and he laughed. To my sorrow, Connie witnessed the exchange. He gave me a few big hits, including one that nearly cost me an eye. That was one of the few beatings of any great consequence that I received during my years as a prisoner.

The men sustained many injuries, most of them accidental or the result of poor equipment. Because of these accidents and illnesses, we always had two corpsmen with us. With only these two, though, and slightly less than eight hundred workers, the corpsmen were quite scattered and a man could lose thirty minutes to an hour trying to locate them. Many of the injuries were superficial and caused by the men themselves so they could get some time off of work. Since the corpsmen got into trouble with the supervisors for coddling the men, they rushed any treatment, and at times seemed insensitive to the men. The corpsmen had little to use to assist an injured man. One of the medicines they had plenty of was Gentian

Violet that they used in place of iodine, although it did not have the bite of iodine. Purple in color, medics used the Gentian Violet for external use for everything but trench mouth and eyewash.

One day while playing railroad engineer, my buddy and I pushed our cart down the tracks. The cart behind me released accidentally. It cut me down and ran over me. I was skinned from head to foot. I was so beat up that two men were allowed to take me to the corpsman. When he saw me, the corpsman told me how sorry he was for what he had to do to me. The corpsman had been putting a lot of astringent in the Gentian Violet to make it sting so that the men would not come back. The medic said to me, "Jones, I'm sorry but this is all I have with me today, and it's going to burn like hell." The corpsman was right. I was a mess and the Gentian Violet really hurt because my shoulders, back, buttocks, thighs, and legs were skinned deep. What had made the injury so widespread was that I had been wearing only a "g" string. (The Japanese issued us these "g" strings. It was a piece of cloth attached to a string that was long enough for us to wrap around our waist. The cloth measured about twelve inches wide and thirty inches long. The "g" string really covered only our private parts.) The only good part of all of this was that I did not have to work anymore that day or the following one. I guess I was lucky that I did not get any infection. When I returned to work, the heat and sweat really bothered me, but I was lucky it was not any worse. I am fair skinned and very susceptible to becoming sunburned. In fact, I used to be a redhead. For some reason, which defies logic, I worked all day in only a "g" string and did not get burned. I really did not tan, either. In the States after the war, I could and did burn easily.

Doctors were at Las Pinas along with, as I recall, only two or three medic corpsmen. We had sick call between breakfast and when we had to fall in line for work. The doctors confronted the same problems at this camp as they did at all of them. The Japanese did not want any man to have the day off while the doctors tried to keep men who were really sick off of the work details. As at Cabanatuan, the guards beat the doctors if they pushed too hard to excuse the men from work for medical reasons. Always low on supplies, the doctors also tried to obtain more medicine and food for their patients.

After we had the huge field fairly level, we next had to dig huge drainage ditches. Depending upon the elevation of the field we were working on and the height of the nearby fields, the depth of these ditches could be anywhere from nearly ground zero to over six feet deep. We worked in pairs, with each pair given the task of digging down ten feet on an area about four feet wide. The task lent itself to trouble. With two men working together using picks and shovels, it became very difficult to do the work without injuring your partner, getting the work done, and making sure all fifty men kept the depth at the same level. It was only natural that you talked to your partner. It helped pass the time and made the work easier. What did we talk about? In my case, my partner and I did not know each other before the war although he, too, was from Clovis. He was in a different age group and we did not go to the same schools. We discussed our backgrounds, what we had done in civilian life, drinking, girlfriends, food, education, and life in general. Because we were from diverse backgrounds, our discussions became an education for both of us and we worked well together. Except for this time together in Las Pinas, we had not been together since the surrender. To my regret, we separated when we left this camp. We never got together again, either during or after the war, even though both of us survived.

We nearly received a terrible beating in one incident. We had been digging this deep ditch and got to talking and resting too much. When the noon whistle blew, we had unearthed an area about two feet shallower than the areas dug by pairs on either side of us. The area we were digging in had a foot or two of hard ground, a couple of feet of soft dirt, and then harder dirt. My partner and I were lucky since Connie and our Japanese overseer took a longer lunchtime than usual. With that extra time, we worked and were almost caught up with the other pairs before Connie came along to check us out. As we tried to catch up with the others, Connie gave us several good swats on our back from his stick, but it would have been much worse had he been his usual sweet self and made his inspection before lunch. Writing fifty years later, I am making light of his swats. He hit us with a club that was some thirty-six inches long, about the size of a pick handle. While Connie seldom broke any bones, his swats gave us many bruises. We especially had problems with him after he took a day off. I think he came back with a hangover. With the hot sun on top of that condition, he took it all out on us.

We gave the junior supervisor, the young teenage boy from Taiwan, the nickname "Rabbit Ears" since he was always listening to us. I think he did this to learn the language more than for any other reason. Most of the time Rabbit Ears was not mean to us and because of this, Connie got on his case and made him hit us harder. Connie demonstrated by hitting us himself, to show the kid how to do it. Our punishment thus doubled. The treatment we received while we worked depended on the overseer each of the fifty men had. Some like Connie were mean S.O.B.s, but others were not too bad.

Actually, the Americans were their own worst enemies. The equipment we worked with was very poor. A few good American-made shovels and picks were mixed in with the tools, but the majority of them were made out of such thin material that it became hard not to break them. To make matters worse, if you damaged an implement, you received a beating, and if you tore it up, damaging it so much it could no longer be used, they really laid into you. Nearly all of us at one time or another broke a pickaxe or the tin shovels. As such, we reaped the consequences. The situation with the tools got so bad that as soon as the first work group out of the nearly eight hundred men reached the work site, the group ran to pick out the best made tools. In a few days, as my group approached the site, some men in the back started running so they could get good tools. The Japanese thought we were crazy. Many others, including myself, agreed.

The American officers had to go to the site to keep us working. They also were there to keep the overseers from beating and working us too much. The officers tried to keep the crazy ones, those who ran for a tool, back and in line. The Japanese, however, would not let them stop the men. The Japanese thought it was ludicrous. The American officers tried to talk to the men in the camp to warn them not to run, but they never were able to stop it.

When the rainy season arrived, it was too muddy and sticky to dig ditches or level the ground, so the supervisors put us to work building revetments. These were to be square "U" shaped, about fifteen or eighteen feet high with a wide base at the bottom that narrowed down to about one foot in width at the top. The revetment was just high enough so that if a bomb dropped nearby, its dispersion would not hit the plane inside unless the bomb landed right in front of revetment. The Japanese gave us little baskets with a depressed center; they were shaped a little like a giant shovel, about twenty-eight inches wide and a little longer in length. As some men passed by with the baskets, the group shoveling would put dirt into them. Once they were full, the baskets were used to build the revetment, like the Egyptians had built the pyramids. One man dumped his basket, then another did the same, and then another until the desired height was reached.

Because of all the rain, the dirt was like liquid mud. By the time you reached the spot to dump your load, half of it had leaked through the basket. We spent all morning trying to build one revetment, fifty men in a constant stream, like a bed of ants carrying food to their anthill. By noon we had built one revetment about six feet high. We climbed on the pile of mud and I guess we managed to pack it a little, but the pile kept getting wider at the base. Finally I convinced Connie to approach the task by a different route. The men made a long line and the first man dumped his load into the second man's basket. That second man then dumped what he had just received into the third man's basket. This continued on up to the top, or to the last man. This method kept the base from widening and expedited the building of the retaining wall. In this way, we saved a lot of steps and we were not as tired as we had been just standing in one spot. It did not speed up the process by a single ounce of dirt. When the last man received the mud from the man behind him, he only got a handful of mud. One day of that convinced the Japanese that it would be much better to wait until the rains stopped and the ground dried out a little.

There were very few days that the Japanese allowed us to stay in camp because of the weather. When we marched home from the airfield, as we neared the camp it became our custom to start singing. We marched a little faster and held ourselves more upright, just to make the Japanese mad. This sometimes backfired, however, because they worked us harder the next day. As I mentioned earlier, the labor I did at Las Pinas was the hardest I had ever worked. In the summer between my freshmen and sophomore years at college, I delivered ice. This job required that I lift upright three hundred pound cakes of ice. I even held one hundred pound pieces of ice on my shoulder with my bare hands so they could be slipped into certain types of ice boxes. I began work at 5:00 am and delivered nine or ten tons of ice a day. The work at Las Pinas proved much more debilitating. I have identified it to be the hardest work I have ever done because of the task and the equipment—we were building an airfield with picks and shovels. Coupled with the treatment we received there, and the psychological duress we worked under, our work was extremely rough.

One day one of the men, or his partner, accidentally broke his arm. Contrary to the usual treatment where the prisoner would be treated by a corpsman at the site, the Japanese took this man back to camp immediately so the doctor could set his arm. In a couple of days, the man was taken to Bilibid and a replacement returned in his stead. This gave an idea to a number of the men. In the middle of the morning, it became common for many to approach the medics in the field, claiming they had broken their arm or hand. I do not think the Japanese ever caught onto the scheme to get out of work. Prisoners also wanted to return to the base camp because we were fed even less on this work detail. Men, if they were fast enough, were eating anything that moved, such as rats, ants, and grasshoppers. Some were even eating weeds and grass.

We had at least one man in camp who augmented his income by breaking arms, legs, or hands. He did not take out an ad in the *Manila Bulletin* (the local newspaper, copies of which sometimes made their way into camp with the help of one of the drivers). But word of mouth circulated news of this man's services. His method was to lay the prisoner's arm across two pieces of wood, then hit the arm between the two uprights with another heavy club, breaking the arm. The injured man suffered all night. The next day, after arriving at the airfield and working for a while, he showed his arm to the supervisor. Once on sick call, the injured prisoner was sent back to the camp and then to Bilibid. One man actually drove his pick into his foot to get off of the work detail and to Bilibid.

We had been in Las Pinas about six months when a casual friend approached me one evening. He asked to talk with me in private. We walked to a point between two of the barracks where he turned to me and asked if I would break his arm. I wanted to know why he wanted to do such a stupid thing. I pointed out that I could end up hitting him too hard and crushing the bone. He might not get the proper treatment and he could end up with a permanent injury to his arm. He replied that he didn't care. He could not take the work and treatment by the Japanese anymore. My reply to him was "no" for the following reasons. First, it would put a little more work on the remaining men. Second, if the Japanese caught onto what had happened and he squealed on me, I would end up with a broken bone or two. Third, I thought it was a depraved way to get out of work at the expense of others, even though the injured man went away with the real punishment, a broken limb. I have often wondered what happened to this man. He did have a broken arm a few days later and left camp, supposedly to Bilibid. I hope he survived without any ill effects, but I was not going to help him in the manner he requested.

While in Las Pinas, we received some Red Cross packages, or parts of packages. My notebook indicates that one arrived around Thanksgiving 1943 and another one a month later around Christmas. We also got one in January and one in February of 1944. In April of that same year we received a few items by lot, including butter, raisins, powdered milk, and sugar. The Philippine Red Cross sent us some fruit, nuts, cookies, and beans for each man. We also received some clothing. For each room in each barracks, there were fifty items of clothing, from knitted caps with earmuffs to vests, coats, sweaters, handkerchiefs, and heavy underwear. I suppose each room handled the distribution of these items in the same way. Each item was written on a small piece of paper which was then folded. Based upon the number of men in the room, an individual pulled a number, blind. I was lucky and received a vest. The knitted cap was the pick of the lot because this was the rainy season and the cap not only covered one's head, but it also had earflaps. The American Red Cross had made the caps. In a strange turn of lucky events, the room's 1st Sergeant drew the last piece of paper out of the hat. It was the knitted cap. The man who was the next to the last one to pick a number was sure that he had picked the last piece of paper in the hat. Given my experiences in the military, though, I felt certain that the 1st Sergeant had, with a little forethought, inserted the last paper under the sweatband of the hat.

One of the men in our room was a truck driver, and as such, he worked out of the transportation pool. He apparently had a lot of free time. The Japanese treated him fairly well. After we received the first Red Cross packages in Las Pinas, we asked him if he could bring us a jar of alcohol, which all of the vehicles ran on. The next day he brought in a canteen filled with it. We filtered the alcohol several times through charcoal and ashes from the kitchen. Our Red Cross packages had some sugar and sometimes we were able to buy extra sugar at the commissary. We mixed the alcohol, sugar, and some raisins together to make a rather potent drink. It did not taste too bad. I guess we were lucky that we did not drink enough of it to have any adverse affects on us. As I have said, ingenuity is one of the traits Americans possess.

The truck driver who had assisted us had never tasted coffee. With every Red Cross package he received, he traded his coffee for powdered milk, sugar, or something to eat. The coffee was well received, especially during the rainy season. Upon receipt of the first Red Cross packages at Las Pinas, the kitchen had set up a system so that when we returned from the airfield, we all went by the mess with our canteen cup. We got a cup of water that was almost boiling and returned to our room where we enjoyed a cup of hot coffee. Depending upon one's feelings, many first rushed to the showers and cleaned up from the day's work. We washed out our "g" string, rushed back to the room, donned what little clothes we had and hung out our "g" string to dry. We then sat back and enjoyed the coffee and a cigarette. The hot shower, especially during the rainy season, was one of the highlights of our day, followed by the coffee and smokes.

After listening to us talk about how good and refreshing the coffee was, the truck driver finally asked me for a spoon of coffee. What we had was dehydrated, and sometimes crystallized or caked. It was not very good even by the standards of the early 1940s, but the driver wanted to try it. After getting a cup of hot water, he stirred the coffee into it and added powdered milk. After a few swallows, he was hooked. After watching him mix the various parts, I was afraid that he did not have a very good mixture, so I asked for a swallow to see why he thought it tasted so good. I knew right away that he had put in too much sugar and milk, but since he was happy, I did not discourage him. From that time on, he did not trade anything, saving his coffee.

The Philippine Red Cross also gave us a toothbrush, tooth powder, a razor, seven blades, and a little sewing kit. I am sure you would be surprised to know how highly we valued the sewing kits. Our clothes were originally long sleeved shirts, long pants, and underwear, tops and bottoms. As our long pants and shirts started to wear out, we shortened the long sleeves and used the remnants for patching. We did the same with the long pants. Soon everyone wore shorts. Until we had the sewing kits, threads unraveled from our shorts or pants. How did we use the thread? I do not remember, but we must have found needles to borrow, beg, or buy.

We found ways to add to what we were given. The munificent salaries we received actually stretched a little further than one would surmise as we bought some items we needed. As traders, we also did pretty well, since what one man had as a luxury another man saw as a necessity. In nearly every camp, regardless of its size, we found a tailor, cobbler, tonsorial master, and a music virtuoso; we also had card dealers and dice handlers. Sometimes the biggest problem was getting hold of the necessary supplies to do what we want to. In time, most of us were able to adapt things to our individual needs, to a degree.

Socks were the first to go, followed by shoes. We could do without socks very well, but shoes posed a much bigger problem. Flat, wooden shoes, with a strap across the top and the heel whittled out, was the first footwear created. As with all fashions, mutations soon evolved. The wooden shoe became much less cumbersome and more stylized; the soles were much thinner and the heel not as pronounced. Various materials, dictated by what was available, were used for shoestrings—belt leather, rubber inner tubes, and strips of leather wider than those used in belts. Some men even had real shoestrings. From cast off tires, we made rubber heels and soles. I could not begin to elaborate as to the initial source of many of our supplies. For most of us, sacrificing our belts proved rather difficult to do since we needed them to hold up our pants. We punched more holes in it to make the belt smaller. When all else failed, we even used a piece of rope or wire.

In time, most shorts were made of patches on patches. In many instances, the patches did not match the original material, or even the patch to which the patch was patched. The short sleeves went to half-length, then to the shoulder. Shirt pockets were used as patches, as was the shirt's tail. We had Eisenhower jackets, which were waist length, before Eisenhower was even a general. A slight sartorial change in our jacket occurred when it no longer had the tab that would usually be pulled over at the bottom. Give the General credit for the addition of that tab to the jacket that bears his name. We did not have the luxury of material. Time has erased from my memory the names of who should be given the credit for modifying the shoes, clothing, and hair cuts, but in most instances, I am sure that several different individuals would be responsible for them.

Even though the Japanese paid us fairly regularly in Las Pinas, we could not, of course, buy the clothing we needed, but food was another matter. As I mentioned earlier, privates received .10 centavos per day and non-coms .15 centavos. I never understood how the Japanese knew how much to pay each man when they could not count. With few exceptions, every time we lined up for the morning *tenko*, or the evening count before we left the airfield, or the count after we got back to camp, the guards had to do the roll call more than once. Maybe the problem was our lack of cooperation or our attempt to confuse them. For whatever reason, several roll calls or count offs had to be done before the Japanese were assured that we were all there. This happened regardless of the camp.

I averaged about four pesos per month from twenty-eight days of labor. At our commissary, we could purchase tobacco by the kilo and long, thin, dark brown cigarettes that were usually very good. Sugar, coconuts, and bananas helped with our meager rations, as well as our mental well-being. Las Pinas also had a library with an interesting supply of historical novels by authors such as Kenneth Roberts, James Hilton, and Lloyd C. Douglas. Surprisingly, many men hoarded one or two books, reading them over and over; they also loaned the books to others.

One of the biggest morale boosters was when men received a package or letters from home. In Las Pinas, we received a package in March 1944. A few days later, numerous cards and letters arrived. I had received some letters from my parents the year before. I had recorded the dates they were written and received in my notebook. I got one, dated May 24, 1942, on July 28, 1943. On September 25, 1943 I received one that they had written on May 23, 1943. Obviously, some letters took longer to arrive than others. I was able to save these letters and others that arrived later. In 1944 on August 15th and 19th I received eleven more cards and letters from both my parents and from friends. While some of them were Christmas cards received months later, they were still well received. I still have these, as well as the several cards I was allowed to send home.

My mother had carefully saved everything she had received from me.

During my years as a prisoner, I only received one package from my parents although they sent more than that. The package was welcomed because even though you knew people back home had not forgotten you, you now knew that your loved ones were still alive. My package contained personal care items such as toothpaste, a toothbrush, shaving gear, playing cards, and a cribbage board since my parents knew how much I loved that game. A jigsaw puzzle was also in the package along with a pipe and tobacco. Three pairs of under shorts were welcome since after a shower in the warm season I could wear them. The package contained no food since I think my parents were under the impression our captors would feed us sufficiently. In the package, my father had included a list of the items he was sending along with what they had cost, which amounted to just over $16 American. I received all that he had listed, with nothing taken by our hosts.

I was always amazed how some of the men squirreled away food for several weeks and how others used their package up in a few days. To each his own. In my case, I guess I would put myself between the two extremes, carefully hoarding some of the food that would not spoil but understanding that an opened can of sardines or other fish had to be eaten that day. Most of us shared a can with a buddy to prolong the experience.

One day when the airstrip was about half finished, we heard a bee-like buzz gradually growing louder. We finally spotted a flight of small planes coming in for a landing. They were two-seater, bi-planes, evidently used for training. As it turned out, the day became one that was out of the ordinary, one that created quite a bit of excitement. In addition to the planes, we heard music from a band celebrating a funeral in the nearby cemetery. These events kept our troubles in the back of our minds for a little while. At least the funeral was not for any of us, even though we were halfway under the ground digging drainage ditches. The planes amused us almost everyday for many days. These two-seaters took off with the pilot/teacher in the back seat and the trainee in the front seat. After a few days of take-offs and landings, the trainee was ready to test his wings and would be given full control of the plane. If the trainee did not execute a good landing, the teacher hit him over the head with what appeared to me to be a brake club. Such a tool was used on the railroad to set the brakes on a boxcar. In length, the club measured about two feet or thirty inches. We were amused to see the teacher beat the trainee on the head, and he did not use love taps. We saw the club bouncing off of the trainee's head. The crash landings amused us even more. We clapped and yelled our appreciation, to the chagrin of the supervisors and the guards.

  As a rule, amusement was in short supply. Usually, we did not even have one day off every week. We believed that the number of days we worked was regulated not only by the demands of the higher ups, but also by how poorly we made use of our time. Even when we were not working, amusement was not easy to come by. On our rest days we repaired our clothes and rested our bodies. We also visited friends in other barracks, especially after we received mail, to see if the other men from Clovis had any news. The library had a few books that contained small maps the Japanese had not found. We eagerly scanned them for information as to where our rescuers might be.

  We received most of our information or heard the newest rumors from the truck drivers, or from an occasional short conversation with a Filipino. That was how we kept abreast of the war's progress. Occasionally, an issue of the *Manila Bulletin*, printed in English, was smuggled into camp or it made its way into the hands of a truck driver. The truck driver in our room let us read the paper, but we could not take it out of the room. While we had it in our barracks, we had a lookout at the door. More commonly the truck driver got information by talking to a Filipino when the driver's guard was not around. This news, however, was always suspect, although we believed anything if it was good news. We heard that the Americans were shelling Leyete. We knew the location of that island since it was in the Philippines, not too far south of Luzon.

I am sure that all of us tried to be less productive than we could have been if we had wanted to do the jobs the Japanese assigned us to with some expediency. For example, when we dug the drainage ditches, we spent time making sure that the sides of the ditches were as smooth as we could make them, which actually had no bearing on the construction. While running the railroad and knocking down the hills to fill the valleys, none of the ten cars in each group could move until all ten were filled. We came up with a method of loading the cars that involved some scheming. Some men filled part of the cars quickly, so they rested. Prisoners loaded the remainder of the cars slowly, and always with one car loaded even more slowly than the others. That way all of the men got some rest except for those who loaded that one last car. We took turns being the last car to fill up. Those who worked the last car might catch a hit or two from the supervisors. But by taking turns to insure that the last car was not always the same one, we got by with this subterfuge.

There were other ways we created work slowdowns. We stopped working if one man in a group needed to go see the medic, or if one person needed to use the *benjo* (toilet). We also felt that sabotage was one duty required of us. Breaking a tool was always good for ten to twenty minutes of not working while the man who broke it went to the tool shed to try and find a replacement. But if that happened, the prisoner always endured a beating for breaking the tool, but usually the beating was not too bad if the supervisor was in a good humor. Many of our beatings depended on the supervisor's mood. If we made him think that we were doing a good day's work, he would be a little easy on us. Connie often had a hangover, and if it was a bad one, he left Rabbit Ears in charge while he went off to sleep for an hour. It was easy to make Rabbit Ears think we were working harder than we really were.

At his best, Connie was a bitch to work for. He was considered about as bad as any of the supervisors. He often marked off how deep he wanted us to dig and demanded that we reach that depth regardless of how the day went. Connie was seldom at his best, meaning when he joked and laughed. He usually had a scowl on his face and murder on his mind. But as bad as Las Pinas was, we all felt we were lucky that we had not been shipped to Nichols Field. I know that when we passed that place en route to this camp, I heaved a big sigh of relief. I am sure most of the men felt the same way. The "White Angel," a Japanese supervisor at Nichols Field who wore a white hat, seemed to take particular pleasure in beating up Americans. Without doubt, that detail was the worst on Luzon.

I must have been in pretty good shape to endure the time I spent in Las Pinas. I know we were all hungry most of the time. Some of the men ate anything they had. All of us caught colds, accompanied by fevers, because we worked in the rain so much of the time. I had several huge boils while in this camp. The doctors or medics could not do anything to alleviate the problem until the boil became "ripe," or ready for lancing. The boils were very painful, particularly one that precluded me from sitting or sleeping on my back. The good part was that when it was ready to be lanced and the cut was made, the poison shot out. The relief from the pressure pain was enormous. The medic dressed the incision and after a week or so it healed.

Wading knee deep in the mud, we learned the first day to

preserve our clothing, especially our shoes. The weather determined if we took our shoes to work or if we left them in our room. The goo from the mud pulled our shoes off, or if we had tied them well, the mud pulled the soles off. The weather also dictated what we wore on the detail. Most of the time we worked in our "g" strings, not only to save our clothing but also because of the tropic heat that we lived in for most of the year. There was one man who was so fair that he had to wear a big straw hat, a long sleeved shirt, and long pants. He even wore gloves. I do not recall his name, but I do remember that his nickname was "Rosie" because he had freckles, a very red face, and red hair. I do not know where he obtained all of his clothing since there was not a clothing outlet by the name of "Big and Tall," and he was that.

Las Pinas was one camp I was in that did not seem to have any problems dividing up the rations. I do not recall a single fight because Prisoner A received more food than Prisoner B. This was most unusual. Fights were not uncommon, though. They broke out over the most inconsequential reasons. We came in from work tired or perhaps sick, and a wrong word, even from a friend, could begin a fight. Fights were not allowed in the rooms, but they could take place between the barracks buildings. By the time the two men got out there and swung a few blows, mutual friends stopped the fight and all was forgiven. In most instances the fights did not come to much. The men were so overworked, underfed, and undernourished that they could not hurt each other. At times there were some rather bloody fights, but these usually occurred after we received the Red Cross packages and the men felt stronger.

Stealing was one of the big reasons for bloody fights. When a man was caught stealing, the person he had stolen from was allowed to fight with the thief in any way he wanted to. If the wronged man was too small or fragile, others were allowed to mete out the punishment. A progression of men was even allowed to beat on the thief. After the punishment had been given, everyone ignored the man. While we did not condone stealing from each other, stealing from the Japanese was. We encouraged it, seeing it as our duty to do so.

The leeches were another problem. As far as I know, none of the men tried to eat them. The leeches were a big nuisance, and they were painful. If you tried pulling them off, their claws remained in your skin. The easiest way to dispose of the leeches was to bring a little heat near them. A cigarette or a match could be used. Feeling the heat, the leeches instantly released their hold on a leg or an arm. As I recall, once we drained off all of the water and did not walk in the nearby stream, the leeches were no longer a problem.

Another creature provided us with a source of wonderment, huge anthills. The ants built these huge mounds that measured five or six feet in height. A big base of mud was at the bottom and as the hill rose, it tapered off to a thin cone. I do not remember the ants creating any problems for us. When we knocked down their hills, they disappeared.

Knocking down the dikes was a much harder task. It was more difficult than we had anticipated. Since they had been there for years, the tropic sun had baked them into brick. I am sure that the poor Filipino who owned the land was properly reimbursed for its use, probably by being beaten to death as he begged for his property.

At one point, and I am sure it was during the dry season or just before the rains came, for nearly two months we worked without a day off. We did have help on the job from a large group of men and boys brought in from Formosa. They worked at night with only the light from flaming torches powered by coconut oil. The amount of work they accomplished must have been very little. We received first class treatment in comparison to the Formosa crew.

According to my notebook and my memory, September 21,

1944 was a big day. For some reason, I was not working. Instead, I was in the barracks, but when I heard machine guns and airplanes, I rushed outside. I saw some strange looking planes shooting at other planes that had the rising sun painted on their sides. The planes winning this air battle did not have the star in a circle emblem on them, as I remembered American planes having. They obviously, though, were U.S. Navy planes. I think I went to the airfield again on the 22$^{nd}$ to watch another raid by the American Navy. For several days after this, however, until October 1, 1944 when I boarded a ship, I have no recollection of what happened in Las Pinas. The time span of some ten days is a blank. But we must have been transported to Manila and the dock by truck sometime in that period. When we passed, but did not stop at Nichols Field on our way back to Manila, we must have heaved a sigh of relief. I felt Nichols Field must have been out of action because of our Navy planes. When we passed Bilibid and went directly to the dock we had very mixed emotions.

I felt a huge disappointment. The Americans were so near, and yet so far away. I stood on the dock facing a tub of a boat, and I knew it could have only one destination. Before this time, I do not think I had known of any prisoners going to Japan because when a group left Cabanatuan, we were never sure of its destination. I guess we must have thought that many men had been sent to Japan because so many had left that camp. Most never returned to Cabanatuan, nor were they ever heard of again. What was amazing was the bamboo telegraph that reached into many camps. Men left, and weeks, usually months later, some men returned to camp, sick or injured, and word got around about a friend being in some location. We heard what they were doing and how the camp existed. Some men came back in fair health, returning from a detail that had folded. I guess I assumed many had taken this cruise, but I never gave it much thought. Again, we had lived day to day.

At Las Pinas as our work detail had folded, the Japanese had told us that we had done a good job and we were going to be given a rest. On that dock in Manila, though, we had no idea where we were going or what was going to happen to us. The spider was rushing around the web, excited. The status quo was changing, and the spider saw an opportunity to perhaps pull us into its web even more.

# 21

# Haro Maru

It did not matter much as to where we were going. It was just another cruise. Hopefully, the accommodations would at least be adequate. What a dreamer I was!

The Japanese marched us up the gangplank and then across a short deck. With much haranguing, wild motions, and shouts of "speedo" (the Japanese term for "hurry"), the guards forced us to climb down a long ladder. At the bottom of it, we landed on a pile of coal slack (small pieces of coal). Since I was not an expert at that time on coal, I am not sure if it was anthracite or bituminous. We did find out that this coal was not soft.

We were further made to walk to the opposite corner of the hold where the Japanese had us stand shoulder to shoulder with our backs to the bulkhead until the line was complete. The next line stood in front of this first group, with their backs to our chests.

Since very few prisoners had chests or stomachs that bulged, it was man touching man. This continued until about five hundred men filled the hold. Only then were we allowed to sit down. I just wrote "sit," but how much space is provided for sitting when the man in front is touching you while you are standing?

The hold measured about forty feet by fifty feet, jammed with five hundred prisoners. Nearly all were enlisted men. The cast of characters also included a few officers (one or two of lower rank) and a number of doctors. One of the doctors I knew, Julien M. Goodman, later published a book in 1972 entitled *M.D.P.O.W.* on his experiences and included a chapter on this cruise. His pages are more detailed and graphic than are mine. My version includes only what I was aware of.

One of my best faults has been to look on the bright side of any situation. I did this even when I was in the military. When I began this cruise, for example, I saw a bright side to it in that our accommodations were located at just about water level. Since I have always been susceptible to motion sickness, I was glad that we were close to the water line because a person experiences less rocking closer to the water.

I guess this ship or boat, whatever you want to call it, was a small freighter with two holds. Prisoners were put into both holds. As it turned out, my group of five hundred men was the lucky one. As I mentioned, we had to contend with coal residue since that had been the cargo in this hold on a prior cruise. The men in the other hold, however, had to contend with the remnants of its prior passengers, horses.

The ship was loaded to capacity during the afternoon of October 1, 1944. The guards put heavy wooden beams over the hatch. We moved out that evening but went only a short distance. We lay idle the next day. Before sailing, many of the men received mail in the hold. On October 3$^{rd}$ I received three letters from my parents, dated December 23, 1943, December 24, 1943, and January 16, 1944. I also received six Christmas cards from family friends, all of them dated October and November, 1943. Although the letters and cards were almost a year old, I was happy to get them.

When the ship finally moved out on October 3$^{rd}$, the Japanese really battened down the hatch. They tied down the heavy beams, about four inches apart, with steel cable to make escape impossible for us. The heat was intolerable. The men stripped down to just "g" strings. We were crowded together like a bunch of ants. Lying down was impossible. Instead, we sat down with our legs on the person in front of us. My salvation, if there was one, was the fact that I ended up against the bulkhead. Only a few men were between the ship's side wall and me. The wall and the bulkhead were almost too hot to touch. In the corner opposite from where I was, there was a small opening above the ladder. While I am sure they received a little more air and oxygen than the rest of us, pity should be given to the men in that corner. For them, the worst part was yet to come.

The Japanese delivered food and water to us via a long rope. They lowered food, in what was usually a five-gallon can, down by rope. We received our water by the same method. The bad part of this for the group around me was that we were about the last ones to get food and water. The bad situation for the group under the ladder was their proximity to the toilet outlet. This, too, was a five-gallon "honey" bucket passed around to the men who yelled for it when they needed it. There was a constant call for the bucket. When the bucket filled, we passed it back to the corner where the ladder was. From there, the guards pulled the bucket up by rope. The movement of the ship determined how much reached the top and how much slopped over, back to the bottom of the hold. The Japanese used the same rope for the toilet bucket as they did for the buckets that carried food and water.

Never one to enjoy the "Chick Sale" outhouses, my personal

comfort became my first consideration. I had a hard time visualizing how, with the movement of the boat, I could hit a swaying object, namely the toilet bucket. At the same time, I thought of the need to keep the area I used as a sitting room and bedroom clean. I also considered the damage to my sensitive posterior. After much thought, I decided to abstain from using such facilities as long as I could. Of course, this resulted in a big case of constipation. At the same time, the small allotment of daily food and the miserly distribution of water reduced my need to yell for the latrine to a bare minimum.

When the Japanese loaded us on this ship, the smokestack was clearly marked with a red cross and the number "2." As we pulled out from Manila Bay, they painted over the red cross and made the "2" into an "8." We learned this from the doctors who took turns on duty topside. As men became sick, and I do not mean just seasick, but so sick they almost became terminal, the Japanese allowed a few men to be placed on the hatch. While this proved to be good for those who were ill, it was not for those underneath where the sick men had been positioned, especially if the latter had dysentery. All too often the men were not allowed topside long enough to recover from the heat and conditions in the hold.

The heat under normal conditions would have been unbearable. Certainly, these were not normal times. Temperatures in the holds must have reached 110 degrees. Since we were being transported to Japan to become laborers there, thus releasing more Japanese to fight the Americans, one would think our captors would at least allow halfway tolerable conditions during our transportation. But the Japanese would not even allow sufficient air into the hold. The doctors and the C.O. tried to prevail upon the Japanese to give us more air, but the more the doctors and the ranking officer protested, the more harshly the Japanese treated them. Sometimes during the daylight hours the guards removed a few planks that were over the hatch. Our captors would not give us more food, water, or medicine, even though later, after we reached our destination, the Japanese insisted that more medicine be given to the doctors.

Suddenly, on the third or fourth day out of Manila, an explosion occurred not far from our ship. An Allied submarine was attacking something. (Until this happened, I did not know that our ship was part of a convoy.) The Japanese sped up the zigzag course they had been following, making it even more pronounced. Down in the hold, we heard another explosion and machine gun firing. A few hot casings dropped into the hold and injured some men, but we still cheered the submarine's attacks. The guards pushed the Americans who were topside down the ladder, securing the hatch. It was hotter than ever. What were we thinking, cheering the Yanks and hoping an enemy troop ship would be hit? What about us being the next victim? In the daylight hours, such an event did not seem so bad. In fact, many were ready to see our ship sunk in order to get out of their misery. Maybe we would be next to catch a torpedo, but at the same time, thanks to God that we were a very small ship. No red cross marked the smokestack. I am sure that we were saved because we were not big enough and not deep enough in the water to be worth a torpedo.

Night proved to be the hardest part of this cruise. Men were weak, crazed by illness and a lack of oxygen, scared, and halfway out of their minds. Like a pack of wolves, one man started yelling or crying and soon half the hold joined in the outcry. The chaplain tried to calm the men by praying and talking quietly to them. This worked for a few nights. If the chaplain could get the men quiet enough, he started the Lord's Prayer. The men soon joined in and their good senses took over. Some of the men in the hold were Navy, and a night or two after the first torpedoes, they talked about our ship being "pinged" by the submarine's sonar. I never heard any pinging, but then I was in an Army group trained to shoot down airplanes, not blast ships out of the water, which was what Navy men had been trained for. What do you think that pinging sound did to the half-starved, waterless men? During this voyage, chaos was a mild situation in comparison to what would happen in the middle of the night to those of us in the hold.

Because of the unsanitary handling of the food and water buckets, after a few days dysentery and diarrhea broke out. This only compounded our problems. As our trip continued, the usually inconsistent Japanese, who did not always allow sick men to leave the hold, at times allowed up to twenty men and one doctor on the hatch. One man had been sent topside because he was ill. The next day, after a couple of hours, the Japanese sent him down into the hold again. Several times a man in this condition soon died. When the body was sent back up, the Japanese blamed the death on the American doctors for their failure to treat the man.

One tends to forget the bad things that occur in one's life, remembering only the good events. I am afraid that this is what occurred as a result of my trip on the *Benjyo Maru*, otherwise known as the *Haro Maru*. In Japanese, *maru* refers to a boat or ship. *Benjyo* is the Japanese word for toilet, so we came to have three names for our ship—*Benjyo Maru*, *Haro Maru*, and Hell Ship. And it truly was a Hell Ship as well as a toilet ship. Because of the unsanitary conditions, it became one huge pile of coal and defecation. It is truly a wonder that anyone survived.

We did make jokes, however, about the Japanese. This trip was the only time we did not have to stand roll call several times a day. The guards did know how many prisoners they started with, and they probably counted us as we came up the gangplank and again as we climbed down the ladders into the holds. The Japanese insisted on having the dog tags of every man who died. Other than the "g" string, that was the only other thing we wore.

Because the Japanese counted us so many times, we all learned to count in Japanese. Many resisted learning their language, but in most cases it was best to know it. I am sure that in the end, everyone at least learned to count in Japanese. During our time as prisoners, whenever the Japanese transferred us to a different camp they issued us a new identification number. At times we had to recite this prison camp number in Japanese, so it was not just a matter of counting up to ten or one hundred because camp numbers could be four digits.

As I mentioned earlier, the nights were pure hell. With Navy men calling out the pings on the hull, the men as a group were going crazy because of the lack of water. Many men urinated into their canteens and then tried to drink the urine. Many others stole another person's canteen, and if it contained no water, they urinated into the canteen and then threw it away. When the canteen was thrown, it hit someone and that started another riot aside from the ones that the pinging sound could incite. Some men even urinated into their own canteen. They then let another prisoner steal it, watching him drink what the thief thought was water.

The officer in charge and his appointed helpers, be they an officer or a non-com, tried their best to see that whatever little food and water the Japanese sent down into the hold was evenly distributed. This in itself was a huge undertaking. I have to commend everyone for trying to maintain order amidst this chaos. Of course, in the daylight the crowd could be more organized, but at night it was strictly hell, unadulterated hell.

When we loaded up the ship, most of us had personal belongings with us. We carried a canteen and a knapsack that held a mess kit and other personal items. During this trip, I was able to retain the bag and its contents. Many men were not able to even do this. When a man died, those closest to him in the hold took what remained of his belongings. It would have been impossible to find the man's friends. It was dog eat dog. During these days and nights, I asked myself many questions—How long is this trip going to last? Where are we? What is our destination? Can we make it through this?

One morning, after another night of hell, we found men who had cut their wrist in order to obtain liquid. In those hellacious nights, some of the prisoners turned into animals. During our incarceration, that had lasted for over two years so far, this sea voyage was by far the worst part of our time as prisoners. It was worse than the Death March, the beatings, conditions at O'Donnell, and the lack of water we experienced at more than one point. Men died everyday on this ship. Even more men fought each other every night, hurting each other.

On October 11th, we finally reached port. Ten men had died. I wondered where we were and if the Japanese would allow us on deck. We soon learned that we had arrived in Hong Kong. As I remember, I was on deck twice during our ten days in this port. The first time was when the Japanese washed us down with a fire hose, showering us with salt water. The second time was when we were allowed to use the toilets built on deck. In comparison with other toilet accommodations, these were extremely comfortable. You could sit down, but you were hanging over the side of the ship, with only bay water below you. This was my first trip to the toilet since we had left Las Pinas on October 1st, and this was now October 20th. My trip to the toilet was successful, but it was also very painful. In fact, it was extremely painful.

By this time, I was almost out of my head with rectal pain. The doctors received some drugs in Hong Kong, so I was given something that night that gave me hallucinations. For the first time, I was really out of this world. I thrashed around all night long. I thought someone was trying to steal my belongings, so I fought, it seemed to me, all night long. I was probably not as delusional as I thought, but at the time I was really wired. I do not know what the doctors gave me, but I have never wanted or had anything like it since. This was undoubtedly the worst night of my life. Much of the pain I experienced was caused by the breakup of what was causing my constipation.

We got under way several times in the evenings, but by morning we were back at the dock. Aside from the two times we were allowed on deck, the only other bit of excitement occurred on October 16th. Shortly after noon that day, all hell broke loose. American bombers out of China hit the dock areas. A few minutes later, low flying bombers swooped over the area. They strafed and sunk several ships. The planes set several others on fire. When the first run of high level bombers hit the dock area, the Japanese got their guns limbered up. When the second group of planes came through, the Japanese let a lot of firepower loose. I do not remember that they downed a single American plane, however, but the attack sure shook up the Japanese. Again, we were thankful that we were on such a little ship.

We finally set sail, for real, on October 21st and left Hong Kong. Seven more men had died since our arrival at that port. For the next three days and nights, we zigzagged to avoid American ships. Several more men died on this short leg of our journey. Dysentery was rampant, and ulcers developed from lying on the coal. Nights continued to be the most dangerous and longest periods for us. Men continued to go mad from lack of water, and fights occurred again at night when it was impossible to control what was happening. One of my acquaintances, Carl Deemer, died. He may have been killed by one of the other men. I knew him because his father worked for the railroad in Clovis and Belen, New Mexico. Carl was such a nice man. On the hell ship voyage, a fight had broken out and someone hit him over the head with a heavy canteen filled with some kind of liquid. I thought he was all right, but the next day I saw him taken up the ladder. Carl never returned to the hold. I do not know if it was the lack of food and water, illness, or the blow to his head that killed him. I had been very lucky. I knew all of the men around me, and we tried to take care of each other. Except for that one night when I was out of my head, and thought that someone was trying to take my belongings and canteen, I had endured.

The next two days after we had left Hong Kong were better than the first one. We had two meals and a full canteen of water. We were still below deck, but the Japanese had taken some of the lashing off of the huge beams over the hatch. That allowed a little more light into the hold. It was also not as hot in the daytime and the nights were cooler. After three days at sea, we finally landed at another port. I wondered where we were now. We all prayed that we had reached our final destination.

It turned out that we had arrived in Takao, Formosa, but we still lived on the ship. For sixteen more days we stayed in this stinking hold. No one could imagine how filthy we were, not only from the coal residue but also from the personal filth of so many men crammed in such a small area. We especially felt bad for the ones near the ladder since the "honey" buckets continued to be lowered and raised through the small hole over the ladder. Those near the ladder still received more air, though.

The guards brought us up once or twice to have glass rods inserted for smears, firmly, not gently, into our rectum. Despite this rather odious duty, the Japanese who did it seemed to take a perverse pleasure in ramming the rods in. I hope they found something in those smears, but I do not know what. A few days later, the Japanese had so much fun with the glass rods that they decided to repeat the brutality. The ineptness of their procedures, however, apparently failed to divulge any high level medical information. Their repetition of this reminded me of how much the Japanese loved to give us shots. Nearly every time we changed camps we had been given smallpox shots. One inoculation resulted in four shots, all administered at the same time, in a little square configuration. My notebook contains a record of the various shots I received, sixteen for smallpox. Just like the Japanese liked to count us again and again, they gave us shots again and again.

In those sixteen days our ship was docked at Takao, everyday or two the Japanese told us that we would unload tomorrow, but again, this proved to be just a teaser. We put out of port a couple of days, but I do not know if this was due to possible air raids or if they could not decide what to do with us. More men died daily. Finally, on November 8, 1944 we disembarked. We came to understand that thirty-nine men died on this trip, which coincidentally lasted thirty-nine days.

These deaths, I guess, were the Japanese way of weeding out the weak. They certainly did not try to obviate the mortality in any way. The brutality the sick suffered on deck, and the treatment given all of the malnourished men in the hold, continued until the last man was off the ship. When the Japanese unloaded us, if a man did not act quickly enough as the guards ordered us to move, punishment followed. They doled it out even to men who were incapable due to their mental condition or because of physical illness.

As in every case when men in a large group are moved around, one never knew whether the new grouping would be good or bad. In very few cases did we have an opportunity to be with our friends. In some cases we ended up with old buddies, but at other times we ended up in the middle of a group we had never seen before. We all had the same problem, so in most cases we made new friends. The buddy system was crucial to survival. In every situation, such as illness, beatings, and despondency, you pulled someone through it or they pulled you through it. The original members of the 200th from New Mexico, and the draftees we received, tried to stick together as close as possible so we could help each other. I am sure that is the reason why many of us survived.

Our six-hundred mile or so cruise from Manila to Hong Kong, and then the less than four-hundred miles from that port to Takao, Formosa, could have been much worse if you had not had friends and buddies who helped you in some way, perhaps with a little food or water, perhaps with their strength and faith. For example, had members of the 200$^{th}$ who knew Carl Deemer been near him when the fight broke out in the hold, I am sure a buddy would have prevented what happened to him. As it was, I think he was more or less alone in the middle of the pack, a bystander in a fight that resulted in a bad concussion and later his death. This trip on the *Haro* or *Benjyo Maru* was the only instance I know of when Americans took advantage of other Americans and violence occurred. To the best of my knowledge, no man from the 200$^{th}$ was involved in harming another person, other than a Japanese, during our entire time of captivity.

There were many instances when men returned to an animal-state, especially because of the lack of water. Some used any trick in the book to obtain water, medicine, or food, often to the detriment of others by underhanded and nefarious plans. It is my observation that adversity is a great teacher to many. To others, it is a return to animal life.

We endured so much. In the pitch-black hold of a ship, men became deranged by the lack of water, insufficient oxygen, and the maddening heat. We heard the sounds of ships being blown up with at least two different submarine attacks on the convoy. Even while in the port of Hong Kong, we experienced a bombing and strafing attack. Only your buddies, friends, and God could help you.

For those men who had survived the Death March, this voyage was much worse. While they did not have to contend with the sights of Japanese brutality that had accompanied that march, the thirty-nine days and nights, especially the nights, would never be forgotten. Crammed into the hold of this ship, shoulder to shoulder, with no room to actually sit down without bothering another person, one learned to put up with one's neighbor, regardless of body odor, excrement, language, and other filth, including coal dust. The spider caught a few more within its web.

## 22

# Formosa

After we finally were kicked off of the *Haro Maru* on November 8th, the Japanese divided us into different groups that went different ways. From the time we had been loaded in Manila on this "Hell Ship," we had sat in three ports for a total of twenty-six days and had actually sailed for thirteen days. I wonder why I worried about getting seasick.

In Takao, a port on the southern end of the island of Formosa (now called Taiwan), my group ended up in some elementary school buildings. According to my diary, we were in or near a small town that I called "Injin" for some reason. I do not know now how I acquired that name for the village, or even if it is the correct name. We were in this school grounds and buildings from November 9, 1944 to January 12, 1945. This is another of the blanks in my book of memories. I have the impression that the food was not too poor, and the treatment was better than usual. I do not remember any beatings. All in all, I do not think this camp was that bad.

Somewhere in the back of my mind, it seems like we had a rather big and unusual problem, the stealing of food or something on that level that created quite a variance in our everyday life. I do not remember the circumstances, but there was a problem within the camp among the Americans. I just cannot pull out of my memory bank who was involved, what it was about, or why it occurred.

At this schoolhouse, we did not have too large a group of men. The accommodations were not bad. I am sure we did not have beds. I guess we slept on the floor in the classrooms. For the first week or ten days, I do not remember doing any work. What work I remember doing after that was not very laborious. A part of the school backed up to a hill. Apparently the land had been cleared and leveled to create room for the buildings and the playground. The back end of the principal building was up against a vertical embankment, but there was not enough room between the building and the hill for a person to squeeze between the two. The part of the hill that was exposed at one end of the building was not fenced in. It was too high to enable us to escape. The fence around the entire enclosure began at the point where the hill leveled off.

Our job was to enlarge the schoolyard at the point where the bare bluff was exposed. Pebbles and small rocks saturated the face of the bluff. We had to pick the rocks out of the soil, piling them according to size in different locations. After doing this, we hauled the dirt to another part of the yard. Basically, we knocked down a good-sized hunk of earth, sorted out the pebbles from the larger rocks, tossed them into the proper pile, scooped up the remaining dirt, and shoveled it into the big pile. This was pick and shovel work. It certainly was not hard work, especially compared to Las Pinas. Guards were in sight to give us moral support, but I do not remember any incidents with them. Nor do I remember them prowling the interior of the camp.

Perhaps because we were only in Takao for only a short time, the Japanese did not start us on any big projects. They only seemed to want us to keep busy, maybe to keep our mind off of our situation. Compared to the other camps I was in, I know we had ample time to be idle. I recall playing bridge. One of my friends, Edward Mehegan, who was from Pennsylvania, was a bridge nut. He had originally been in the Air Warning Service. Ed was the type of bridge player who could tell you the day after the game what had been in your hand and how you should have played so that he could win with the cards he had.

We were in Formosa over Christmas and I recall that we had a church service, even though we did not have a chaplain. (In fact, I do not remember having any officers in our camp. We had just enlisted men. The ranking one was in charge of the camp.) The church service included Christmas carols. We did not receive any Red Cross packages while in Formosa although I think we received more food in this camp than in the others. I think we received mostly rice. In my notebook, I recorded that I weighed one hundred and fifty pounds in Las Pinas and one hundred and fifteen in Formosa. I do not know how I knew these were my weights at those points. If the numbers were accurate, they would indicate that I had lost about thirty-five pounds in the thirty-nine days on and in the *Benjyo Maru*. I must have had a belt left, or a good piece of rope, to help keep my pants up. About ten days before we left this camp, I recorded my weight to be one hundred and thirty pounds, so I guess they fed us a little bit so we would be able to do more work when we arrived in Japan.

I never looked as bad as many of the prisoners did. I guess I had a big advantage on these men since I had weighed about two hundred pounds before the war began so I could afford to lose some weight. Many of the men, before they had became prisoners, had not weighed over one hundred and fifty pounds, fully loaded with their backpack. They could not afford to lose any weight at any time. Picture what they must have looked like after losing fifty or sixty pounds. Many did not have enough meat on their frame to hide their ribs and their thighs looked like just bone. They were only skin and bones, with the skin stretched very tight so that every bone could be counted without touching the man.

What clothes we had were all summer weight tropical. We wore shirts without sleeves and shorts. The only warmth we had with them was in strategic points where we had sewed patches over patches. Very few men had regular shoes; they wore mostly homemade clogs.

We never got out of this camp from the day we entered until we left it. In most camps you would leave on some type of work detail, but here all of the work was within the camp. Since I was only one of some one hundred and fifty men, though, and my only work detail consisted of making piles of little and big rocks, I might not have known if anyone left camp. My feeling is that if they had left, it would have been someone who worked in the kitchen, mainly to bring food into camp.

We saw only Japanese guards, and outside of the Japanese who had invaded Formosa, the rest of the island's population was Chinese. The countryside was rather nice, as was the climate. The weather was not cold but semi-tropical. That was another factor, aside from the work and availability of water, that makes me rate this camp as about the best one we were in. (Water was always our number one concern regardless of where we were.) The fact that the Japanese guards did not mistreat us and that the food we were given, while not sufficient, was adequate, are other reasons why I rate this as my number one camp.

What about news of the outside world? While in Formosa,

we received none. We had been without such news for over one hundred days and were starved for information. On the *Benjyo Maru* we certainly did not receive any news. That was quite a change from when we had been in the Philippines. Usually the large camps had clandestine radios and news from them spread throughout the camps. Truck drivers brought us news in other camps. Our only recent source of information had been the bombing of our ship when it had been docked in Hong Kong. Because of that attack, we knew the Americans were not too far away because of the cover that the fighter planes furnished the bombers with. (Fighters had limited flying distance so they had to come from an American base or from an American carrier.)

We also had a strong, gut feeling that the Americans were still advancing from the south because of the movement of our ship out of the harbor in Takao after we had first arrived there. We did not hear or see anything else to give us hope. We still lived on faith in God and in the Americans. We all felt that we were going to make it, but we did not know exactly when we would be free. By the time we were in Formosa, we had spent close to three years in this hell. Unknown to us, the spider was weaving an even bigger web.

# 23

# Melbourne Maru

On January 12, 1945 we finally left our schoolhouse camp in Formosa. The Japanese took us back to Takao and loaded on us another ship, the *Melbourne Maru*. What a change in transportation, both in bad ways and in good ones. The fact that it was a much larger boat was a negative aspect. The *Melbourne Maru* would thus be more of a prize for a submarine attack than the little tub we had existed on for thirty-nine days and nights. On the positive side, the ship was much cleaner. It appeared to have been a troop transport, at least the part of the ship we had booked for this cruise had housed troops.

The *Melbourne Maru* was undoubtedly a top of the line cruise ship. The configuration in the area to which we had been assigned did not require us to sleep on the deck. Bays had been built around the perimeter of the hold with an open space in the middle of the deck. The Japanese assigned us the bays to sleep in. These were very commodious in comparison with all of our previous accommodations. The bays were crowded, but even in that aspect there was no comparison even with our bedrooms at Cabanatuan.

We did not leave Takao immediately although the Japanese had loaded us on the ship, after their usual multiple counting of prisoners, as soon as we reached the port. While not a big port, it was crowded with ships. It was while the *Melbourne Maru* lay in the harbor that we received news of the war's progress. In the first two days we were on board, the Americans bombed the port. Since the guards had put us below deck, we could not tell whether the planes were big bombers or Navy bombers. We did, however, hear the loud noises and explosions that resulted from these war efforts by our fellow Americans. We were not nearly as frantic, though, as we had been during the torpedo attacks and bombing while we had been at sea. In those instances we knew we were at the mercy of the sea. If our ship had have been hit in open waters that would have been it for us. If the ship would have been hit while we were in the harbor, however, we could have had a chance to survive the attack. Unless it was a direct hit, we might have been able to reach the shore.

Again, the news that accompanied this attack was both good and bad. On the positive side, we had not been hit. On the negative side, though, another ship loaded with American prisoners had been. Apparently all of the men on board had been killed, including someone from our regiment. Col. Luikart was on that other prison ship. He was the Commanding Officer of 2nd Bn. Headquarters, 200th CA (AA). Luikart had carried my mattress and helped me move from Camp O'Donnell to Camp Cabanatuan. He had lived only one block from my home in Clovis, New Mexico. I knew his family very well. It was extremely hard for me when I heard of his passing after the war was over.

We shot out of Takao harbor during the bombing raid and headed for the high seas. Within a few days, we noticed a change in the weather. While it was getting chilly, we were not uncomfortable. It had been somewhat stuffy in the harbor at Takao, so we were rather happy to have it a little cooler.

The American officers in charge assigned men to go topside for our food and water. The Japanese on the ship handled all of the cooking. Whether we received two or three meals mattered less to us on this trip than on our previous cruise because we had better accommodations and the Japanese paid less attention to us. As I mentioned, the weather did not bother us, especially me, until the day I was assigned to go after the food. I then realized that I was not sure of what we were getting into. When I reached topside, it was bitterly cold because of a strong head wind. While it was not raining, it was very overcast. I realized we would have a problem because a huge coat of ice made the railings of the ship very thick. What had been a one-inch cable was now about four inches in diameter because of the wind, the below freezing temperature, and the ocean spray that hit the railings. After my trip topside, I was not too excited about being on the detail to get the food. I hoped that I would never be so lucky as to get that job again. Ordinarily, that would have been a choice work detail.

All of us wore every piece of clothing we possessed, but we had only threadbare shorts and sleeveless shirts. As I mentioned before, very few of us had any kind of shoes, only homemade clogs made of one-inch thick wood. While we had modernized these clogs over the months, they gave us no protection from the extremely cold weather. Our feet froze. After more than two and a half years in the tropics, it shocked us to now be in the type of weather I had experienced on deck. We were miserable during the last week of this cruise. While we had food and water, the cold weather made us hope that we were nearing Japan.

# 24

# Japan

Finally, on January 25, 1945 we landed in Moji on the island of Kyushu, which is Japan's third largest island and located southwest of the main island. It was extremely cold. The Japanese immediately ushered us into a large building that was at least fifty feet by fifty feet, if not bigger. It contained several hundred scantily clad prisoners. The building had only one piece of furniture, a small pot bellied stove. If there had been plenty of wood and if the room had been insulated, this stove would have amply heated a room about twelve feet by fifteen feet. As it was, only those who had entered the building first and sat close to the fire were not overly warm. Aptly named "the icehouse," we lived in this building for two days. I am sure we received food in that time, but our need was for warmth.

We were never satisfied during the entire duration of our

hellacious experience as prisoners of war. When the Japanese held us in the Philippines, we received brutal treatment. They gave us little food and water. Filth and blowflies surrounded us. Regardless of the camp, we labored strenuously and we lived in extremely poor accommodations. On the Hell Ships, the lack of food and water continued. We sat on coal, surrounded by bodily excretion. During our time as prisoners of war, we endured either extreme tropical heat or intense cold rain. In Moji, it was bitterly cold. We were never satisfied, and we were extremely hard to please. You would think that we were paying for our accommodations and cruises.

As I mentioned, we languished in this "icebox" for two days. On the morning of the third day after our arrival in Kyushu, the Japanese loaded us on ferryboats. They took us to Shimonoseki, across the water, so we went just a short distance from Moji. Shimonoseki is on the southwest tip of Honshu, an island just across the channel north of Moji. We boarded a train that was quite similar to American trains except for its size. These seats were shorter and closer to the seats opposite them. The guards made two of us sit in one passenger seat. Two other men sat opposite the first two prisoners. Even in our emaciated condition, it was a little crowded with two of us sitting on the same bench-type seat. Our knees also intertwined with the knees of the men opposite us.

While we sat there, the Japanese ordered us to pull the shades down. Once the trained started to move, however, we were allowed to raise them and view the countryside. Before the train arrived at a major city, the guards ordered us to again pull the shades down. Later after we left the city, we could raise them. The country was very pretty. Here it was the 27th of January and our first view of Japan, outside of the cities, was one of pine trees and trees loaded with oranges. We were surprised to see snow on the ground. The patches of snow, which did not completely cover the ground, enhanced the beauty of the landscape.

The train was warm, heated by steam. The only orders we received from the guards concerned lowering and raising the shades. It proved to be a very slow trip, but with the treatment we got, we were not in any hurry to get to wherever we were going. The Japanese gave us two meals, served in little *bento* boxes. These held self-contained meals, ready to eat. Made of very, very thin wood, like balsa wood, the boxes were flat and not very thick. They had little partitions to keep the various items separate. Our meals usually consisted of rice, a pickled vegetable, and a little something that tasted sweet for dessert. The boxes also included chopsticks for our use. In retrospect, the train may have traveled much faster than I had first thought. It must be over five hundred miles from Shimonoseki to Tokyo, factoring in the many bays that jut into the lower part of Honshu. It certainly is not a straight shot between the two cities.

We finally stopped in a place we later decided had to have been Tokyo. It was nighttime and after the guards unloaded us from the train, we wended our way for a considerable distance, through one tunnel after another. It had to have been a big city to have such an elaborate underground system. During this march through the tunnels, we stopped at one point and the Japanese issued us clothing. Remember that this was the middle of winter and we had been wearing only shorts and sleeveless shirts. The Japanese gave us long pants, a shirt and an overcoat. The coat I received was either Australian or British-made. It was rather generous in fit. While these items were not winter gear, they were much warmer than our old clothes. We almost froze from the time we had left the train until we had received this clothing.

After continuing through the labyrinth of Tokyo's underground station, we finally reached a point where the guards loaded us onto another train. This one was similar to the first train except for the fact that the Japanese instructed five men to sit in the same sized area that four had occupied in the previous train. Additionally, this train was not heated as the first one had been. Even though we wore new clothing, and more of it, we were still cold. We tried to combat the cold by having five of us huddle together, one man sitting on the floor surrounded by legs. We piled our five overcoats on top of us. While it was not the best arrangement, it served its purpose since we all fell asleep in this distorted position. Eventually the train started moving. We had not slept much in the past sixty hours, and in our weakened and exhausted condition, at first we did not realize that stream from the engine began to permeate the train. After some time, we finally awakened to the fact that we were sweating. We gradually shed our overcoats. It was as if we were coming out of our cocoons.

During the entire trip, we did not see any civilians. In fact, we saw no one except the guards who accompanied us on the first train and on our journey through the Tokyo underground. We had never been allowed to see any cities of any size, nor did we see any evidence of American bombing of Japanese cities. The morning after our late night departure from Tokyo, the guards allowed us to raise the shades. To my amazement, the countryside we saw was not that much different from any other country's landscape, aside from the construction of some buildings. We looked out on lots of land, rice fields, and paddies. A considerable amount of that ground was under cultivation.

The second train looked very similar to the first one, with the exception of being crowded for a few hours. We assumed we were going north because of the sun's position. After we were given another *bento* meal, we detrained. The guards walked us across the street to another train. Apparently the train we just unloaded from was not going in the right direction for our final destination. We were a little concerned as to our destination because of the overcoats issued to us. We feared we were going from one extreme in temperature, the heat of the Philippines, to another, the cold of Japan.

This was the 28th of January. We had been on trains for over twenty-four hours. Since we had been treated well, we were not complaining. In fact, we enjoyed the scenery. In many places the view was extraordinary. After going through a tunnel, we came to a huge steppe or tableland. Snow covered the distance from where we were to the surrounding mountains for nearly as far as we could see. The only evidence of habitation was the peak of a few houses. We saw these peaks and it appeared that a door or window had been opened in these homes so that an entrance and exit existed. Smoke emerged from the chimney. We could see no other parts of the houses; we did not know if they were one-story or two-story homes. The sight was beautiful. Nothing disturbed the brilliant, white, virgin snow.

A few hours after we left on this train, we went through another tunnel in the mountains. As we exited it, we saw another beautiful scene, with snow again piled as high as the peaks of the houses. We could not guess the snow's depth, but we could see seven or eight houses. They had a path beaten from the window or from the door in the peak of the house. The path led from the opening until it disappeared in the snow. Smoke came from the chimneys. My thoughts centered on a return trip over this same route, but in reverse and in the summer so that I could find out the depth of the snow.

At mealtime we stopped at some little town where the guards loaded on *bento* boxes. From daylight when we had left Tokyo, we had been able to raise the shades and look out the windows. As I mentioned earlier, five of us were crowded into the space for four smaller-bodied people. After the first change of trains sometime in the morning, we were allotted a little more space. Now two seats only held four men.

For the remainder of the day, the guards allowed us to look out the windows. I was quite shocked to realize that Japan was not a flat country. As we discussed the topography we were seeing, some of the men voiced their belief that the Japanese islands were no doubt the result of volcanoes rising from the ocean floor. The further north we went, the more mountainous the landscape became.

At one point we changed trains again. This time we walked over about one block to another train. It headed in a slightly different direction. Because of my railroad background, I was very interested in the equipment. I noticed that each time we changed trains the new one belonged to another railroad company. The equipment was painted differently, and while I could not read the characters on the sides of the cars, they appeared to be different, especially in length. The engines were also painted in different ways and in different colors.

The guards accompanied us on these little walking excursions, but we gave no thought to escaping. I think we were more concerned with looking around at what few civilians we saw, especially the children. No doubt we had given up any idea of escape. Where would we have gone? What would we have done for food and water? So far, the trains had ample water and we eagerly awaited the *bento* boxes. As I mentioned earlier, we always carried spoons wherever we went, just in case we needed them. The *bento* boxes always contained a short pair of chopsticks. Most men had learned to eat using that item, but there were a few who could not eat fast enough with chopsticks so they always used a spoon. Since Cabanatuan, I had been carrying a set of chopsticks in my pack. My friend Lester Morrison had made them for me when we worked together in the kitchen at that camp. He had carved these chopsticks out of bamboo. Over ten inches in length, the top three inches were carved with a square top and various carvings, some round and some square. The carvings also took the shape of spindles. These decorations were all painted red and black. I have forgotten what Lester used for paint. I still have the chopsticks, and while they are usable, much of the paint has worn off.

We spent another night on the train and the guards gave us a *bento* box for breakfast. It always contained a small portion of rice and sometimes a daikon, which is a long, white pickled radish. (A daikon is also called an iceberg or icicle radish.) The box sometimes contained something sweet, usually a cookie of some sort. To keep us off balance, at times the guards made us pull the shades down, while at other times they allowed them to be raised.

We saw quite a few civilians at the stations but seldom any military men. In the mornings, at noon, and in the late afternoon we saw many children, all dressed in school uniforms. Different outfits seemed to indicate different schools. All of the children had backpacks. They waited for the trains that took them to and from school. The majority seemed to be six to eight years old. As young as these children were, no adults accompanied them. As we changed trains in one village, a group of about thirty small children detrained and boarded another one, all without instructions from anyone.

I never saw so many snotty-nosed children. While we were comfortably warm on the train, the adults and children we saw all had red cheeks. It must have been very cold outside. A guard rarely opened the door at the end of the car to allow a breath of fresh air to enter. Even if he did, it was cold air. It was clear to us that the civilian population was suffering some hardships. Their clothing did not seem to be that comfortable and none of it seemed to be new or adequate in respect to the cold weather. The children especially looked undernourished. The adults' faces appeared more or less the same, with no smiles, just very grave and somber. Their eyes seemed dull. Even the children did not respond to the sight of "round eyes," or white people. They all seemed to be aware of who we were but they were not, in any sense, excited.

Because of my railroad background, I was very interested in observing the railroad activities when we stopped in a town. I never saw a switch engine. Workers moved all of the cars by hand and by back labor. Men and women both pushed one car at a time from one track to another. Probably the most intriguing phase of their railroading concerned the coupling mechanism. They used the old link-and-pin method. That method had been outlawed many years ago in the United States because of the numerous injuries and deaths associated with it. The end of a car had a link, or eyehole. As two cars were pushed together, the two eyes or links would meet each other, one over the other. A pin, threaded on the bottom end, would be dropped through the eyes, and a nut would be screwed on the pin. That held the two cars together. Many men had been killed as they had tried to drop the pin in the two eyes while the switch engine was still pushing the cars together. If they did not get run over, they often lost a foot, leg, or arm. With the invention of the automatic coupler, safety took a big step forward. With it, as the switch engine shoved the cars together, the automatic coupler on the end of the cars meshed together, just like your two hands couple when you clasp them together sideways.

As we traveled on the trains, we did not see any evidence of war. The guards were very careful to pull the shades down. They also made sure that we did not peek out of the sides of the shades while the train traveled through areas we assumed, or should I say "hoped," had been bombed. We had heard of General Jimmy Doolittle's April, 1942 raid on Japan, but that had been long before we had left the Philippines.

After we changed trains at least twice a day for two days, we finally reached our destination about midnight on January 30, 1945. We had been on trains for a good three and a half days. I am sure you are wondering how I knew what time it was. I have no idea on the exact hour. I am sure no one had a watch since we had lost those early in the captivity. I know we had received an evening meal in the form of the usual *bento* box. It had been dark for several hours. We had bedded down for the night when the guards woke us up and told us to gather our possessions and detrain. After we reached a camp, the Japanese assigned us our barracks where we went back to sleep. I just picked midnight as the hour.

# 25

# Kosaka

Our train trip ended in a little town, at least it seemed to us to be small, which was about five hundred miles, more or less, north of Tokyo. We later found out the town was called Kosaka. We were not too far from the northern end of Honshu, Japan's main island. The nearest large town, Sendai, was on the eastern coast of Honshu. After we detrained in Kosaka, our small group of one hundred men walked from the station through a small village that appeared to be a ghost town. We did not see a single light in any house or business building as we wended our way through the village, which is another reason I thought it was about midnight. The snow was at least hip deep to a reindeer, and a rather tall reindeer at that. After we were quite a distance outside of the town, we came to a path that went up a hill. Guards had been stationed along the right side of the path. A wall of snow formed a natural barrier on the left.

I was about the second or third man leading the charge up this steep, icy path. Because many of us were slipping down as we tried to ascend, some, including me, tried to step off the path to the area where the guards stood. They forced us back on the path, however. I finally reached the top of the hill, but in the middle of the pack because of my slipping downward.

The weather was cold, even with the clothing that had been given to us in Tokyo. Somewhere, maybe in Tokyo, we had been given shoes. I have no idea exactly where we got them. So many occurrences have slipped my mind completely, and yet so many others are as fresh as if they happened yesterday. I do recall working in Las Pinas barefooted. Yet I must have had shoes on as I walked up the snowy, ice-covered hill into our camp at Kosaka, or I would have frozen my feet. Even with them, I had a case of frostbite on my toes and ears.

Our barracks resembled our accommodations in the Philippines. It was a long, two-story, wooden building. Windows could be opened on both stories. Bunks stood on either side of the center aisle way with a pot-bellied stove in the center of the first room. As we had seen before, ladders were used to climb to the second floor bunks. Overall, the barracks was a little wider and a little more commodious than those in the Philippines, especially in respect to headroom.

A similar room stood behind the first one, with the toilets behind this second room. We had no toilet paper, however. No grocery store or a Sears & Roebuck catalogue was available to us. Toilet paper was a necessity but it was most often overlooked when it came to our basic supplies. Think of the profit a man in O'Donnell or Cabanatuan could have made if he had had the knowledge or forethought to tie up the market in toilet paper when everyone had diarrhea and dysentery. For some reason, my parents included a roll in the package I received at Las Pinas.

After the war, I never thought to ask them why.

I chose a bunk on the second tier near the center of the room, not too far from the stove and near the ladder. As we laid in our bunks that first night of our arrival, we tried not to think of freezing to death. While the Japanese had given each of us a blanket when we went through the Tokyo underground, they were what I call sheet blankets. Made of cotton, they were nearly threadbare. The blankets were much too thin to provide us with any warmth.

The next morning, the Japanese gave us some wood for the stove, but it was a very small amount. We quickly decided to allow any prisoner who brought in wood to sit near the stove. Cold as I was, I became very energetic in trying to locate something combustible. I found out that as I braved the elements to find firewood, I apparently came to the attention of our only officer, Captain Davis. He had been my room and work commander in Las Pinas. The captain must have thought that I had energy as he observed my activities.

In shape, the camp resembled a squared "U." The two barracks and a small hospital were located at the bottom of the "U." A covered walkway, about six feet wide, lined the sides of the "U." The walkway was open and accessible to those of us in the camp from the inside of the "U." As you faced the camp from the outside of it, on your right as you entered was a small guardhouse. A small jail stood beyond the guardhouse, with the camp headquarters and guards' quarters past the jail. On the left side of the camp was a storeroom. The kitchen stood a few feet past that building and a doorway at the rear of the kitchen led to the bathhouse.

We received our first bath in this camp on our second day there. It had been a long time since we had had one. The guards ordered us into the bathhouse in groups of ten or fifteen men. The big tub measured about twelve feet by fifteen feet. It was not a sunken bathtub, but one raised about three feet off of the floor. Four

Japanese women met us as we walked in. The only way to discern that they were women was by their headpieces. They had long hair, with a large, napkin-like cloth on their head that was very colorful. The women appeared to be wearing four or five layers of clothing with straw slippers on their feet. Using sign language, they indicated to us that we were to disrobe. This seemed a little odd to us, but we were so happy to have a good, hot bath that we did not argue with them. I admit that we were, at first, a little embarrassed to undress in front of these women, but the need for a bath overcame modesty.

As we took off all of our clothes and started to get into the tub, the women again used sign language to show us how to dip the water over our bodies. They gave us soap to lather up with and then, using little pans, they doused us with water from the tub. After we rinsed off all of the soap, the women motioned for us to step into the tub. The water felt extremely hot. The women indicated that we should sit down. As we relaxed, we enjoyed the warmth and rest.

In respect to work details, there were none for the first few days after our arrival. I think it was on the fourth day that Captain Davis called Lester Morrison and me into his office/bedroom, which was a room at the entrance to our barracks. The captain told us that he had an opening for one more man to work in the kitchen. Lester and I could flip a coin, draw straws, or decide between us any way we wanted to as to which of us got the position. Being without coins, we drew straws. I won the draw. While both American and Japanese officers supervised the crew, working in the kitchen was always the plum job in any camp. While your honor was at stake not to take food for yourself, it was hard not to eat a little more than the other men. Overall, the kitchen crew turned out to be very hard workers.

Captain Davis, the other three men selected for the work detail, and I reported to the kitchen. There we met the Japanese who was in charge of that area, Sergeant Ogata San. He was a gruff-talking Japanese who nearly always sounded angry. Again, I found that all armies are the same. Ogata San asked which of us held the highest rank. One of the men, Glasscock, identified himself as a Staff Sergeant and a Mess Sergeant in the American Army. I said that I was a Staff Sergeant but Sgt. Glasscock could be the kitchen honcho (boss). Ogata San wanted to know the dates when we were promoted. As it turned out, I had been a Staff Sergeant for one week longer than Glasscock. I thus became the man in charge of the kitchen. The Japanese obviously worked the same way the U.S. Army did, on seniority. Sgt. Ogata San set down the ground rules of what was to be done and how it was to be done. He had the key to the supply room. Only he and I were to go into that room for food.

There was ample room in the kitchen. The building was at least twenty-four feet wide and very long. Although it was just a one-story building, it was as tall as the two-story barracks. Basically, the building was just a very high room. Large doors at each end of the kitchen led to the outside walkway. A small door at the opposite end of the kitchen led to a small breezeway and then to the supply room. Another small door at the other end of the kitchen led to the bathhouse.

Twenty very tall windows were along one wall. They were all covered with what I would describe as tarpaper. It looked the same as the black paper that lay under the shingles used in roofing back in the States. This side wall was built on a concrete foundation, with about six inches of the foundation exposed. Three feet from the wall and foundation was a bank of twenty concrete fireboxes in a continuous row. Each firebox had a large, round hole in the top and a small, iron door down below where wood could be inserted. A large, iron wok sat in each round hole. These huge woks were very heavy and it took three or four men to lift one off of the stove when it was full of rice. The row of stoves stood about thirty-six inches high on the cooking side because of a depressed walkway, and about twenty-four inches high on the opposite side.

A water fountain or hydrant stood near the door to the supply room. Water ran in a continuous stream into a box approximately five feet by ten feet. The water had to run continuously to insure that the water pipes did not freeze. It certainly hurt all of us to see water go down a drain, wasted. In fact, it still pains me to see water squandered. It is such a precious commodity. Without water, people become animals. One of the biggest sins is to waste water.

Since I was not a cook, I immediately appointed Glasscock and the third man on the detail to be the cooks. Because Dempsey Ford, a fourth man on the detail, did not know any more about cooking than I did, he and I decided that we would chop all of the wood, wash all of the woks as well as any other equipment, and keep the kitchen clean.

Ogata San asked me where I bunked. I led him to the barracks and pointed out where I slept. He told me that he or a guard would wake me every morning by 4:30 am, or shortly thereafter. At that time we would go to the supply room and draw the food for breakfast. They would never furnish any supplies aside from the ones for the following meal.

We soon found out why the Japanese had brought us to Kosaka. They needed our labor in the town's copper smelter. Within a week of our arrival, prisoners were working in the smelter. It proved to be not only hard labor, but also dangerous. Since I never worked in the smelter during our visit to Kosaka, I only know what the men told me about their tasks. Copper ore was run through a process that resulted in pure, or nearly pure, copper coming out of the furnaces. It was then poured into molds, or "pigs," which, when cooled, would be shipped elsewhere for future use. The men received a noon meal, but I do not know what it consisted of or how they got it. I do not remember if we cooked rice for them or if the smelter fed them. I think it was the latter. In the beginning, the men worked eight hours a day. It is my recollection that at first they received the weekends off. This was doomed to change, though, as time progressed.

    I remember that one of the first jobs the kitchen crew did, aside from cooking dinner that first day, was to cut a path across the top of the "U." It went from the kitchen to the camp office and the guards' quarters. The snow in the middle of the "U" was a good six feet deep. As we dug and shoveled snow, the depth of the walkway we were digging measured over seven feet. It did facilitate movement from the kitchen to the camp office.

    The first kitchen task Dempsey and I did was to chop enough wood so that the cooks could prepare a dinner. We found this to be a considerable chore. The wood came from large cuts of trees that had been floated down a river to Kosaka. A great supply had been stored in the inner walkway by the kitchen. The wood was water-soaked and frozen. The Japanese had furnished us with two axes, but the job was not as easy as one would think. Cutting frozen tree trunks required very intensive labor. At first, only flakes of the bark came off as we chopped. We finally cut a large enough gash in the end of the log to insert a spike. Once we pounded that in, the log split in two. Dempsey and I finally chopped enough firewood for dinner and for breakfast the next morning. We did have the foresight to stick as many logs as we could into the warm fireboxes to thaw them out. This was to insure that our labor the next day would not be as difficult. Dempsey and I soon realized that we had the wrong end of the bargain when it came to kitchen tasks. The cooks could stand behind the stoves, with the fire keeping them warm. In fact, the two cooks laughed at us as we tried to chop up the firewood. It took us two days to work out a technique so that we did not have to work as hard on future wood chopping tasks.

    Early the next morning, long before daylight, Ogata San woke me up. He told me to immediately come to the kitchen. As soon as I got my clothes on and washed my face and hands, I did so. Ogata San took me to the storeroom and pointed out what I must take out of it for the morning meal. Returning to the kitchen, he gave me two matches with which to light the fires. Dempsey and I had not looked far enough ahead to splinter enough small pieces of wood to use for that task. The matches Ogata San gave me were very thin, with little heads. It was easy to break the stem, and it was hard to get the end of the match to catch on fire because it had very little phosphorus. After going through six matches, Dempsey and I finally got a fire started, but we earned the wrath of Ogata San. He indicated that in the future, we could only have two matches a day.

As a rule, I would get the supplies as doled out by Ogata San and then wake up one of the cooks. He, in turn, would wake up the rest of the crew. Once the four of us were together, we tried to start the fires. Even though the firewood had warmed in the stoves after the embers were out, and even though we had splintered slivers of wood to start the fires with, it proved extremely difficult to get a fire going. As I mentioned earlier, the Japanese had covered the twenty tall windows, each about three feet wide, with tarpaper. It acted as blackout curtains. We found that the tarpaper was an excellent aid in starting a fire. We tore off a small piece and built a teepee around it. Once we lit the paper, it in turn lit the slivers of wood. We gradually placed larger logs on the fire. Whenever we could get the fire started with one match, we carefully hid for future hardships the other match that had been furnished to us.

The existence of blackout curtains in the kitchen gave us some hope. We certainly did not receive any news of the war, good or bad. For years we had teased the Japanese with questions that revealed they did not know much about geography. We asked them, for example, if their ships had sailed into Chicago harbor, or if their submarines had entered the harbor in Des Moines, Iowa. They always answered yes. Most of the interpreters in the Philippines had gone to school in the United States. However, as I mentioned before, they spoke limited English and they pronounced poorly what they could say. Most of us had learned a little Japanese, enough to keep us, most of the time, out of trouble. Because I worked closely with Ogata San, I started to pick up a little more of the language. I was not fluent, but the two of us could understand each other. The other guards at Kosaka were not too bad. The lieutenant in direct charge of the Japanese was a little mean. He liked to show off his rank. One or two of the guards were rather sneaky, but Sgt. Ogata San turned out to be very nice.

We still dreamed of home and our release. We still had faith in God. We knew we would eventually get back home, but since we were so far removed from any action, we just took it day by day. Actually, what else could we do? We kept our hopes alive.

Sometime in the latter part of April or in the early part of May fifty more prisoners arrived from the Dutch East Indies. Except for the officers, they were natives of Java. Some of them spoke a little bit of English and the officer in charge of them spoke even more, but they tended to keep to themselves. Their toilet preparations were very different from ours and struck us as strange. Not having American amenities, specifically toilet paper, or access to a Montgomery Ward catalogue, they all carried a little can. They filled it up with water before going to the toilet. Many of us could have used that system in O'Donnell and Cabanatuan. I have the feeling that the Americans were not too close to the Dutch. I do not recall any friendships developing between the two groups, but I also do not remember any problems between them. About this same time five British subjects also arrived in camp. Among the one hundred Americans at Kosaka, sixteen had been in the 200th CA (AA). While a few of them were draftees, most had been original members of the organization. Several of these were from Clovis, such as Lester Morrison, Jack Aldrich, and Clarke Smith. All had been in Las Pinas.

> Dear Mr Jones yes I no your son tommy you see he was in the same btry. as me + when we were sent to the 315Th we were together all thru the war + up to 1943 in prison camp no 1. then he went out on detail someplace don't no if he went to japan or to a inner island Detail but maybe I can find out for you he was pretty sick during 1942 + then he got OK it was weighing around 155 pounds when he went out on detail or to Japan so if I here more from the prisoners at santa fe I'll let you no my address will be Bruns Gen. hosp. at santa fe N.M.
> O E Drummond 15715 37

Orville E. Drummond and I served together in the same battalion. We lost track of each other when I went to Las Pinas and Drummond remained at Cabanatuan. Army Rangers rescued him, and other prisoners, from that camp late in January 1945.

Once he returned to the Clovis area, my father appears to have asked Drummond if he had any information about me.

This is Drummond's reply, post marked May 16, 1945.

Even when the Dutch arrived, snow still covered the ground, as it would until the middle of July. The weather had been nice in the few months before that, but even in July there were spots where the sun did not hit the snow. The fence around the entire compound must have been ten feet high, so in long stretches the tall fence shadowed the snow. When the snow started melting, we finally found out why the guards would not let us off the path that went up the hill the first night when we arrived in camp. There was a big drop alongside the path. If we had left it, we would have fallen quite a distance down the hill. While we would not have been hurt because of the snow's depth, it would have been a job to get us back up the hill.

A couple of weeks after we had arrived in camp, Ogata San, Dempsey, and I went into town to pick up some supplies. As we walked into the center of town, we passed a public toilet. Dempsey and I just had to see what they were like. The Japanese commodes at that time were holes in the floor, with about a three-inch, raised tile around the hole. There was nothing to sit on. The toilets were co-educational, with partitions between each unit. There were no urinals as we knew them, just a direct input into the hole. As Dempsey and I used the facilities, a woman entered and she proceeded to use the adjoining stall. The only way we ascertained her gender was by the scarf that all of the Japanese women seemed to wear. Most of the men in Japan at that time seemed to wear a military type of cap. Ogata San had waited patiently for us. Once Dempsey and I were done, we all proceeded to a wholesale fish distributor. We climbed down about six steps cut in the snow and entered a door at the bottom of the steps. We then walked up six steps to the floor of the building.

Six months later, Ogata San and I went to town for fish. This time we climbed up six steps to the front door of a building. After we entered it, we climbed up six more steps. I finally recognized that this building was the same one I had entered in February. The difference was the absence of eight or ten feet of snow that had melted. Both times we had actually entered on the building's second floor. The snow had been that deep in town.

Initially, it appeared that I would go to town quite often. But after I made about three trips in two weeks, all of our groceries and other supplies were delivered to the camp. I do not believe that the Japanese wanted us to see their misery. Most of the supplies that were delivered, such as wood, food, or other items, would be dumped just outside of the camp's front doors. The guards then called upon us in the kitchen to bring them in.

As a rule, we only saw one outsider. He was "the Honey Bucket Man." To us, he appeared to be elderly. Daily, the man entered the camp with two large buckets, one at each end of a pole. He went to the toilets, filled his buckets, and with the long pole over his shoulder, the man walked out of the camp with a peculiar gait. We had learned while in the Philippines that a long pole with a load at each end was a rather easy way to carry something fairly heavy. One had to walk a little differently, however, or shuffle, to balance the load properly. Ogata San told us that the residue from our toilets carried away by the Honey Bucket Man would be used on vegetables as a fertilizer. Since we might prepare these items later in the kitchen for the meals, we were to always wash them and cook them well.

As more laborers arrived, things changed drastically. The men in the copper smelter, for example, went on three shifts. This impacted us in the kitchen. To prepare the meals, we had been using only three big woks, one for hot water to be used to make the coffee or tea, one for a soup or a vegetable, and one for a mixture of rice and barley. Times were getting hard for the Japanese, which resulted in augmenting the rice with barley. When cooked, the two ingredients mixed well together, and they also tasted good. The barley took up a little more space, though, and made it look like we were getting more food.

We expanded our kitchen crew because of the increased work required by the additional shifts. Soon we were using all twenty of the stoves. In the morning we cooked breakfast for one shift as it went to work, then a dinner for those from the previous shift who came back to camp soon after that first shift had left. In the middle of the day we made breakfast for the men who worked the 3:00 p.m. shift. In the late afternoon we prepared breakfast for the third shift, dinner for the first shift, and later another dinner for the second shift. I draw a blank as to how the men, while they worked, received their noon meal. I do not recall cooking a meal that the men could take to work. I think they may have been fed at the smelter. I might be wrong on that, but I do not know. I am sure of one thing, though. Dempsey and I kept very busy chopping wood.

We had a few deaths in Kosaka. Ed Mehegan, with whom I had become friends at one point during our time together as prisoners, passed away. I think it was from pneumonia, or perhaps he was just worn out. We had played bridge together many times. Ed told me tales of driving for an hour across his hometown of Philadelphia to pick up his date. I could not imagine such a trip or such a large city. In Clovis it took only a few minutes to go from one end of town to the other. An hour's drive that began in my hometown would have put me in Texas. I think that altogether eight men died while in this camp, which was not too large of a number. It was a shame their life ended here, though, after going through so much earlier in their years as a prisoner. With these deaths, the Japanese shipped a few more Americans to Kosaka.

One of the new men came up to me a few days after his arrival to tell me that he had heard about me. I could not imagine what he had heard or from whom he had heard it. How had my fame or misfortune preceded me? This new arrival told me that "the old man," Bud Kiely, had told him all about me. I asked him where he had met Bud. It turned out that they had been in a hospital together somewhere in Japan. I do not know how many hospitals Bud was in, but he kept coming back to the camp.

In Kosaka, a number of men who worked in the smelter sustained injuries. The camp had a small dispensary and hospital room. The doctor tried to take care of all the men, but as usual, there was little medicine or help from the Japanese. Lester Morrison suffered one of the worst injuries. When one of the copper pigs at the smelter exploded, he received some terrible burns. The doctor saved Lester's life, and he ended up with only two big disfigurements on his face and arms. Around the time Lester was recovering from the accident, the Japanese allowed us to add more men to the kitchen staff. Lester was the first new man, and soon after him, Pete Espinosa joined us, but for a different reason.

From the area near Gallup, New Mexico, Pete had been with that unit of the New Mexico National Guard. He spoke Spanish fluently, as well as Japanese. We added him to our crew because he had been barred from the smelter and the town. He became too friendly with the Japanese. Because he spoke their language so well, the Japanese were afraid that he might learn things that he should not know. They made him stay in camp all of the time. I may be wrong on this story, but I know that something similar happened to another man who I will tell you about later in this chapter.

Our work in the kitchen intensified. We labored in the kitchen until after midnight. In any twenty-four hour period, there would be only four or five hours when the kitchen was not in use. With more men and three shifts to prepare meals for, our routine and the food we made changed considerably. The Japanese gave us small sharks to serve the men. We called them sand sharks because their skin was like sandpaper. We had to skin them. The Japanese also gave us squid, which, again, we had to de-sack. Our hosts wanted us to chop the squid up and eat them raw, although we could serve soy sauce with them. The men wanted them cooked since we were not into the present-day craze of eating raw fish.

One day the Japanese picked up a number of us and took us to the railroad where they directed us to several flat cars. Skeleton heads from some kind of huge fish were on each of the cars. They were so big it took two men to carry each head. We assumed they were whales but we did not understand the Japanese term for the fish. When we got back to the kitchen, we chopped up the head with axes and boiled the meat off of the bones. We made a rich fish stew with plenty for everyone.

The Japanese always kept us off balance, usually in the wrong way. One time they brought in some apples. There was a box for each prisoner. The box contained between twenty-five and thirty apples packed in sawdust. The boxes were not like the ones we had in the States because of that sawdust. After consulting Captain Davis, we decided to make a dessert of applesauce from all of the apples that were starting to go bad. We intended to then equally divide the remaining apples among each man. Even Ogata San thought this was a good idea. As the applesauce was almost done cooking, I asked Ogata San for some sugar to sweeten it, but he told me that he did not have any for us. I asked him to get the lieutenant in charge of the camp to come over. I explained to this officer what I had done and how much we needed the sugar to finish it. By this time, I could carry on a conversation of sorts in Japanese. But after I explained the situation, the lieutenant told me that he did not understand me. I repeated myself, but this time after each phrase I asked him if he understood. He replied *hai* or "yes." When I was all done, I again asked him for the sugar. He responded by telling me that he still did not understand me. To make my point clear, I picked up a couple of spoons. I gave each of us a taste of the applesauce with them. To my great surprise, it tasted sweet. It had been so long since we had eaten an apple, and these were so sweet that the applesauce did not need any sugar. I offered the lieutenant and Ogata San some, but they declined. They told me that they were not allowed to eat any of our food. This in itself surprised me. As planned, we divided up the remainder of the apples. Each man received over twenty. It may have been close to twenty-five, but I am not sure. The apples had been a pleasant surprise.

Two or three times Ogata San entered the storeroom without me. I think he got a bottle of sake when he did this. That was all right with me because when the guards partied, we heated the sake for them and ended up enjoying the drink with them but they never knew that. They brought the sake over in a little teapot. As I heated it, one of the guards remained with me until it was just the right temperature. He was there to make sure we did not take any of the sake. After the guard left, I had to remain in the kitchen until they returned for a refill. The Japanese like to sing when they drink. Usually by at least the third refill the singing was so loud that before the teapot got hot, the guard told me to bring it to him when it was ready. He then ran back to the party, afraid that he would miss something. He did. As soon as he left, we poured about one-third of the sake out and refilled the teapot with water. As the evening progressed, the guard brought the full teapot over and returned to the party. On each trip he made, we took out more and more sake and put in more and more water. Such a party happened about once a month. The Japanese never caught on to what we were doing.

One day one of the lowest ranking guards came over to me and told me to accompany him to the storeroom. He apparently had stolen the key. The only item he took from the room was a bottle of sake. After he drank a couple of swigs from the bottle, he asked me where **we** could hide the bottle. I knew I had him then.

I suggested that we tie a string to the neck of the bottle and make a loop on the other end of the string. We could then slip the bottle over the hydrant and drop it into the end of the water trough. Since the bottle was clear, as was the liquid, unless a person specifically looked for the bottle, it would not be seen. The guard followed my suggestion. As soon as he left, we drained out one-half of the sake and refilled the bottle with water. We then returned it to its hiding place in the trough. The guard returned several times until he had emptied the bottle. While he thought he had been had, he could not do anything about it. He knew that if he beat me, I would tell on him. He would then be in really big trouble. So as we said in the old days, it was a Mexican standoff.

After we had been working in the kitchen for several weeks, all four of us on the crew ran out of smoking material. A few of the beams at the top of the kitchen had cedar bark on them. It was what a kid smoked before he could get hold of a cigarette. One of the men climbed up to the beams and tore off all of the cedar bark. We had smokes for several days. The bark was so old, however, that smoking it just about scorched our lungs.

At this same time, we spotted a package up in one of the rafters. The Japanese wrapped everything in large, multi-colored pieces of fabric. In this one we found a large chunk of frozen rice. Apparently it had been left there, forgotten by a worker who had helped put the building up. We let the package thaw out and ate the rice.

As I mentioned earlier, we were issued the food we had to prepare a few hours before each meal. One afternoon Ogata San and I went to the storehouse to pick some items up for the evening meal. He gave me a bag of beans. They looked exactly like pinto beans to me so I took them back to the kitchen where I told Glasscock and the other cook that these beans were for the next day. I knew that pinto beans needed to be soaked overnight to soften them before they could be cooked. I then returned to the storehouse for the rice and barley needed for the evening meal. I asked Ogata San what else we would have with the rice and barley. He told me that the beans were for tonight's evening meal. I replied that he was crazy. We could not cook them so they would be edible by then. Ogata San was again upset with me, but he showed us what to do. It turned out that these beans were not pinto beans. They were a different type of bean than what I had thought and they cooked quickly.

One of the dishes that the Japanese liked was dumplings with beans. We had been issued flour and beans one afternoon, but we did not understand what we were to do with those two items. Ogata San showed us how to make dumplings out of the flour and cook them, with the beans, in sugar. To us, these meals proved to be quite a treat, but we had them only two or three times during our stay in Kosaka.

One of the vegetables the Japanese gave us was called *fuki*. It looked a little like a cross between celery and rhubarb. It was to be pickled when used. In anticipation of our staying another winter in Kosaka, the Japanese brought in a large vat. It measured about seven feet deep and five feet in diameter. They also gave us a large supply of *fuki*. To pickle this vegetable, it is washed well in hot water and then the rib-like strings (similar to those found on celery) are pulled off of it. In the next step, the *fuki* strings are wrapped around ten or twelve pieces of the vegetable. To do all of this, Ogata San instructed Dempsey and me to wash our feet before we climbed into the vat. Bunches of *fuki* were thrown at us. We placed them on the floor of the vat and covered them with a layer of salt. We repeated this with other layers of *fuki* and salt until we had the vat filled. The *fuki* stayed in the vat until it was pickled and ready to eat. To me, it was rather tasteless, except for the salt, but the *fuki* was filling.

Many times during the long, cold nights, before we ran

the kitchen almost twenty-four hours straight, Ogata San would look for me and we would go into the kitchen. We sat on the little ledge behind the stoves, with our backs against the wall. We had long talks and soon learned to communicate with each other fairly well. We spoke about the war, our past life, and our families. He expressed the same feelings about the war that I had, that we did not want war. We both would have preferred to be home rather than where we were. I learned that Ogata San was from a town called Yonezawa, in the prefecture of Yamagata. Yonezawa was south of Kosaka, some seven hours by train. Ogata San had worked in a bank before the war and his present job was more like that of a home guard than that of a regular soldier. I think he was about my age, or maybe a year or two younger. (I was twenty-nine at that time.) I think he was married but he did not have any children.

Ogata San wanted to know all about the United States and what I did for a living. He also asked about my family and wanted to know if I had any pictures of them. He showed me pictures of his family. The Japanese are big on pictures and family. Every Japanese we got close to pulled out his family pictures. Ogata San and I became very well acquainted. He wrote his name and address, in English with my help, in my notebook. He also wrote it in his native language, using one of the Japanese dialects. It may have been *katakana* or *hiragana*, but I am not sure of the spelling. I also wrote my name in my notebook using that same dialect. Although we had these visits, he never showed any friendship toward me when we were around others. When Ogata San was with others, he sounded gruff and short, but he was very nice to me when we were alone. I am sure that the lieutenant in charge of the camp would not have liked it if he found out that Ogata San was friendly with a prisoner.

When spring finally came, the Japanese ordered us to build a water tank on the kitchen's roof. They gave us enough tools and lumber to build a nice-sized storage tank, about in the middle of the building. It was not a tough job. The real work came when we had to fill the tank with water. We carried the water up the ladder to the top of the roof in one-gallon buckets from the kitchen. The trip proved to be very time-consuming. I think we had only four buckets. After about ten trips up and down the ladder, we changed our method of getting the water into the tank. We had one man bring water to another who stood partway up the ladder. Another man was at the top of the ladder and the fourth one near the tank, dumping the water into it. It took us two good days of hard labor to fill up the tank.

All of this effort proved to be a good investment. By summertime the shingles, which were not much thicker than a very thin piece of cardboard, started to curl up. Anticipating a fire, we kept a ladder leaned up against the building. We had a rather big stove on the end of the kitchen next to the wall that divided the kitchen and the bathhouse. We maintained hot water for bathing and on this particular day, I guess we had the stove too hot. Someone noticed the long tin pipe that went through the roof had started smoking the shingles. I immediately ran out of the kitchen and up the ladder to the water tank, only to find out that we were not very good Boy Scouts. We were not prepared since we had not left a bucket up on the ladder to dish out the water.

As soon as someone yelled, "fire," the Japanese came running out of their building. They screamed all kinds of orders at us, none of which we understood. In the meantime, I had shouted to Dempsey for a bucket. With the arm of a major league pitcher, made stronger by chopping wood, Dempsey threw a bucket to me, very accurately, all the way to the tank. The fire went out with only two or three buckets of water. It had singed about
five shingles, not enough to even replace them. After this little experience, I hung the bucket on the tank, and in a few minutes I

climbed back up to add a second bucket. Immediately, I caught both hell and thanks from the Japanese for allowing the fire to start and for putting it out. They never realized that we had not left a bucket up on the tank. We did not know it at the time, but the Japanese are deathly afraid of fire. They have had many catastrophic fires in their cities and towns. Their homes are so poorly built and are so close together that when once a fire hits, many houses are destroyed, not just one.

As I mentioned earlier, our barracks had windows with pull down shutters or doors, on both the lower and top level of bunks. When we had arrived at this camp, we could not open the windows on either level because the snow was so deep. Once spring came, the snow melted enough to open the top-level windows, and as summer appeared, we finally could open the windows at the bottom level.

When the Dutch and British prisoners had arrived in camp, an American Navy Lieutenant had accompanied them. With his help and instruction, we were able to invent a washing machine, vintage 1800. It was hand-operated, but it did give us a way to wash our clothes and the rags we used in the kitchen.

The Japanese operated the camp in a rather low-keyed way. Guards accompanied the men to work in the smelter. Japanese boys, in the early years of high school, helped the guards by acting as supervisors. There was really no place to go even if we had attempted to take off.

Ogata San never told me anything about the progress of the war, either good or bad. He did say that things were getting pretty rough for the civilians. The Japanese people lacked food and clothing. They certainly did not have any luxuries of life. Eventually we learned a little about the war from the one Scotchman in our camp. It seems that he had been taken as a prisoner in Hong Kong when the war had begun. His English was horrible, but we learned that we could understand him more when he spoke Japanese. It turned out that the Scotsman had become fluent in that language. If he went to the smelter, he listened to conversations between the Japanese and then passed such information on to us. The guards finally made the smelter off limits to this prisoner.

For several months, I had been barred from going to town for supplies. I never understood why because I was not very fluent in Japanese. One day, however, they took me unexpectedly to Kosaka, and on that trip I learned something, but it was not about the war. While in the town, we passed a wire enclosure that was at least eight feet high. Behind it were a large number of Chinese men with vacant stares. They were thin, emaciated skeletons. These Chinese were in as terrible a shape as we had been in O'Donnell.

One night we were suddenly made conscious of the war. Apparently the Japanese had received an air raid warning. The guards and Ogata San ran into the barracks telling us to pull down the blackout shades. We were totally ignorant of what they were referring to. Before we instituted those consecutive work shifts in the kitchen to accommodate the three shifts at the smelter, we had destroyed up all of the black tarpaper by using it to help us start the fires in the cook stoves. The Japanese never figured out what had happened to the shades. We, in our ignorance, were not of much help. I do not remember if we had to turn out all of the lights in the kitchen. As it turned out, all of the excitement that night was for naught. No air raids occurred and no planes appeared. That night saw only quiet skies.

# 26

# Senso Owari

Finally the day came, August 16, 1945, when the men did not have to go into the smelter. The Japanese did not explain why.

The following day I was told to send some men into Kosaka for supplies. Thinking that we might be able to learn something, I sent the Scotchman to accompany them; as I mentioned earlier, he was fluent in Japanese. I told him to keep his ears open. I was quite surprised that the Japanese allowed him to go into town. When the men returned to camp, they told me that the war was over. They had heard the phrase, *senso owari*, "the war is over," several times. The Scot said he had heard people talking about a big bomb, but he heard no specific details.

How did we feel? We were excited, of course, but until we could be certain that it was true, we did not really believe the news.

We felt it was probably true, but we were still officially prisoners as far as we knew. I think all of us went into our own shell. We felt relief, exhaustion, and introspective. We were excited, but we were also not sure that the war really was over.

A day or two later, the Japanese gathered everyone together on the parade grounds. They told us that we were no longer prisoners, but they did not say that the war was over. They made no announcement that the Americans had won the war. They did not say that the Japanese had lost the war. They simply said that we were not prisoners. The Japanese warned us not to leave camp. For our own protection, they would stay and watch over us. Fear existed, no doubt, that the civilians might harm us, and for good reason. Surely, many of the civilian population had lost parents, sons, and children, as well as other family members, in such a long war. Even as prisoners removed from the front lines of the war, we knew that the Allies had the ability to wage a widespread assault on many islands in spite of the large mass of water separating these islands. The bombings, which we were sure had been intensive, must have affected nearly every Japanese family. The American officers immediately took over the camp. They issued the orders and the Japanese guards respected their orders.

I am not aware of any physical retaliation against the Japanese in our camp by any of the prisoners. There was some verbal retaliation and we made the Japanese bow to us. I do not believe that anyone took any of their swords. I confess that I considered taking Ogata San's sword. I would have liked to have owned such a Samurai-type of sword, but I did not want to embarrass him. He had been good to me, and I did not want to hurt him in any way.

I mentioned earlier that the camp had a small jail. It probably would not have held more than three men at a time. When the war ended, one Air Force man by the name of Foster was in the jail. He had gone over the edge just three or four days before all of this happened. Intermittently he had shouted, "Clear the runways! Here they come." He would do this over and over again for a short time but then be quiet. The Japanese had incarcerated him because of his irrational behavior. They feared he might hurt someone. The Americans transferred him to the hospital when they took over.

During our time in Kosaka, I do not remember the Japanese treating anyone harshly. If someone committed a minor infraction of the rules or stole something at the smelter, I think there were several instances where a man had to stand all day at attention. He also received some blows for punishment as well as a few days and nights in the jail, but in comparison with other camps, the one at Kosaka was a haven.

I have to acknowledge, though, that because of my position in the kitchen, I was not aware of everything that happened at the smelter or inside the rest of the camp. I had a kitchen, which was open practically twenty-four hours a day, to run. It was my responsibility to draw supplies, chop the wood, prepare for another winter, and oversee all of the other details needed to keep the kitchen functioning. Most importantly, I had to preclude any suspicion of partiality between the kitchen crew and the men working in the smelter. It really was a hard job. Everyday between 4:30 am and 5:00 am Ogata San or a guard would wake me up. For the entire time I was in this camp, I was the first American up each morning. I would not leave the kitchen until 7:00 or 8:00 at night. In addition to these long hours, I tried to get more food for the men every time we drew supplies. Trying to stay on the good side of all of the Japanese and Americans in the camp added to my exhausting work.

Do not misunderstand me. I would not have traded my job for that of any other man, but I am sure that any man in the smelter would have been happy to trade jobs with me. I am sure that I did not labor under the same conditions as the men at the smelter, but I am proud to state that there was never any serious censure of the kitchen crew by the officers or the men. I am certain that, at times, some of the men bitched. Captain Davis never even suggested that we in the kitchen had failed to uphold our moral duty of being fair to all when it came to the allocation of the food. I have great respect for the job that the entire kitchen crew did at Kosaka. I interject this only to brag a little about a hard working kitchen crew that did its best to make life a little easier for the rest of the men.

As for me personally, I entered my weight in my notebook at different times during my incarceration. As such, I know that I went from over 190 pounds when the war started to as low as 120. I am sure I weighed close to 100 pounds a couple of times. When the war was over, I weighed 158 pounds. I was in very good physical condition due to all of the wood Dempsey and I chopped.

I do not believe I have mentioned that we in the kitchen also cooked for the Japanese. We used a separate little stove for this. Their food came from several sources. They also ate quite a bit of the same food we were given. The Japanese also had goodies aside from items taken from the supply room. They also cooked other food in their quarters.

All of my responsibilities came to an end, however, in mid-August. Why did the war end then? All we knew was that there had been a terrible bomb, one bomb, in a large city, and many people had died. The Japanese told us that they were expecting orders as to what we should do. They would tell our officers what they heard by radio and telephone. The Japanese impressed upon the officers that we should all stay in camp because these were the instructions they had received. In spite of this, two or three men did take off. I do not know how, but they arrived safely in Tokyo. I can guess, though, how they did this. A few days after we had been told that the war was over, I went to town by myself for a haircut. I found a barbershop where I had my head shaved. The barber was a woman. Using Pidgin English and hand motions, I told her to take all of my hair off. After she was done, I thanked her and walked back to the camp. I did not pay her. I am sure that the Americans who left camp did not pay for anything on their way back to Tokyo. I do not believe that any of us had money.

Some of the men wanted to go to town to get acquainted with the people there. Actually, they wanted to spend time with the ladies of the night. I think they were boasting or thinking wishfully. While they discussed this with the guards, I do not know what they actually did. Although the guards protested, men left the camp, but except for those three who went to Tokyo, everyone else returned to camp.

One of the civilians who had accompanied the men to and from the smelter was a kid of high school age. We called him Rabbit since he scooted around very quickly. One day he invited three of us to his home for a visit. We accepted and enjoyed an hour or so with him and his mother. She served us tea and some small cookies. We discussed with Rabbit the possibility of visiting some of the town's establishments, but he advised against it. "Don't do that," he said, "They are all diseased and you will get sick." We accepted his advice and thanked him and his mother for their hospitality.

Japan's "Rising Sun" was setting, and with it, our work for the "Greater East Asia Co-Prosperity Sphere" was done. The spider's web was now small and the spider itself weak.

# 27

# American Food

About a week after the Japanese told us that we were no longer their prisoners, they ordered us to paint a big "POW" sign on the roofs of the buildings and on the ground outside of the camp. Such indicators would allow us to receive drops from airplanes. The former captors furnished the paint. There was not a problem obtaining applicants for the work since many men were eager to change jobs. On August 25th we were informed that food would be dropped the next day. When this happened, we were to stay in the barracks to insure that we did not get injured from the drops.

The next day, when we heard airplanes in the vicinity, I climbed up on the kitchen roof to see better and stood by the water tank. When the planes came over, I could nearly touch them. The planes dropped cases of food. When I was close to a free American, so close that I could see his face, it really hit me that the war was over. In fact, tears come to my eyes as I put this down on paper over fifty years later. It was extremely emotional then and it still is emotional now. I must have shed tears then, too. Carrier planes from the *U.S.S. Bennington* made these drops. They gave us mostly canned goods and notes. I later wrote the Commanding Officer of the *Bennington* to thank him and in turn received a nice acknowledgement.

On the 28th of August we received drops from B-29s, planes that the Japanese dreaded. They called them "B ni-ju-kus." As I had done with the first drops, I climbed to the top of the kitchen by the water tank in case a drop started a fire. The accuracy of the drops left a little to be desired. This time we received two fifty-five-galloon drums welded together. Parachutes guided them down. Clarke Smith, who was from Clovis and had been with the original group of the 2nd Bn. Hqtrs., also climbed up on the roof. Unfortunately, one of the double drums landed on the kitchen roof, going right through it. Clarke fell through to the floor of the kitchen on top of the drums. The drop came within ten feet of me. I thought I would fall, too. As the big, long double barrel wobbled towards me, I held onto the tank when I saw that the parachute did not open all of the way. I felt relieved when I saw it fall a few feet short of where I stood. I did not realize that Clarke was not holding onto anything. He received a concussion from the long fall. While Clarke seemed to recover a few days later, the effect of the fall lingered with him until his death many years later. On a positive note, Clarke lived another forty-eight years. On a negative note, however, his two older brothers, one the C.O. and the other the 1st Sgt. of 2nd Bn. Hqtrs., died in the Philippines.

In addition to magazines and medicines, the B-29 drops included "C" and "K" rations. Many of the drums broke apart since the parachutes did not fully open. The men took what they could. The doctors diligently warned us not to eat too much, too fast. Instead, they told us to eat often but in small amounts. All of the men were careful not to gorge themselves, except for one man whose last name was Evans. Whether it was his physical condition, the items he ate, or the amount he consumed, Evans came down with a severe stomach blockage. The doctors diagnosed the problem but they could not do anything for him. We promptly took Evans to the local hospital but he could not be saved. What a way to die. After starving for three and a half years, freedom was on his doorstep. What happened to Evans shocked all of us and it was a horrible end for him and his family. But put in the context of dark humor, Evans did have one last, big meal.

I know many men who ended up with stomachaches, but they had to suffer with them. Anti-acid pills were not included in the drops. I thought that the chocolate bars and the canned peaches tasted best. We continued to be given rice and barley that we cooked. This supplemented food items in the drops. One of the dishes we had several months earlier contained beans, sugar, and dumplings. This had tasted so good to everyone that I decided to make it again one evening for all of us. The men ate very little, and I understood why. It tasted terrible after the stateside food. We gave the rest of the meal to the Japanese. We tried to give some of our American food to the Japanese. By that time, however, most of the guards had disappeared and the ones remaining did not eat much of our food.

The coffee was extremely well received by all of the men. The original "C" rations coffee was usually solidified and terribly bitter. The instant coffee in the Red Cross packages was much better, and the "K" rations coffee even more so. The coffee we had been making out of burnt rice or barley proved a very poor substitute, while the tea we received in Japan was a good substitute for real, American coffee.

The spider was gone, but the web was still there. It continued to hold us since we were not yet completely free.

## 28

# Another Free Cruise and Old Friends

On September 11th, twenty-six days after the war was over, American officers instructed us to go that evening to the train station in Kosaka. By that time, the guards had disappeared. We marched down to the train station carrying what little we had and boarded a train that, this time, had ample room for all of us. I do not remember what time we departed, but early the next morning the train pulled into a place we later learned was Sendai, on the eastern coast of the northern island of Honshu. We had been sleeping, but a bullhorn woke us up. A Marine major barked orders for us to detrain and, as he put it, become soldiers once again. As we unloaded, other Marines directed us to some LSTs, or some other type of personnel carriers, that took us to a hospital ship in the harbor.

We were deloused and given a cursory examination. Those men who were in bad shape were admitted to wards on the ship. The ambulatory men were taken, again on LSTs, to a troop transport. I was in this latter group. After showing us our bunks, we were lead to the ship's mess. As we started through the chow line, the Chief Petty officer announced, "I am sorry, but we just ran out of turkey. We have lots of ham left, if that is okay." We devoured the meal. I really was not aware of any men on this transport other than those from our camp. But in retrospect, I am sure that men from other camps had traveled with us. Since we only had about one hundred and fifty-five men in our camp, that number of men by themselves could not have consumed all of the turkey. When I think back upon this time, I am sure it had been a big logistical problem to gather all of the POWs from many camps, some small and some large, spread out all over Japan. There had been one camp, much larger than ours, where men had worked in copper mines in a town called Hanawa, which was near Kosaka. We had finally destroyed the spider's web, but the spider had gotten away.

The following morning, September 13th, we were loaded onto destroyers for another leg of what had become a very long journey. Two United States destroyers and one British destroyer were tied to the transport. I ended up on the *U.S.S. Taylor*, an American ship. I was later grateful that I had made this leg of the trip on an American ship since that meant American food, including coffee. The men who sailed on the British destroyer ended up with tea and, according to them, a poor substitute for a lunch. While on board the *Taylor*, we saw for the first time some strange helmets. We had been issued the 1918-type helmets, which were flat with a little bulge for your head. The new ones were much bigger and came down lower on the head to protect the ears. Even more of a shock was the huge helmet used by sailors who wore telephone headpieces. The crew certainly looked strange to us, and young. Of course, when we had joined the military we were young, too. In fact, we had had at least one sixteen-year-old from Clovis in our regiment. I do not know how he got past the recruiters.

That afternoon we ended up in Yokahoma harbor. From there, trucks took us to the Atsugi airport outside of Tokyo. Between those two cities, we saw other towns and it was devastating to see the results of the firebombing. Nothing but rubble, with an occasional smokestack that jutted up from the rubble, broke the monotony of ruins. It was sickening to see the obliteration of so many cities. What happened to the occupants of the buildings and homes? All of this immediately brought to mind the Civil War statement by General William Tecumseh Sherman, "War is hell." His affirmation still sticks in my mind. I am sure that the others with me had the same feeling I had, that we were lucky to have been so far north. Kosaka was such a little town that Americans did not know about the smelter there. The planes obviously did not have the need to go that far north for targets.

I later found out that many POWs had labored in Japanese coal mines, on docks, in steel mills, and other areas targeted by the American military. Some had been in Hiroshima and Nagasaki. Did they survive the bombing? What it must have meant to these men to go through three years of "Hell," and then, as the end of the war approached, to endure the bombing that the Americans were unknowingly throwing at them. After the war I also learned about POWs held in southern Japan who became guinea pigs in Japanese medical experiments. What became of them? I was lucky throughout my entire three and one-half years. The good Lord looked after me and answered my prayers.

Inside of the airport, we were each assigned a cot in a huge hanger. There were hundreds of cots and hundreds of men. Many were too exhausted to mingle, and many were too excited to rest. Either on the hospital ship or on the transport, we had been given two barracks bags of clothing and two pairs of shoes. When we had arrived in the hanger in Tokyo, we received two more bags of clothing and two more pairs of shoes. When we got the second bags, we abandoned the first ones. We continued that practice throughout our trip home. I had developed a huge boil on the top of my right foot. It was so large that I could not get a shoe on that foot. Somewhere I found a pair of low-cut tennis shoes that I was able to wear, although I could not lace the right shoe.

As transportation became available, I was finally assigned to depart Tokyo on September 15th. We boarded C-47 cargo planes, and I landed in Okinawa that day, late in the afternoon. We were assigned to tin buildings that I think were called Quonset huts. A record typhoon hit Okinawa while we were there. Many of the ships in port had to go to sea, and some sustained severe damage during the storm. While in the Philippines living in straw huts, we had been through a number of typhoons, but we had felt very secure. As the typhoon neared Okinawa, we were all grounded for the duration of the storm. That turned out to be four days and nights. The rain hit the metal huts, keeping us awake at night.

During this time my boil "ripened" and I felt great pressure from it. I went on sick call and the doctor thought it was appropriate to lance the boil. As he sat on a small stool, with my foot between his legs, the doctor cut open the boil. He regretted doing that. When the sharp knife pierced the boil, the mess popped out. It went all over the doctor and even hit the nurse who stood behind him. The pain from the knife was also very great, but the relief from the pressure immediately overcame the pain. For some reason I had a number of boils during my years with the Japanese. I still have a scar on my foot, my butt, and my wrist from these incisions. I was a little surprised that the doctor in Okinawa had not deadened the foot before he pierced the boil.

On September 19th I boarded another plane, this one headed

for the Philippines. When it landed, a bus took us to a replacement depot outside of Manila for repatriated POWs. Seeking out old friends, I found Bud, or he found me. We had a joyous reunion. It was great to see him. In prison, those who knew Bud had called him "the old man." His hair had turned white, his face was drawn, and he was as skinny as could be. In camp, one would not have expected him to survive. It was also great to see so many men who had been shipped to different camps during the three and one-half years since the war had begun. It was very sad, though, to hear about the ones who had not made it.

Bud told me that Major Cash Skarda had departed that morning for the States on a plane loaded with POWs. Cash was the 1$^{st}$ Lieutenant who had volunteered me to be a bugler, and he had also volunteered me to fill out the Government Bills of Lading to move our battalion from Fort Bliss to San Francisco. Bud and I learned that Cash's group was the last one to return home by plane. The rest of us went by ship.

We spent a week at the replacement depot, but we had no desire to go into Manila. We had seen enough devastation to last us. Again, we were showered with two more barracks bags of clothes and two more pairs of shoes. As with the shoes we had received in Tokyo, one set was a pair of dress shoes and the other a pair of combat boots, the likes of which we had not seen prior to the first issue of barracks bags. While we were anxious to get home, we did enjoy the liberty, the availability of food, and the PX (post exchange store) in case we wanted to buy something.

While in Manila, and on all of our future stops on our way home, the military gave us an advance on what it owed us. I usually took $100. When we all had entered the Army, we had been allowed, if we so desired, to take out an allotment that would be sent to a particular individual. Most married men allotted a portion of their pay to their wife. The single men could identify their parents as the recipient if they wanted to do so. When the war began, quite a few of the men changed their allotments and increased them. While on Bataan, the military command made it mandatory that all of the men designate an allotment to their wife or to their parents. They did not have to send all of their pay to that person, however. I had half of my money sent to my parents.

Life insurance premiums, which were low, could also be taken out of our salary. Before the war started, many men had not opted for this. But on Bataan, we made sure that every man had taken out the maximum amount of insurance and had designated a beneficiary. It was my responsibility on Bataan to obtain signed papers, from each man in the battalion, for the maximum insurance allowed. After I returned to civilian life, I had to make a sworn statement that I had overseen the necessary insurance paperwork for all of the men under me. The Army had kept records on what was due us, what had been allotted, and what had been the deductions for the insurance policy. At the replacement depot, the Army was willing to give us as much money as we wanted against our account, but most of us just took "walking around money."

Seeing one of the original men of Battery E who had not gone with us to the Philippines was one of the most exciting surprises I had while we waited in Manila to go home. I mentioned earlier that before we left the States, one of the men, Thompson, had done everything he could to keep from going with us. He gave himself a high fever that landed him in the hospital. He swallowed a sack of Bill Durham. Finally, I think he even went AWOL (absent without official leave). Who did we run into digging a latrine ditch at the replacement depot in Manila? Thompson. According to the story told by one of his friends who did accompany us overseas, Thompson went AWOL at least two times. He was a goof off then and it appeared that he continued to be so even afterwards. That explained his assignment to permanent latrine duty. Thompson was alive, though, and well fed. Many of those who had gone overseas with us had not come back. Those of us who did had not been well fed in our years as prisoners. Who was the smartest? In the end, one has to live with oneself, and I am sure Thompson had his reasons for acting as he did.

While we stayed in Manila, Uncle Sam had also set up a communications unit that allowed us, by wire, to contact our families. Of course, I immediately sent a telegram to my parents to tell them of my arrival in the Philippines and that I was well. Unknown to me at that time, my mother had saved all of the cards I had been allowed to send home from the several camps. She had put them in a scrapbook along with newspaper articles on my regiment and some of its men. She also included any other information she had received as to my whereabouts. The scrapbook also contains stories about many of my friends who served in different theaters of the war. I read all of this with great interest upon my return home.

While at the replacement depot in Manila, we had another cursory medical examination. Doctors listened to our heart and pounded on our chest. Someone also looked at our eyes, ears, and throat. As we waited to be shipped home, it was great to see our old buddies, but a little sad, too, that we were soon separated once again. The military shipped us out based on the barracks we had been assigned to. Lester Morrison and Jack Aldrich were in my barracks, so we could make the trip home together. Bob Stephens showed up before I left the replacement depot. I was extremely happy to see that he had survived. My friends and I had talked Bob into joining our regiment while we were at Fort Bliss. I had always felt extremely sorry that we had done that to him. Bob and I had lived next door to each other in Clovis before we went into the service.

In essence, most of my story, with a few changes in respect to names, dates, and camps, could be the story of any of the prisoners who had lived through part, or all, of more than forty-one months of degradation. During that time, the Japanese had subjected us to a physical and mental hell. At any point in those years, we were all sick, hungry, and without water. We all lived through bad and better times. All of our stories were quite similar.

# 29

# Our Last Free Cruise

*I* arrived in Manila on September 19th and departed eight days later on the *U.S.S. Howse*, a troop transport ship. The military command shipped us out based upon our physical condition and what barracks we had been assigned to. The various ships had different destinations. The one Bob Stephens caught docked in Seattle, while the one I went on docked in San Francisco. The cruise on the *Howse* was not unduly bad. All of the men were POWs and ambulatory, although many were still pretty skinny. The overall condition of the men varied from those who could barely walk to those in fairly good health (although only in appearance). We were a happy but exhausted group. The euphoria of being free and heading for home overcame any negative aspects of the voyage. It was interesting to listen to the ship's intercom system that advised the sailors "clean sweep, fore and aft." We bunked four and five high and the food was adequate. The ship went through a storm for a couple of days. During that time, when we went through the chow line (part of it was on the bottom, outside deck), as the ship swayed from side to side, you could actually reach out and catch some seawater. It was that rough. I was very happy that I did not get seasick. I guess I had so little in me that the rough seas did not affect me.

We arrived in San Francisco on October 15th. That first view of the Golden Gate Bridge was a sight I and the other prisoners had been dreaming of for many months. Tokyo Rose had told us we would never see it again.

The other ex-POWs and I spent six days in Letterman General Hospital in San Francisco's Presidio. Only those who were too sick, or too worn out to walk, received any thorough medical assistance. The doctors gave the rest of us another cursory examination, similar to the other three or four exams we had received at our previous stops in the Pacific. They weighed us, but I failed to record any of those numbers. I had tried to keep track of my weight while a captive, but I had stored my notebook on our trip home so I did not enter any notations on my weight after our release. At Letterman General every tenth man was shunted aside to another room where, I was told, he received a more thorough examination. I am not sure we were even x-rayed. The doctors did not seem to have any idea of what we had been through. To them, we were just more bodies passing through. We did not complain about these superficial exams. We were anxious to get home to our families, so we did not bring up about any health problems. If we had done so, we would have been hospitalized. Most of us felt that we were the walking wounded, but our wounds were psychological ones. At no time, however, did we receive any psychological or psychiatric examination, although I am sure that many men would have benefited from one. We believed that home would help us the most.

While we stayed at the hospital, most men spent their time either lying on their cots or in town. We did not spend much time in the city. Too many military men were on the streets. I do not know who had been fighting the war. San Francisco's streets had more soldiers, sailors, and Marines on them than we had had on Bataan and Corregidor.

I received a letter from my parents when we reached Letterman General. In it, they told me that they had moved from Clovis to Amarillo, Texas because of a promotion my dad had received with the Santa Fe Railroad. My parents also wrote me about the death of my grandfather. They told me that they did not have a telephone at home because of the lack of phone lines (copper, used in such lines, had been redirected to use in the war effort). But my parents included in the letter the phone number of my father's office and indicated I could call there. As soon as I could, I placed such a call. My mother answered the phone. I was so surprised to hear her voice that I choked up. I could hardly speak.

I later learned that Dad had told his boss that I was on my way home and that man believed I needed to talk to my mother as soon as possible. At that time, the railroad had its own phone system, which stretched from Chicago to San Francisco. It included all points that the Santa Fe covered. Upon hearing of my expected arrival home, my father's boss immediately ordered the communications department to install a phone at my parent's home. It was an extension of my dad's office phone. This action by the railroad was certainly way above what was necessary for the Santa Fe to do. When I called the number my parents had put in their letter, it turned out that my father was out of town, but the phone also rang at their home.

I should interject here that friends and relatives of all of the POWs were intensely interested in those of us who returned. Their telephone calls and letters to our relatives comforted our families.

At the same time, however, unless there was news to give them hope for the return of their loved ones, their despair could deepen.

Shortly after I called my parents, I sent a telegram to an old, family friend in Washington, D.C., New Mexico Senator Carl A. Hatch. I wanted to share with him my thoughts from the last three and one-half years. Senator Hatch was from Clovis. Since I knew him well, I thought my Washington contact should know what I thought of war. The telegram, very short, simply said, "Sherman was right. War is hell."

On October 21st a bus took us from Letterman General to the Southern Pacific Railroad station where we boarded a train. To our amazement, it was a hospital train. We were again separated from our friends as we boarded different trains. This time we were being sent to the hospital nearest to where our families lived. Since my parents were in Amarillo, Texas, I was sent to Brooke's General Hospital in San Antonio. Most of my friends were sent to Bruns General Hospital in Santa Fe, New Mexico. Santa Fe was actually closer to Amarillo than San Antonio, but I am sure that by this point in my story you know how the military works.

The trip on the hospital train was another delightful experience. Next to the windows, the cars had bunks, two high, which ran the length of the car. A wide aisle went down the middle of each car. Each car also had a little kitchen and refrigerator for snacks. Meals were served three or four times a day. A beautiful nurse was in charge of one or two of the cars. Our thoughts still focused on food, however. At each station stop, cheerful and helpful Red Cross ladies met us, offering us donuts, coffee, milk, and apples. Throughout our trip, we received royal treatment by the Red Cross and especially by the nurses on the train. This train trip took only twenty-four hours even though we traveled further than we had on our 1941 trip from Fort Bliss to San Francisco.

After the train arrived in San Antonio, a bus took us to

Brooke's General Hospital where the staff told us that we would be their guests for a week or so depending upon our condition. Immediately, a storm of protest erupted. Everyone wanted to go home. In the midst of this uproar, the Commanding General came through to visit with some of the POWs. It turned out that he himself had been a prisoner for a short time during the war. The Commanding General immediately turned to the doctors who were with him. "Get these men out of here as fast as possible. Their families can do more for them than you can." With that order, we all endured another rapid and superficial examination. Before noon on the following day, a great number of the men were given ninety-day furloughs. Some of us were also given travel orders. As soon as we finished lunch, everyone who had received the furlough headed for town. Others, such as myself, promptly went to the railroad station to buy tickets for home. I do not remember now, but I am sure that those of us who would be on the train overnight were given sleeping accommodations.

When I finally got up to the ticket window, the clerk told me that I could not get a sleeper until the next day. Since I did not want to wait that long, I bought a ticket for the chair car. I think the train left about 7 pm. It was to arrive in Amarillo about 12:30 pm the following day. We were told that the military would be boarded first, followed by the civilians. The clerk warned us to be in line to board the train before 6 pm. He emphasized that. I thought he was crazy, but I did not know about gas rationing or about the heavy traffic on the buses and trains.

Along with some of the other POWs, I wandered downtown to see where we could spend some money. This was something new to us. After a few beers and some window-shopping, we headed back to the train depot. Just as the ticket clerk had predicted, a large crowd had already shown up even though it was only 5:30 pm. This particular train was made up (that is railroad talk for "originated") in San Antonio, with a final destination of Denver, Colorado. Its route took it through Lubbock and Amarillo, Texas. Promptly at 6 pm, they started loading the train. We had been standing in line for nearly one hour. An employee directed us to the cars reserved for passengers going to Lubbock and Amarillo. The military personnel boarded first, followed by the civilians. By 7 pm, our car, and all of the other cars, was standing room only. When the train started, several of us soldiers could stand it no longer, and we got up from our seats. We offered them to some of the many ladies of all ages who had been standing. Being polite was quite a change for us. In prison, that was seldom an option. Many of those who were still standing, including several in the military, spent the night on the floor or in the aisles, trying to get some shuteye. To we former POWs, this proved not to be a hardship.

While on the train, I met a soldier from the "Lost Battalion," a unit from the Texas National Guard that had been en route to the Philippines when the war started. Eventually, the Japanese had captured them on some of the small islands in the South Pacific. I do not remember how we became acquainted on this trip home. I think it was his destination, Lubbock. As we visited, I discovered that I knew his father, a railroader in Slaton, a terminal of the Santa Fe just south of Lubbock.

# 30

# Home At Last

After a long, hard night, that I spent on the floor, and a good breakfast in the dining car, we finally pulled into Amarillo about 12:30 pm on October 23, 1945. It had been over two months since the Japanese had surrendered. Forty-six months and seventeen days before, I had left home. To avoid the draft, I had enlisted for what I thought would be just twelve months of military duty.

What a surprise to see my parents and a few friends on the depot platform! My mother and the other ladies were dressed in long, formal dresses. My father wore a tuxedo. I couldn't imagine what had prompted such outfits, but after all of the hugging, handshakes, and greetings, they told me that they had been attending an Eastern Star Grand Chapter assembly for the state of Texas. My mother had been the Grand Matron of the Eastern

Star in New Mexico and my father the Grand Patron for that same state. These are the two highest state officers of the Eastern Star. The organization itself, open to both men and women, is an offshoot of the Masons, a fraternal male organization. At Amarillo, my parents had been honored guests at the meeting due to the offices they had held.

Because of this assembly meeting, my mother had not made lunch, so we went to the Silver Grill, a well-known cafeteria. I am afraid that I embarrassed my mother as I went through the line. I saw all of the goodies I had not seen in so many, many months. I do not remember what I ate, except that when we reached the bread station, I saw some Parker House rolls. They were just ordinary pieces of bread made into a roll. I told the lady serving the food that I would take "half a dozen" of those rolls. My mother said, "Oh, you do not want six rolls." But I did. I took them and ate them all.

Even though the war was over, meat was still rationed. After I had been home a few days, I applied for and received my meat stamps. The next day Mother and I went to the grocery store. Walking by the meat counter, I saw a ham that looked rather delicious. I spent a month's worth of my meat stamps just on that ham. Fortunately, the meat rationing was discontinued a few days later.

After a couple of weeks, my parents and I returned to my hometown, Clovis, New Mexico. We visited old family friends and had dinner with some of them, including a few who worked for the railroad. One had a son who had been killed in Okinawa. A few days later, I returned to Clovis by myself. At that time, when it came to the selling of liquor, New Mexico operated under local options. Clovis was a "dry town," meaning liquor could not legally be purchased there. The nearest bar was some sixty miles west of Clovis. Since Amarillo was a "wet town," I thought

I would take a bottle of scotch to my friends and fellow ex-POWs in Clovis. There was a liquor store across the street from the Santa Fe Railroad depot in Amarillo. I stopped there to purchase a small supply, and, to my surprise, the lady running the store was an old acquaintance from my Clovis days. After a little reunion, I explained to her my plan to take some liquor to Clovis. First she advised me about the problems of purchasing good liquor. Supply and demand were two major factors. An ample supply of rum, gin, and cheap whiskey existed, but it was suggested that in order to buy a good bottle, you had to buy a least one, and sometimes two, bottles of the cheap rotgut. Then she pointed to an M.P. who was walking around the depot. She told me that he had the authority to appropriate any liquor carried by a military man in uniform, such as myself. After I told her that I had been a POW, she offered to take care of me anytime I wanted something from her store. Because of her warning, I passed on my initial plan to take some scotch to Clovis on this trip since I was in uniform. Since I did not own a car, and because I knew many of the railroaders, I used both the passenger and freight trains to go between Amarillo and Clovis. I wore civilian clothes.

World War II and the Vietnam War were, of course, two very different wars. I have heard that Vietnam veterans did not receive any parades when they returned home. Nor did we. In my case, the war was over for nearly three months before I arrived home. I was really not interested in a parade. I had played in my high school and college bands, so I had my fill of parades. I do not know of any buddies of mine who wanted a parade. In fact, I do not remember ever giving it a thought at that time. I only thought about it years later because of remarks by Vietnam veterans. I do not know if there were any big parades after WW II was over. I do remember seeing movies of parades after WW I.

When I arrived in Clovis, everyone who knew me was

happy to see me, and I was happy that I had made it back. One's fifteen minutes of fame can be quickly used up with a few newspaper articles and a picture in the paper. But I could not tell the newspapers what I had gone through. Such treatment of prisoners of war had never happened in modern times. No one would have believed what my life had been like in the last years. Since I was traveling back and forth for the ninety days I was on furlough, I missed some of the events in Clovis that had recognized the return of my buddies and me. I do not remember any of us discussing the true story of our experiences with anyone, be they friends or reporters. We had already found out that Army doctors did not believe our problems. If they did not understand, why would civilians? We received no parades or heroes' welcome. We were not heroes, only survivors.

What proved very difficult was talking to parents and wives of the ones who did not come home. Somewhere, at one point, we had been advised not to tell any family members of these men the details of what had happened to their loved ones until Uncle Sam had made the proper notification to their parents or wives. I dodged Billy Deemer, Carl's father, until the government formally notified him that his son had not survived. Finally, I had to meet him and share what I knew about how Carl had died. That was the hardest part of being a survivor. In addition to Mr. Deemer, I spoke with other parents about their sons. There were so many unsaid questions as to, "Why my son?" None of these parents actually felt I should have died instead of their son, but I think that all of us returnees received this impression many times.

I had another hard day when I spoke with John Shields' parents. When I had played the clarinet in the high school band, John had been on drums. His parents had aged greatly because of the trauma they experienced from John's death. They wanted actual knowledge of how he had died, but I was not with him when it had happened. I did not know how or where he had died since the men from Clovis had been so scattered during our years as prisoners. I was equally embarrassed if, when I asked people about their son, wife, or husband, I was told that they had passed away in my absence. It became so bad that, although I knew I was displaying poor manners, I did not ask.

During my ninety-day furlough, I made arrangements to transfer my records to Bruns General Hospital in Santa Fe, New Mexico. It was closer to my parents' home than the hospital in San Antonio. I also wanted to be with many of the men who had been with me during the POW years. While on furlough, I went back to work for the Santa Fe Railroad in Clovis. Because of some technicality that I have long forgotten, I worked one day in 1945. After that, I checked into Bruns. At the hospital, the doctors gave me a more detailed physical than the other ones we had experienced since our release. After that checkup, I received a week's pass to spend the holidays with my parents.

It was a great event for me to share Christmas with my parents. The past five Christmases had been extremely difficult for me. In 1940 both my mother and father had been in the hospital with, I believe, influenza. Bombs were dropped on Manila on Christmas, 1941. I spent Christmas in 1942 in Cabanatuan. I was in Las Pinas in 1943 and Formosa in 1944. Each Christmas was different, but those of us who had experienced them were grateful that we had been alive to do so.

After the holidays, I returned to Bruns for a couple of months where I was fattened up. I do not remember any major disabilities I suffered from that the hospital treated. Most of us were called "the walking wounded." We displayed no apparent physical difficulties, even though my records should have indicated the following—beriberi, dengue fever, malaria, an unsteady gait, and bloody urine from beatings in the kidney area. My joints, legs, and feet also swelled up. In addition to these ailments, I suffered from skin disease, pellagra, vitamin deficiency, sunburn, skin ulcers, boils, nausea, diarrhea, dysentery, vision problems, jaundice, teeth cavities, worms, sores in my mouth, bleeding gums and teeth, hearing problems from being boxed on the side of my head, swollen glands, pneumonia, neurasthenia, and malnutrition. I am sure that the food I received aided in my recovery from many of these physical problems.

It was still a very small world upon my return. Cash Skarda, now Major Skarda, was also in Bruns. As it turned out, the oldest and youngest daughters of Colonel Luikart, who had been killed on a prison ship in Takao Harbor in 1944, lived in Santa Fe. Before the war, the Luikarts had originally lived only a block away from me in Clovis. Cash started squiring Annabell, the Colonel's youngest daughter. Soon they became engaged. When they married in Santa Fe, I had the honor of being Cash's best man. The Colonel's oldest daughter, Jerry, was Annabell's maid of honor.

In an earlier chapter, I mentioned the bamboo telegraph we used during our war years. It was weird how information spread. Cash ended up in a Manchurian prison camp. I think it was Mukden. When he was released, Cash wrote his father and told him in that letter that Bud and I were both alive, in Japan. Most of us, when we had the opportunity, tried to pass on information about each other to our relatives, knowing they would get that information to our families. I never asked Cash how he had learned that Bud and I were in Japan. I am sad to say that he passed away about four years ago. There were so many questions not asked.

For most of us, our stay in Bruns consisted of the staff taking our temperature and fattening us up. We spoke with no psychiatrists or psychologists. No one dug into what had happened to us. I am not aware of anytime during our convalescence that a POW received a psychological evaluation. Nor was there any type of debriefing.

Such practices were not in vogue at that time. The staff at Bruns just checked our outside, so to speak, for evident signs of problems. We POWs did not complain. We wanted to get our health back and return to a life of work and, in many cases, marriage.

I am not aware of anyone telling our friends or relatives what he had actually gone through. In my case, I felt so bad because of what my parents had endured. They never knew if I was alive or not. My mother and father still wrote many letters and sent packages, but they never knew if I received them. Mother worked very hard with the Red Cross. Dad tried to make a living and worked extra-long hours. Friends constantly questioned both of my parents to find out if they had heard anything about me. This went on throughout the war. Yes, they received a few cards from me. These cards were more or less multiple-choice forms of communication. The cards had lines where we crossed off what was not applicable, leaving, supposedly, lines that were—I am well/good, or I am being treated well, etc. On one line we could write something more personal, but it had to be phrased in such a way that it got past the censors.

I only told my parents that we were under-nourished and that the Japanese worked us hard. I never spoke of ill treatment, beatings, torture, or any other atrocities. It got so tiresome to be asked, by parents, relatives, and friends, "How are you?" I automatically responded, "Fine," regardless of my condition. As newspapers started to recount some of the atrocities that had occurred in the Pacific war, people constantly asked those of us who had been prisoners if a specific brutality had happened to us. We usually replied that we had heard of such acts, but not everyone experienced such treatment. We made sure we told our friends and family that inhumane treatment happened to others, not to us, and it did not happen everyday.

My father and I in a photograph taken late in 1945.
The photographer was employed by the Santa Fe railroad and
he took this picture in my father's office in Amarillo, Texas.

People who had not been prisoners of war, or internees, could not understand the feelings of those who had been in that position. Prisoners experienced prolonged periods of depression and, most of the time, prolonged periods of helplessness. In our particular case, the intimidation, the beatings, and the mental anguish we endured, as well as what we saw inflicted upon others, created psychological problems that we could not explain to persons who had not gone through such a situation.

The information the United States military and civilians received prior to our release, and even after that, was hard to believe. At the same time, I understand that the military hid the truth about our treatment for many months from the general population. I can comprehend how hard it was for anyone to believe that the Japanese could treat other human beings the way they had treated their prisoners of war. No one could understand the filth we had lived in during the first few months of our years as POWs. Even more difficult for others to grasp was our lack of food and water and, when the Japanese did give us something to eat, the strangeness of the food for us, not accustomed as we were to the diet of our "hosts."

With very few exceptions, all of my friends from Clovis who had shared the POW experience with me returned to a normal life once we arrived home. If they had not married before the war, they did so after it. They returned to some type of work, many to the same jobs they had held before the war. Like most others, Bud Kiely, Lester Morrison, Bob Stevens, and Jack Aldrich, along with his brother Bob, all returned successfully to the workforce. They had children and lived their lives without noticeable problems. Looking at most of us, other individuals could only see the outer person, not the inner person who went through this hell.

We knew the concerns our friends had for us. They repeatedly asked us questions about whether or not we had endured the "water treatment" (where water was poured down a person's throat), if we had been forced to kneel with a stick behind our knees, whether we had been hung by our thumbs, if we had stood motionless for twenty-four to forty-eight hours, and if we had been stuck in a little jail, unable to stand erect with only enough room to assume a fetal position on the floor. Regardless of how much we appreciated their concern, it did become embarrassing and tiresome.

So many friends wanted to know more about our experiences, and yet we refrained from being the least bit graphic. We were afraid they would not believe us, or they would think we were bragging or complaining. It was just better to let the sleeping dogs lay, or lie. Equally as bad were the stories friends told me about how hard it had been on my parents. They had worked and worried, never knowing during those war years what had happened to me. I know it must have been a tremendous burden for them over those many, many months. Mother and Dad saved so many letters, wires, and cards that they received from friends and relatives. I am sure such communications only increased their worries because the messages brought home to them again and again my unknown status, but I hope they also were comforted by knowing that so many people were also concerned about me.

As usual, the income tax collectors were right on the ball during WW II. When it had been time to file the 1940 taxes, I was stationed at Fort Bliss, living on $21 a month and keep. Since I had not felt very rich, I had submitted a 1040 Form, writing across it that I would send in a completed form at the conclusion of hostilities. In 1942 my parents started to receive correspondence addressed to me from the New Mexico Income Tax Division, requesting that I pay state taxes that were due. My father replied for me, informing the director of that office that I was in the service and would pay when I returned to the States. Soon after, another letter arrived. It advised my parents that if I did not pay my taxes by a certain date, the state would come and get me. My father's reply to that letter concluded with a paragraph informing them that I was a prisoner of war in Japan and that he would be very pleased if they would go and get me. Shortly thereafter, my father received a nice letter of apology for the unnecessary correspondence. The IRS wrote that it would await my return. Luckily, I did not own a home or the agency could have taken that. Once I arrived home, I prepared my tax form for 1940 and mailed it in. I think I owed less than ten dollars.

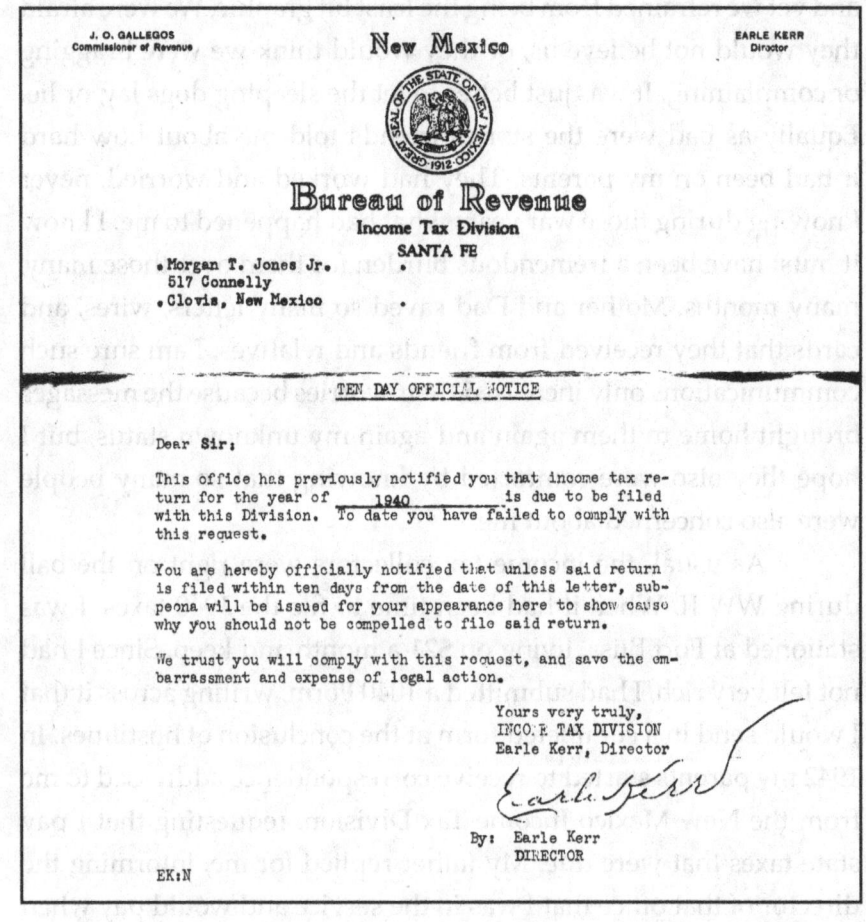

The 1942 letter my parents received from New Mexico's Income Tax Division.

> Clovis, New Mexico
> September 4th, 1942
>
> Mr Early Kerr, Director,
> Income Tax Division,
> Santa Fe, New Mexico
>
> Dear Sir:-
>
> This will acknowledge receipt of your form letter to Morgan T Jr. regarding filing tax return for 1940. This is the first form he has received for the state tax.
>
> If you could get him here with a supeona, we would certainly be glad because he has been in the Philippines for over a year with of course no word from him for months.
>
> Seriously, though, we would be glad to cooperate with you in this matter. At the time he was at Ft Bliss, he made out his Federal return for the year 1940 and said that he sent it in with the information that he did not have the money to pay the tax at that time and would pay it when the war was over. If you could get those papers and we could make out the state tax returns from them, we would be glad to pay both the Federal and State tax for him.
>
> Yours truly,
>
> M T Jones

**My father's reply to Mr. Kerr.
Note his humorous remark in the second paragraph.**

When we were released from Bruns, the Army gave us two weeks of R&R (rest and relaxation) at several different places in the Midwest and in the southwestern part of the States. We could take our family with us. For some unknown reason, I chose Galveston, Texas and took my parents. I thought the trip would be good for Mother and Dad as well as me. This happened about the second and third weeks in May 1946. I do not recall the name of the hotel in Galveston, but I do remember that it was a big one with a number of business offices in one of the towers.

The day after we arrived, I looked the place over and

recognized the manager's name. After I spoke with the person at the front desk, I became sure that I knew not only him but also his wife. Again, it is a small world. The manager's last name was "Hubby." When I had entered the service, he had been working at the Hotel Clovis. I knew his wife because she was one of Colonel Luikart's daughters. As children, she and I had attended the same school. A few days after I spoke with Hubby and his wife, they invited us to their home for dinner. We enjoyed our reunion and I was able to tell his wife more about her father and her youngest sister's wedding. One evening Hubby took us through some of the business offices. They belonged to big shots in the oil and cattle industry. I could not believe how lush and expensive these offices were. After two pleasant weeks, we started home. I stopped off in Dallas. I caught a plane there to Fort Bliss where I was discharged on May 25, 1946. It turned out that the one year of military service I had signed up for in December of 1940 became five years, five months, and five days.

Between November 1, 1945 and May 25, 1946, I had been in and out of Clovis, especially around the railroad offices, numerous times. My good friend Elmer Reamer, who had trained me on many different railroad jobs, introduced me to a Texas lass, Marguerite Coffey, who worked in the clerical section. She was on the same shift, off and on, as Elmer, and he was interested in introducing me to her. Marguerite finally agreed to go to a dance with me after which we started dating rather regularly. When I finally returned to work with the Santa Fe, this young lady lost her job. During the war years, the railroad, like other industries, honored the seniority of those who served in the military so that we were still, in essence, "on the job." Because of the seniority system, my employment meant that the person with the least seniority lost his or her job. That person was Marguerite. She was from Crosbyton, Texas, a little town about thirty-nine miles east of Lubbock. As often occurs in this small world, I was well acquainted with her uncle who worked for the railroad. I also knew her brother from my years at Texas Tech before the war. Her brother and I were not good friends, but we were acquainted with each other.

Even though I had caused Marguerite to lose her job, she was industrious and needed money, so she worked part time with the Santa Fe Railroad. My health declined as a result of her schedule. My shift was from 8 am to 5 pm. Marguerite usually worked from 3 pm to 11 pm. I picked her up after work or sometimes later that night. I took her home to her apartment after our date. Then at 8 am I had to be at work. This short night business got tiresome, and we finally married on August 24, 1946. In spite of my war memories that negatively affected my disposition, here it is fifty years and two children later, nine moves and nine different homes and cities, and we are still married. What a gal! Marguerite put up with a lot of what is now called Post-Traumatic Stress Disorder (PTSD). It affected my temperament to such a degree that I did not have my usual, positive disposition that had characterized me before the war. Since I did not share with her the details of my life as a prisoner, for years she dealt with an enigma (me). On top of all of this, there were the moves necessitated by my job transfers.

I actually went back to work on the railroad in February 1946, although I did take some leaves of absences to go back to the hospital for a week and two weeks of R&R in Galveston. It was about this time early in 1946 that I found Ed Mehegan's home address in my notebook. As I recall, he was not married and his parents were decreased. I had the address of one of his sisters so I wrote her. I explained who I was and the fact that I had been in the same camp Ed had been in when he passed away from pneumonia, malnutrition, and hard work. I shared with her what I knew of his life for the three years he had survived before his death. I also told her about some of the things we had talked about as prisoners—our desire for food, home life, and civilian jobs. Ed had spoken about how he, or his sister, had worked for the Nestle Chocolate Company and how all of us in camp would have enjoyed the products Nestle produced. I later received letters from two of Ed's sisters thanking me for telling them about Ed's final hours. At Christmas time in 1946, I received a huge box containing at least one of each chocolate product Nestle made. It was a thank you from Ed's sisters for my letters to them. We kept up a correspondence until I finally lost touch with them because of my moves or their deaths.

Since I stopped making entries in my diary or notebook when I returned home, some of the following dates may be a little off. I believe it was in the late fall of 1947 that I had a serious breathing problem. I could not seem to get enough oxygen in my lungs. I went to the Santa Fe hospital in Clovis. After several tests, the doctors decided to send me to the main railroad hospital in Topeka, Kansas. In my first day there, an old doctor told me that if I quit smoking and drinking, I would be okay. The following morning, I was assigned to a young doctor. After he examined me, he suggested that I go across town to the Winter General Hospital. This was the Army's psychiatric hospital run by the famous Menninger Brothers.

The young doctor at the railroad hospital arranged for me to be admitted to Winter General. I stayed there for six weeks. My problem turned out to be my nerves, caused by my attempts to bury my war experiences in my mind. It was suggested by a doctor at Winter General that when I had a breathing problem, I should see a psychiatrist or an Episcopal minister, individuals who were trained in listening to people's problems. (This doctor especially valued the listening skills of Episcopalian men of the cloth over other denominations, for what reason I do not know.) "Tell your story," the doctor said. "Don't try to hide it." Fifty years later, I still have breathing problems whenever I start thinking about some of my war experiences. This especially happens if someone starts to question me in depth and I have to relive some of those experiences.

I received my first in-depth psychological examination at Winter General since the main thrust of my treatment there was to settle my nerves. They did not look into any other medical problems I might have had. The doctors asked me detailed questions about the war. They even hypnotized me. I am sure the doctors knew what they were doing, but I lost some faith in them when I asked them about their opinion of "goldbricks." In the Army, a goldbrick is someone who goofs off in order to get out of his work or duty. The doctors told me they believed that a goldbrick must be sick to some degree or he would not act in that manner. There is some logic in that thought.

When my breathing problem first acted up after I returned home from Topeka, I called a psychiatrist. He quoted me a charge of $50.00 per half hour. I recovered quite rapidly without a visit to his office. I still have reoccurrences, but I have been able to control the problem somewhat. Over the years, I never again went to a Veterans Administration hospital because of the attitude it displayed to the majority of the POWs. The staff at the V.A. all seemed to consider us as trying to get something we did not deserve for free. In other words, they made us feel as if they did not believe our story or us.

The V.A. continues to stonewall on anything it thinks is going to make the government agency lose face. Take Desert Storm, for example. After four years or more of claiming that no war-related situations caused a great number of veterans to be ill, the V.A. finally admitted that it had known for four years about some chemical problems that caused veterans of that war to be sick.

In the early 1980s the V.A. wanted to conduct some "protocol" examinations on all POWs. Like many others, I did not respond at that time. Over the years I had undergone two arthroscopic operations on my knees, one brief hospitalization for a suspected heart condition, many, many trips to a dermatologist for several different types of skin cancers, and a gall bladder operation, After all of these, I finally went to the Long Beach V.A. Hospital, the one nearest to my home in Redondo Beach, for the "protocol" examination. Before my visit there, the hospital sent me a four-page questionnaire to fill out. I was to bring it with me to my appointment. One of the questions it asked was, "Despite the negative aspects of your POW experience, were there any positive ones?" I replied, "Yes." I saw those years as a learning experience and a time when I came to appreciate what it meant to be alive. What does not kill you must be a learning experience. I thought that time was an extremely rewarding and beneficial experience for the survivors, but not an experience one wished to repeat, or to have others endure. But my conclusion on my years as a POW was applicable only to those who survived.

My decision to go for the protocol examination was due to considerable pain I had in my knees, even after the previous successful surgeries. I thought the V.A. would discover the source of my problems. Once I arrived at the hospital, I underwent the usual preliminaries such as x-rays and blood tests. I also spoke with a psychologist. Another doctor spent two hours questioning me, testing my reflexes, and listening to my heart and lungs. He concluded by saying, "Okay, that's it. You're fine." As I mentioned before, the main reason I went for this exam was to get something done about my knees. The V.A. doctor did not see that as his job. I finally got him, however, to arrange an appointment for me with an orthopedic physician. The first such doctor told me he could give me a cane. I replied that I walked nine holes three times a week on a golf course. I didn't need a cane. My knee problem was something deeper. On my next appointment, I had a different doctor. He had me walk back and forth for a few minutes. After observing me, this doctor told me that I was not walking properly. If I corrected my walk, that would help my knees. He was right. After about a year of not trying to protect my knees so much when I walked, much of my pain disappeared.

My next visit to a V.A. hospital was after I moved from Los Angeles County to San Diego County. I felt I needed a knee or hip replaced. I went to the V.A. in La Jolla, the hospital nearest my home in Lake San Marcos. I had tried to get an appointment with an orthopedic doctor by phone. No, I was told, you must present yourself in person and go through the administrative process. Ten hours passed from when I left my home until I returned to it. In that time I had succeeded in getting a prescription for ibuprofen and an appointment, in two months, with an orthopedic doctor. On this visit I had only seen an intern.

Not satisfied with that, I called my civilian doctor for an appointment. I received one within the week, visited him on the appointed day, and was home again in two hours. His office was also in La Jolla. In this civilian process, I ended up with a hip replacement with no assistance from the United States government. In addition to this surgery, over the years I have had two knee operations, a gall stone operation, and innumerable treatments for skin cancer. I paid for all of these medical expenses, not the government. Do not misunderstand me. I am sure that many former military have had excellent service from V.A. hospitals. I understand that many former POWs living in New Mexico have had great relations with the V.A. Hospital in Albuquerque. Maybe I was just disgusted with the whole scene and did not want assistance from the V.A. After this incident, just thinking about the Veterans Administration got me off on a tangent and I went many years before I used their services again. The persons who worked in the V.A. hospitals I went to were always very nice to everyone as far as I could see. I know they were courteous and gentle with me. The doctors, in particular, have always seemed nice but defensive and unbelieving. It was as if I was trying to get something for nothing. I have spoken with other POWs who have had similar experiences. We all agree that the doctors did not seem to believe our physical and emotional problems. I think you can understand the hesitancy of many POWs to go to the V.A. It is so depressing to visit one of those hospitals and see all of the old men. You wonder how anyone won a war. Of course, any hospital is depressing to a point. Apparently, today the V.A. is taking better care of the Vietnam veterans and those from more recent wars.

As time passed, the railroad transferred me a lot as it promoted me to different levels. In 1951 I went first to Richmond and then to Oakland, California. From that city I went to Gallup, New Mexico. I returned to California with a promotion to San Diego and finally to Los Angeles. With each transfer, I lost more and more contact with former POWs I knew. My father had retired and moved back to Clovis shortly after Marguerite and I had married. With his passing in 1956 and Mother's in 1971, my visits to Clovis stopped and I practically lost all contact with those men.

I had no communication with Lester Morrison for nearly forty years. In 1985 I located his name and phone number in a Fresno, California phone book. When I called him, we were able to get acquainted again. Lester was very active in the American Legion and in other veterans' organizations on the local and state level in California. I had joined one or two such groups but I was never active in them. Lester told me that in a few weeks the New Mexico Bataan Veterans Organization was planning a reunion in Clovis. He convinced me to meet him there. It turned out that Delbert Miller, who was also from my hometown and was my boss at that time, planned to return to Clovis that same weekend for a high school reunion. Marguerite and I accompanied the Millers as we all went back to Clovis.

It was an enjoyable weekend. I was very anxious to see all of the men from Clovis who I had served with. It proved to be a good reunion, but at the same time a disappointing one. Many of the men I had know had, like me, also moved around in the years after the war. As such, many could not attend the reunion or did not even know about it. In particular, I had hoped to see Cash Skarda, but he did not attend. There were some surprises, though. David Johns, who I remembered as a little, skinny man from, I think, Silver City, New Mexico, was at the reunion. He had been with us in Kosaka. But at first I did not recognized him. When I was registering for the reunion, I noticed a rather large man whose name badge identified him as David Johns. I introduced myself. David told me that he had asked people about me for several years, but no one seemed to know anything. He confessed that he had not recognized me, either.

    I enjoyed the reunion, seeing quite a few old friends, but missing many more who I would have liked to have seen. Lester was there, as well as Marlett Byars, Harold Knighton, Burren Johnston (a former bugler), Clarke Smith, Otis Yates, and W.A. Noffsker. Bob Stephens, my old neighbor, was there in spirit, a faint spirit. He was hospitalized and could not attend the reunion; he passed away a few weeks later. Others I had known came to the reunion from all over the state of New Mexico; at the same time, I was not close friends with them. It was worth the trip, but I have not been too gung ho for such meetings. As I mentioned, Lester was very active in different military organizations. I think he was a little disappointed in me for not being more involved with such groups.

    One group my parents had gotten involved with during the war was the Bataan Relief Organization. Because so many POWs were from New Mexico, and since the focus of the war seemed to be on Africa and Europe, relatives of POWs from my state formed this group for political reasons and to help the POWs in whatever ways it could. Unfortunately, it was all for naught. At the end of the war the BRO was turned over to returning veterans and renamed the Bataan Veterans Organization. Both it and its predecessor accepted membership from outside the state of New Mexico, to first relatives of Bataan POWs and later to any former POW. The BVO in turn eventually became the national organization American Ex-Prisoners of War. Still in existence today, EX-POW accepts as a member any POW from any theatre or from any war. Even some civilian POWs from WW II are members. These many men, women, and children had been caught in the Philippines and imprisoned in Santo Tomas and Los Banos. Unfortunately, food-wise the Japanese treated them as badly as they treated the military prisoners; they did not, however, endure the atrocities the military POWs did. Uncle Sam also deserted the civilian POWs, but they have been welcomed by the EX-POW organization.

After the war, the government paid POWs held by the Japanese initially $1.00 per day for the length of their imprisonment. Later the government increased that amount to an additional $1.50 per day. I think the funds to cover these payments came from Japanese money that had been frozen during the war in bank accounts belonging to the Japanese. Much later our government paid $20,000 to Japanese Americans who had been living on the West Coast and interned in relocation camps during the war. They experienced no atrocities in these camps, but they had been uprooted from their communities and suffered economic losses. Which group of prisoners got the best deal?

In 1972 Marguerite and I took a trip through the Orient. Our daughter Denise had graduated that June from Torrance South High School. Our son, Morgan Thomas Jones III, was studying Chinese in Taiwan on a National Fellowship from Stanford University. As I mentioned much earlier, Ogata San had written his name and address in my notebook/diary. I had no idea if he was still alive or where he lived in relation to Tokyo. Shortly before we departed for

Japan, I wrote Ogata San a letter. I told him who I was, when we would be in Tokyo, and where we would be staying. En route to Japan, we were delayed in Honolulu for five hours to preclude our arriving in Tokyo at the same time a huge storm was due to hit that city.

When we finally got to Tokyo, it was about midnight and we went straight to our hotel, the Hilton. Upon registering, the desk clerk advised me to call Ogata San immediately. I explained that I could not speak Japanese and Ogata San probably did not speak English. I therefore asked the clerk to call him for me. He did so. Ogata San wanted to know what Marguerite and I planned to do later that day, when we would be leaving Tokyo, and where else we would be going in Japan.

The above paragraph gives the impression that the phone call to Ogata San was an easy one to make, but it was more complicated than it appears. After Ogata San posed each of his questions about our itinerary, the clerk asked me the question in English. He then returned to the phone and had another long conversation with Ogata San. The clerk asked me the next question and translated my answer back to Ogata San. Marguerite and I had noticed on the plane en route that the announcements in Japanese were much longer than the same announcement in English.

After this lengthy conversation, it was agreed that I would call Ogata San again the next morning. But hours later, just as I was getting out of bed, the phone rang. Marguerite answered it, expecting our son to be on the other end. She quickly threw me the phone. Marguerite did not understand the *mushi mushi* business. (*Mushi mushi* in Japanese is similar to hello in English.) The call was from Ogata San. I finally made him understand that I did not know what he was talking about. I told him I would call him later. When I located our tour guide, I had him phone Ogata San. It turned out that my old guard lived too far north to come to Tokyo, and since we would not be anywhere near his home while in Japan, we could not get together. Ogata San did tell the guide that we should return in five years when he would retire. I talked with Ogata San, after a fashion, one more time while we were in Tokyo, but we really had very little understanding of each other.

Our son joined us later in the day. He traveled with us through Japan, Taiwan, the Philippines, Thailand, Singapore, and Hong Kong. When we left for the States, Morgan returned to Taiwan. During our tour of Manila and the surrounding area, we visited an old church that had an organ made out of bamboo. The church was in a little barrio named Las Pinas. I questioned several people but no one knew the location of the airfield that I had helped to build during the war. I could share many good stories about our trip, but time allows me to relate only one of them. The tour also took us to the Manila American Cemetery. This stop was not advertised as part of the tour, and I did not know such a cemetery existed. For me, it was one of the highlights of the trip. The rotunda is in a half or three-quarter circle. It is open-aired with no side walls. The seal of each state is in the middle of a walkway. Engraved on the granite or marble walls on each side of the walkway were the names of the men from that state who died in the Pacific during the war. Twenty-four separate arcs stood on each side of the entryway, one for each state. One separation had a large map of the area that identified the major battles of the Pacific war. Facing out from the entrance were the many, many headstones with the names of the men buried there. It was a very dramatic, touching, and emotional experience. To my sorrow, carved in the marble walls I found many names of men I had been with. And to my dismay, I found the names of a few men whose fate had been unknown to me. Marguerite and I also found the name of her cousin, Kenneth Coffey, who died during the war. He was from Silver City, New Mexico.

We also went to Tagaytay, south of Manila, where a large

battle had occurred at the start of the war. It actually is a lake with an island in the lake and a lake on the island. Now Tagaytay is a resort. The one place I would have liked to have visited was Bataan, but we could not squeeze in everything on this trip. While we were in Tokyo, we had dinner one night with the Santa Fe representative in that city. I did not know him personally, but he and his wife gave us a nice tour and a big dinner, with a Kobe steak cooked on a rock at our table. All of that was a very nice touch. Supposedly, to fatten them the cattle from Kobe are fed beer.

After this trip, Ogata San and I maintained a correspondence through the years. We also exchanged gifts. In 1977, five years after our trip, he retired from a position in a bank. One year later, Marguerite and I made a return trip to Japan. This time we did not take a guided tour. Our trip consisted of ten days in Tokyo (which included a half day tour of that city by bus) and ten days in Yonizawa, Ogata's hometown. We had arranged an open return.

This time I personally knew the Santa Fe representative in Tokyo, Harold Williams. During our first seven or eight days there, he took us around the city. Harold and his wife also hosted a dinner party for us at their apartment that included other Americans who worked in Tokyo. Because Harold and his wife had been so kind to us, I asked them to be our guests at dinner and told Harold to choose the restaurant. He suggested the dining room in our hotel since it was noted for its steaks. After dinner Harold took us to a nightclub very near our hotel. Because of the cost, we had intended to have only one drink. We were not in the club for more than thirty minutes, had two very weak drinks, and danced one time. The tab was over $150.

We had been asked by a friend of Marguerite's to deliver a package to her son who had married a Japanese lady. This couple met us at our hotel one evening and we took them out to dinner. A few days later, the young man's wife asked us if we would go with her and their baby to visit her family on the Izu peninsula, south of Tokyo. This proved to be another interesting sidelight of our trip.

## 31

# Return To Kosaka

After eight days in Tokyo, we took a cab across town and boarded a train for Yonezawa at the Ueno station. The train left at 8 am. Marguerite and I had many suitcases. The trains in Japan run on schedule and do not stop very long at any station, except the end of the line. We knew from reading the signs that the next stop would be ours. Before we got to it, the conductor and his helper started getting our suitcases together so he could throw us off at the next stop. The conductor did not help anyone else on the trip, just us. He was not being especially kind to Marguerite and I. The conductor did not want to delay the train. We arrived at Yonezawa about 4 pm. It was not hard for Ogata San to pick us out of the people detraining. Marguerite and I were the only "round eyes."

Ogata San had written me before our departure from the United States to ask us what we would like to do once we arrived.

One of the things he suggested was a stay in a *ryokan*, a Japanese inn. When Ogata San met us, he had an interpreter, Koichi San, with him. That man owned a car; Ogata San did not. First they drove us to Ogata San's home. Apparently most of the Japanese homes have a small, western type of sitting or living room. We had been warned to take our shoes off in any house, which we did. Marguerite and I were escorted in where we met Toshiko, Ogata San's wife. She was a very pretty lady. In their living room, Toshiko served us tea and cookies.

After a short visit, all five of us drove out to the Japanese inn. Taking off our shoes again, we went to the front desk and then to our room. It was about 5 pm. The maid showed us where the bedding was, in a small closet. She later returned with some tea and cookies. Ogata San had told us that we would have a banquet at 6 pm. While we waited, we disrobed, washed up, and rested a short time. Then Marguerite and I dressed for the banquet. About 6 pm we heard a knock at the door and we were escorted into a room across the hallway. The five of us sat on the floor, around a small, raised table. Things were a little strained for a short time and Marguerite finally told me that she could not drink any more tea. In Japan, when a beverage was served the container was never allowed to get more than half empty. It would be refilled as soon as it was nearly half gone. I told Marguerite not to drink so much so fast and that helped. I finally asked Koichi San if Ogata San and Toshiko liked Scotch whiskey. He asked them and they replied in the affirmative. I excused myself and went across the hall to our room where I got the bottle of Scotch I had brought for them. After a couple of drinks, things really warmed up. From that time on, the atmosphere was very cordial. During our stay at this *ryokan*, I noticed that the interior rooms were always spotless, as were the grounds, but the entrance to the inn and the front desk area were dark and ill-kept.

As it turned out, everyday had been planned for us. Ogata had previously sent us a gift of a wooden owl and rooster, each about twenty-four inches high. One day we went to the country to see the man who carved, all in one piece, these tall, wooden chickens and owls. The farmer making them gave Marguerite several small ones as he carved them. Our hosts then took us to a workshop in a town where these figures were painted with details such as the rooster's comb and beak, or the owl's eyes. The small gifts Marguerite had just received were painted for her. While we were at the workshop, we met the owner. He had written a rather famous book about carved figures. He gave us a copy of the book as well as one of the figures pictured in it.

Another day Marguerite and I were taken to a big house where silk kimonos were made. We watched the girls working on the looms. Marguerite was given a beautiful, skillfully woven, large ball, about ten inches in diameter. It could be hung in a showcase box. We also received a silk scarf.

One day a lunch consisted of a stack of wooden trays, each filled with different kinds of noodles, and one night we had a special dinner. As Marguerite and I sat down on the floor, someone brought in a wooden sailboat, about two feet long and ten inches wide. The boat was filled with about ten different kinds of raw fish, including octopus, squid, and some fish we were not familiar with but which we did not mind trying. Aside from this treat, it was a typical banquet.

Koichi took us to a nightclub one evening. After we sat and talked for a few minutes, he excused himself. Marguerite and I watched him as he spoke on the phone. About ten minutes later one of his friends came in, dressed in his kimono, to join us. Like Koichi, this man was also a high school teacher. Both men certainly liked to practice their English.

One day after a scheduled trip, Koichi took us to his school and we visited one of his classes. The children were very excited and asked Marguerite and I many questions, so many that we had a hard time leaving. Like their teacher, the children enjoyed practicing their English.

After a few days, Ogata San told us we would be leaving the next morning to return to Kosaka. This was the first time such a trip had been mentioned. Ogata suggested that we leave most of our luggage in our hotel's storeroom. Back in the States when Marguerite and I had bought our ticket and the mini-tour, the travel agent had told us that we must pay for our hotel before we left on the trip. I had agreed to pay for the hotel in Tokyo, but I had not been able to find a Western-type hotel in Yonazawa. The travel agency had not been able to do so, either. Once Marguerite and I arrived in Yonazawa, however, we saw one, seven or eight stories high. That in itself was an eye-opener. Marguerite and I checked into the hotel. Each room had a piece of equipment, that each male guest promptly put to use, to press a man's pants. We saw Japanese businessmen who, after a day of work or play, had taken their suits off to press their pants. They walked around the hotel's hallways in their long-handle underwear.

On the day of our departure for Kosaka, Ogata San picked us up at our hotel about 8 am. Marguerite and I had repacked, so I proceeded to take most of our luggage down to the front desk where I asked the staff to store them for us until our return. There was no problem with my request. The big problem, however, was paying our bill. As it turned out, I was short by about $2.00 American. The hotel would not take a traveler's check or a personal check. The management wanted just Japanese money. When Ogata San arrived, I told him of our problem. He paid what little we owed. Since we left Yonazawa before the banks opened, Ogata also had to pay the cab fare and purchase the train tickets. He also bought us lunch on the train.

When we arrived at our destination (I do not know the name of the town), it was after 3 pm and, again, the banks were closed. Masao Nakamura, who had been the civilian in charge of the Kosaka prison where I had been held during the war, met us. His wife and another interpreter also welcomed us. Ogata explained my money problem to Nakamura and I was told not to worry. But it was embarrassing to be without money in a foreign country. After our seven-hour train ride, our hosts took Marguerite and I to a famous park in that area to show us the lake and other natural beauties. The Japanese people love to show off the countryside. After a long walk and a cold drink, Ogata, Nakamura, and the others took us to the *ryokan* where we were to stay for three or four days. I believe Masao owned the *ryokan*. He lived in a big house about one hundred yards from the inn. When Masao was in the *ryokan*, he acted as though he was in charge.

It was suggested that we might want to take a bath. Ogata and Toshiko offered to come and show us where the bath was located. In a few minutes they arrived and took us to separate areas. (Although the baths were communal, there were separate ones for the two sexes.) Both baths were about the same size, ten or twelve square feet. The water was so hot we could hardly get in. First we poured water over ourselves and then we soaped up good. This was followed by another dip of water poured over us to rinse us off. We then eased ourselves into the extremely hot water. After lounging in the baths for some time, we dried off and returned to our rooms. We had been given kimonos to wear.

On our first night, we enjoyed a nice dinner with our hosts; Masao's daughter and son-in-law joined us. After our meal, Masao suggested that we go to a nightclub. In Japan, the ladies of the house are not included in such exciting outings. After much discussion in Japanese, the interpreter told us that they had decided that Marguerite could go with us, but not the other ladies. Upon entering the nightclub, several Japanese geisha girls followed us to our table. They sat down with us. The one next to me was very attentive to me, ignoring Marguerite. After a few drinks, I excused myself to go to the *benjo* (bathroom). The girl next to me showed me to the room, but she did not enter it. She waited for me and when I was done, the girl escorted me back to the table. Marguerite tried to explain to her that she was my wife and that the girl should keep her hands off of me, but Marguerite's message really did not get through to her. This first night ended after a very long but enjoyable day.

The next day we made another trip to a scenic area up in the mountains, not far from Hanawa. I have a picture of me standing on the highway, one arm extended as high as I could reach, but the snow was still some ten feet above my hand. In fact, some people, in the month of July, were skiing that day. There are many beautiful sights in Japan, among them the parks. It seemed that the educational system was very heavily weighted on younger children visiting all of the parks and lakes. At every park or volcano we saw, there were always busloads of school children there. During our trip, I also noticed that the parks, volcanoes, and other tourist spots were spotless, although the walkway to the volcano was littered with trash. As we traveled, I noticed that the interior of the houses we visited was always clean except for the bathroom. Tile surrounded the tub where one would soak after washing, but because of all of the water, mildew was on the tile. We saw symmetrically arranged gardens that were so attractive that they were works of art. After another day of sightseeing, our hosts told Marguerite and I that there would be another banquet that evening.

There were nine persons at this banquet. The meal was very nice. As soon as we finished eating, the guests wanted to sing. They wanted Marguerite and I to teach them American songs. As it turned out, they knew more American songs than we did. The only song Marguerite and I could think of that we knew all of the words for was, "You are My Sunshine." Masao's daughter and son-in-law knew quite a few popular American songs. They tried to teach us some Japanese ones. Throughout the evening, three women waited on our party and we could not empty a *saki* glass, so it was a long, hard night.

The next morning Marguerite and I were told that we were all going on a long ride. It turned out that we were returning to Kosaka. We arrived at the smelter about 11:30 am at which time we were given a short tour of the plant's administrative offices. After that, our hosts took us into the manager's dining room. Marguerite and I sat opposite the plant's superintendent at a big table. There were five of us. Ogata San, Masao San, Toshiko, Marguerite, and I. We all sat on one side of the table. About six Japanese sat on the opposite side. After a few pleasantries, out of the blue the superintendent asked me in English how much money I wanted. To my knowledge, nothing had been said about money, but apparently I was wrong. I replied that whatever he could spare, a thousand yen or so. The superintendent spoke to one of the men and he left the table. In a few minutes, the boy who we prisoners had called "Rabbit" during the war walked into the room. He was now an adult and comptroller of the plant. His proper name is Tadao Ogasawara. He sat down opposite Marguerite and we had a nice, little visit. I reminded him that I had visited his mother in 1945 before I left Kosaka. Rabbit had several thousand yen and I asked the superintendent if he wanted American money or travelers' checks. He preferred American money. I had been without any walking around money for three days. I was happy to now be able to have some spending money so I could repay my Japanese friends for the expenses. After a large meal and a few drinks, we toured the working end of the smelter. Our hosts gave us copies of a brochure, one in English and one in Japanese, of the plant. After many thanks, we left.

Deep in thought, I was not paying attention as we drove away. After a few minutes, we stopped at an open field a short distance out of town. We all got out of the car. I looked around and asked where we were. Our hosts told me that we were where the camp had been in Kosaka. I should have known that, but I guess, after having seen Japanese men working in the smelter, I was thinking back to the POWs who had worked there thirty-three years before. I was completely stunned by the appearance of the area. No structures remained standing, and there was no evidence that any buildings had ever stood there. Everyone stood by the automobile. I walked over to where I thought the kitchen had been, and then over to the sight of the burial grounds for the eight men who had died there. I was in shock.

I could not believe that terrible things had happened at such a pretty place thirty-three years ago. I thought of the privation and the hard work, especially for the men at the smelter, which had occurred there. I said a little prayer for the ones who had died there, especially for Evans who had lived through it all only to die when the war was over but before we were actually repatriated.

It was an inordinate emotional experience. I think that if our hosts had told me that we were going back to where the camp had been, I would have been somewhat prepared, but to step out of that car onto this little plateau without any warning was just too much for me. Our hosts were thoughtful enough to give me some time to myself, which I did appreciate.

I am sorry that I did not ask Ogata San questions when we were at the old campsite in Kosaka, but I was too emotional at that time. I later learned that Kosaka was actually one of the better camps. For the men at the smelter, life was not easy, but psychologically and physically, it was a better camp than many. Kosaka was far less brutal than any other camp we were in, with the exception of Taiwan. During the war, we were not aware that there were other POW camps nearby. At least one of the other camps, Hanawa, was much bigger than ours. The men in that camp labored in the copper mines, which was hard, dirty, and dangerous work. After the war I became acquainted with one man, Woody Hutchinson, who worked in those mines. He was originally from Las Vegas, New Mexico.

After our stop at Kosaka, the following day Nakamura San told us that we were going to take a long automobile ride. He was correct in that it was long and tiring, but he wanted to show us more of the scenic beauties of Japan. Marguerite and I did enjoy the ride. After that trip, Nakamura San told us that we going back to Yonezawa, but we would depart from a different city than the one we had arrived in. I had found Japan to be a very captivating country in peacetime, not as it had been in 1945.

On our trip, the interpreters were not very good. Koichi was the best. The general problem was that they did not know what to interpret, whether it was translating from Japanese or to Japanese. They usually failed to translate all of what was said. At no time was there any mention of what had transpired in 1945 or in the years right before it. At least no one had spoken about the war to Marguerite and me. Probably some of our hosts mentioned past history when they spoke to each other.

The train trip to Yonezawa was much shorter than our long automobile ride. Marguerite and I could not reconcile ourselves to the anomalies of the country. Food and drinks were sold on the train. When a person finished a drink, usually a bottled one, the bottle was thrown on the floor. Wrappers from candy were also thrown on the floor as was any uneaten food. After the train stopped at a few stations, a person would get on the train, sweep up the debris, and then get off at the next station. Even though items were picked up, the floor was very sticky from the sweet drinks that had been spilled. The floor was not mopped until the train reached the end of the line. When the train had originated at a terminal, it was very clean. At the end of the trip, it was completely dirty.

When we returned to Yonizawa, we checked into the same hotel where we had stayed before. We retrieved the luggage we had left. After a little rest, Marguerite and I went out on the town by ourselves. Yonizawa was a nice sized city with several multi-story department stores. Of course, we had souvenirs to buy, so we purchased some kimonos and some colorful scarves. We also bought some do-it-yourself crafts, but when we got home we found that we could not read the instructions since they were in Japanese. Marguerite and I had thought we had brought enough luggage, with room for the souvenirs we knew we would be bringing home to our friends. But as it turned out, we were showered with so many gifts from our Japanese friends and from the different places where we were honored guests that before we left for home we had to buy another piece of luggage.

Marguerite and I saw only Japanese people during our ten days in Kosaka and Yonizawa. For me, the biggest surprise was the way they responded to us. With the exception of small children, no one seemed to recognize Marguerite and me as any different than they were. The small children were apparently just starting to study English, and they liked to practice on us. Very bashfully, they would say "hello" to us. Most students seemed to fear that they would not pronounce some of the words correctly, and as such, they were a little embarrassed to speak unless spoken to first.

One day we drove out to the countryside where we lunched at a very nice restaurant. As we were leaving, we witnessed the departure of a large group of Japanese, evidently from a wedding. Each couple carried a large, colorful scarf, a common practice in Japan. The scarf was filled with five or six different sized boxes. The largest one was on the bottom and the next boxes, in succeeding sizes, piled on top of it. It created a pyramid effect. We had seen many of the guests arrive without presents. In Japan the newlyweds receive money from the guests. In return, the guests all receive a present, but the same one. That is opposite of what we do in the States, but maybe the Japanese custom is a better one. That same afternoon we walked around town with Ogata San. He took us to the cemetery where his parents are buried. We also saw a few other interesting sights that were not on any tour list.

That evening Marguerite and I enjoyed a very nice dinner in Ogata San and Toshiko's home. We all sat on the floor as we ate. Today Marguerite and I could not handle such a visit as we had in 1978 because we would not be able to get back up from the floor. When we toured their house, we saw a pairs of doors open that revealed their religious shrine, small in depth but about six feet wide. As dinner progressed, Ogata San suddenly left the room. When he returned a few minutes later, he was dressed in one of his kimonos. Ogata paraded around to show it off. He then decided that I should try the kimono on. Ogata only had his long, flannel underwear on under that kimono. He was not embarrassed, however. As I mentioned earlier, we had seen several Japanese men parade around in the hotel hallways dressed that same way. Toshiko picked out one of her kimonos for Marguerite and they took our picture wearing these outfits. It was a very merry, pleasant evening.

Ogata and Toshiko had a son and a daughter. Their son was studying at a college in another city. Masako, their daughter, was about twenty-four years old and worked in a nearby hospital. Marguerite and I did not get to see much of her, but we had brought her a turquoise ring as a gift. She became very proud of it. Masako later married and sent us a big folder with pictures of her wedding.

Throughout my visit with Ogata, we really did not talk much about how we met. I did learn from him that when the war ended, the Americans had imprisoned him two different times for several months. I was very sad about that. When I returned to civilian life in 1946, some government intelligence officer interviewed me in Clovis about my war experiences. I tried to impress on the agent that Ogata San had been good to us. As usual, the left and right hands did not get together on Ogata San. Some of the information I had given the agent on Ogata had obviously not gotten to the proper authority. The American government imprisoned him in Tokyo for about one year, although he did tell me that he had been treated well. The interrogators had not believed him when they questioned him about our treatment in Kosaka.

Toshiko told us that Ogata San had studied English for the past five years in anticipation of our return. I found during our visit that he spoke fairly good English except when he got excited. When that happened, Ogata used some Japanese words, at which point Toshiko corrected him in Japanese. She did not speak any English to us but Marguerite and I thought she understood our language. Both Ogata San and Toshiko comprehended Marguerite's English better than mine because I used more slang expressions. After our ten-day journey to Kosaka, Marguerite and I went back to Tokyo for a few days. That return trip to Kosaka had been truly remarkable and enjoyable, as well as a sort of catharsis. From Tokyo, we flew home to California.

We did not know it at the time, but Ogata San had been fighting cancer for some years. Toshiko wrote us when he passed away just one year after our visit. I thought when we were there that he did not look as robust as he had when he had been my guard, but I never thought he had a serious illness. In her letter, Toshiko told us that our visit had been one of the highlights in Ogata San's life. Just as Ogata and I had corresponded between 1972-1979, I continued to do so with Toshiko. Our letter writing does pose a problem for both of us, however. Marguerite and I write in English most of the time. Several times we have found a Japanese lady who translated our letters in Japanese before we mailed them. Usually

Ogata and Toshiko's letters were in English. (A schoolteacher had translated them.) Toshiko and I still exchange gifts and family pictures at Christmas.

The year after our trip to Japan, Koichi San, the interpreter we had in Yonizawa, visited the United States. He served as a translator for a Japanese group on a tour of South America and the United States. Koichi had written us and promised to call when he arrived in Los Angeles. He did so and Marguerite and I picked him up at his hotel. We asked him what he would like to do. Koichi wanted to see Dodger stadium, but aside from that, he did not have any other requests. Disneyland and other tourist sights were on the tour's itinerary. Marguerite and I took him to a Japanese temple that I knew about in downtown Los Angeles. That same night, we went to dinner at a Xavier Cugat's Mexican restaurant. While we were there, a wandering trio came by our table playing Mexican music. After one song, the three men started to sing in Japanese. Koichi San joined in. After that, Marguerite and I took him to our home in Redondo Beach, then to two local nightclubs in the area and, finally, back to his hotel.

I am not aware of any other men, from Bataan or Corregidor who ended up in Japan, making the type of return trip I did to the sight of their Japanese camp. Many have, however, returned to the Philippines, just as many of the European POWs have gone back to Europe. It was hard, but I feel that my return to Kosaka was well worth the trip.

As I write this, over fifty years have passed. I have long forgotten most of the bad occurrences. Some of the good events have stayed with me. I am still proud of the way the Lord took care of me, bringing me back to raise a wonderful family, as have my children.

To the best of my knowledge, not more than ten percent of the original fifty-four men of Battery E and the twenty-seven in

2nd Battalion Headquarters Battery are still alive. This epistle began over five years ago by my daughter-in-law, Ronna Reed Jones, as more or less a personal chronicle of my military experiences. When I originally dictated this story, I found that I could not express to my daughter-in-law in very graphic terms exactly what had happened to me. If one was not there to see and experience it, one could not believe the full extent of the truth. I am still unable to graphically describe what we endured in respect to the atrocities we experienced as well as the degradation of our bodies and minds.

I started reading the stories of other men who had also been held by the Japanese during the war. Up to that time, I had not read any such books, trying to keep this out of my mind. Each of these stories told about the same tale. The atrocities did happen, though not to everyone, but they did occur daily during the Death March. The Japanese have not rewritten or edited their history books to reflect the whole truth. But I am sure that we Americans have, in many instances, failed to tell the whole story in our history books, too.

Marguerite and I were in Honolulu on Pearl Harbor day a few years ago. I made it a point to question many of the men who were proudly wearing overseas caps inscribed to identify them as Pearl Harbor survivors. The majority of these men were still bitter about the actions of the Japanese. I was not there, so I cannot agree or disagree with their feelings. Many of the men I spoke with, however, felt it was, as usual, the politicians who brought on the war, not the people themselves. As such, these men did not have bitter feelings towards the Japanese people. In my conversations with Ogata San, we had both expressed the same feelings. Neither of us blamed each other for what our leaders did. It was all about the fortunes of war, and as usual, innocent individuals received the wrong end of the stick.

I mentioned earlier that field promotions had been made

while we were on Bataan. I believe that one half of the list was promoted on April 1, 1942 and the remainder was to be promoted on May 1, 1942. Of course, the surrender made it impossible for the last group to be elevated to the rank of 2nd Lieutenant. I had been in that second group.

---

**BRIGADIER GENERAL CHARLES G. SAGE**
THE ADJUTANT GENERAL

OFFICE OF
**THE ADJUTANT GENERAL**
SANTA FE

9 April 1947

T/Sgt. Morgan T. Jones
208 West 6th Street
Clovis, New Mexico

Dear Sergeant:

    Under the provisions of Section 3, paragraph 1, Circular No. 46, WD 1947, former Prisoners of War may apply through channels for appointments as first lieutenants in an appropriate section of the organized Reserve Corps.

    Your name had been recommended as second lieutenant before surrender of Bataan. We have made every effort since our return to the states to have those who were recommended promoted to second lieutenants. The above are the results of our efforts.

    If you are physically fit and otherwise qualified and not drawing any compensation from the government, it is requested that you write us your decision in regard to a reserve commission and we will initiate the proper papers for same.

    Attached is a letter on the subject of appointment of Prisoners of War as first lieutenants in the ORC.

Sincerely,

*Harry M. Peck*
HARRY M. PECK
Colonel, CAC
Asst. Adjutant General

---

**In April of 1947 I received a letter advising me that those men who had not been promoted on Bataan could receive a promotion to 1st Lieutenant in the reserves. By that time, I was married, had a good job, and I also had my fill of the military. With thanks, I politely declined the offer.**

# Addendum

Much has been omitted that really has no direct bearing on this story. Nor is this epistle as graphic as it could be as to the actual treatment and the atrocities that occurred. I did not intend this memoir to become an assortment of incidents to brag or complain about. I simply want to record, as accurately as possible and as well as my memory allows, humorous and degrading incidents in my life during the many months of hell, as well as the consequences of that period for my later life. Our memory subtly forgets many repugnant incidents and, for the most part, we recall the better incidents, if any could be called better.

This book is dedicated to the "Heroes" who did not return. I wrote it on behalf of all of the "Survivors," with our prayers for their souls. It is also dedicated it to my family, who had to bear the consequences of my war experiences.

What about all of my buddies? Of the original fifty-four men in Battery E and the twenty-seven original men in Headquarters Battery 2nd Bn., at least 51% perished during the war and our imprisonment. One, Billie Black, was killed in action that first day. Since the survivors are scattered throughout the country, to the best of my knowledge only about 10% are still alive.

Of the officers and enlisted men of the original 200th called into service on January 6, 1941 along with the draftees from New Mexico, 54% of the officers died. Of the enlisted men, 46% did not live to return home. Many of the officers were on one of the several Hell Ships bombed or torpedoed en route to Japan. None of the ships were marked as Red Cross or prisoner of war ships. One study indicates that the New Mexicans in the 200th and the 515th CA(AA) suffered a casualty rate of 47%.

As I have mentioned several times, and as has been suggested by at least two published books on this subject, had it not been for the buddy system that worked within the 200th and 515th, the casualty rate would have been much greater. Each of the men, whether they were in the original 200th or whether they were draftees, tried to help others. The well-researched books I refer to are Eve Jane Matson's *It Tolled for New Mexico* and Dorothy Cave's *Beyond Courage: One Regiment Against Japan, 1941-1945*.

The spider and the web are all gone. There is nothing to fear.

"Who shall separate us from the love of Christ? Shall trouble or hardship or persecution or famine or nakedness or danger or sword?"
—Roman 8:35